# High On Rebellion

Inside
the **UNDERGROUND** at

# High On Rebellion

## BY Y VONNE SEWALL-RUSKIN
FOREWORD
BY LOU REED

max's kansas city

THUNDER'S MOUTH PRESS
NEW YORK

Published by

Thunder's Mouth Press
841 Broadway, Fourth Floor
New York, NY 10003

Library of Congress Cataloging-in-Publication Data

Sewall-Ruskin, Yvonne.
    High On Rebellion: inside the underground at Max's
  Kansas City/Yvonne Sewall-Ruskin.
       p.    cm.
     ISBN 1-56025-183-2
    1. New York (N.Y.)—Social life and customs. 2. Max's Kansas City. 3. Restaurants—New York (State)—New York—History—20th century. 4. Bohemianism—New York (State)—New York—History—20th century. 5. Celebrities—New York (State)—New York—Social life and customs. 6. Celebrities—New York (State)—New York—Biography.
  I. Title
  F128.52.R87  1998
  974.7'1—DC21                    98-5533
                                    CIP


Design by Pauline Neuwirth, Neuwirth & Associates, Inc.


Manufactured in the United States of America

Mickey Ruskin, creator and proprietor of Max's Kansas City and the father of my children, made several attempts to launch a book about Max's. The kids were getting older and he figured it might help pay for college. Unfortunately, Mickey died before his vision became a reality, leaving it up to the rest of us to tell the story. So here it is, Mickey—a tribute to the four fabulous children that you fathered and the countless others for whom you were a father figure. I hope you're smiling wherever you are.

With love and fond remembrance,
Yvonne

Max's Kansas City was the exact spot where Pop Art and Pop Life came together in the sixties—teenyboppers and sculptors, rock stars and poets from St. Mark's Place, Hollywood actors checking out what the underground actors were all about, boutique owners and models, modern dancers and go-go dancers—everybody went to Max's and everything got homogenized there.

—Andy Warhol

# contents

# foreword: the dark brigade by Lou Reed

**i**t's all really gone now. The laser light that shone from the back room with all its red tables. The chick peas. The bad steak and horrible salad. Warhol, the superstars, the rock-groups-to-be and not-to-be. The poets (and almost everyone was thought to be), the painters—in the front at the bar—and, toward the end, the upstairs where entertainment of a more formal nature resided—complete with a booker. The Velvet Underground played its last gasp up there.

Mickey, thin, hawk-faced, dark stringy hair severely parted and forever hanging over his right eye, was personally responsible for my survival for three years because he fed me every day. While I sometimes showed up for the five P.M. buffet, it was actually the "tab" that made it possible for me and a small army of other artists to exist just to the left of the line that defines more extreme modes of criminality. The difference between car theft and a stabbing, for instance. I remember when Tiny Malice tried to commit suicide after an especially degrading sexual encounter with Leland Rose the critic and the choreographer Little Mouse the Dwarf (another in a long line of self-inflicted degradations). Malice was the publisher of *The Lavender Movie Guide* and an ex–*New Yorker* editor fired for correcting a VERY FAMOUS AUTHOR's prose. Of course she survived, and with the flowers sent by Mickey to the hospital came a note advising her to pay her bill first next time.

And of course, Eric and Ronnie and Jed and the Twins, the Cuban Bananas, the incredible David Hoff, the West Coast Davids, Larry's Winchell and the Spaghetti triplets, movie stars with credit cards, and Dylan's rejects from Woodstock who had mastered a nasal midwestern twang that somehow seemed revolting removed from him. Record-company flacks and writers and PR people galore—the home of many a career-to-be and life-to-end and drug casualties in the extreme, only no one (well, I didn't) knew it yet. Some of these drugs were so new they weren't illegal yet unless you trusted your new best buddy's downtown review of the week in Bellevue. And how was your day?

I myself don't know anyone who paid the tab although there must be someone somewhere. Every seven or eight months Mickey might mention it. We naturally would be insulted—nervous: he could cancel it.

Contacts were made, lives changed. It was the most democratic meeting ground imaginable. It was there Brian Epstein took me to his limo to tell me between drags of pot how if he could "only take three records to a desert island..."

People thought the Velvet Underground really existed, this appendage of Warhol's. But we were broke, totally and completely and always had been. Money went for drugs or drink—not food. And there was never any money.

But there was always Mickey and Max's. We had a home in Mickey's game room, this extension of his psyche, his home. He was interested in artists. He liked them. He wanted them to have a place. He wanted them to survive. Many people in Max's got me into trouble but so many others helped me out. Few of the regulars lived long enough to be a nostalgic memory. It was a speedy world—New York—and revolutions were taking place in it—art, life, and rock and roll. It was palpable and exciting. A young reckless nighttime bunch were we. The dark brigade who never saw the sun.

Mickey didn't lecture us unless the outrage was beyond endurance and then you were temporarily banned until no one remembered what happened in the first place. He made sure you were okay and everyone was still standing. Nodding you in from his perch at the bar or scanning the back room, possibly amazed it was still there. And on those days when you thought the world might have ended and you crawled to Max's shaking, Mickey would send over a scotch and beer, tell a waitress to come over and "take care of..." We wanted to be artists. And Mickey believed and supported us. Who else besides Andy did that?

Later revived, you passed Mickey who waved you out the door with, "Think you might catch that bill in a couple of months?" Laughing. A man's man.

You didn't have to be poor to appreciate what a great guy he was. But I don't think money people ever got it. Genteel journalists and critics could pontificate forever about the exploitation of people, by Warhol, by Max's. But those people wouldn't understand a good time if it kicked them, nor greatness if it sat across from them in a crowded booth and stood them to a good meal. For myself it's scary to think what would have happened to me without Mickey Ruskin in my life. We made a big family all of us.

And Mickey, I think you'd get a big laugh at where it all ended up.

preface

There were so many colorful personalities that clung to Max's as a second home, a home which drew its remarkable energy from an amazing mix of smarts, talent, daring, and originality. I feel so privileged to have been part of the family. We were a constellation of sparkling stars. As for those members of the family whom I was unable to reach, it surely wasn't for lack of trying. People scatter, people change, and, as we all know, they leave, but those red tablecloths, steak, lobster and chick peas, surf 'n' turf, the salad bowl, the baked potatoes with sour cream, the snowball...are an important part of your history too. So I hope that these pages evoke the fondest of memories, and resonate with the fabulous familiar spirit of the one and only MAX'S KANSAS CITY—DOWNTOWN ON PARK AVENUE SOUTH.

—Yvonne Sewall-Ruskin

**t**here were so many people who offered their support and inspired this very long journey back to Max's Kansas City, and the birth of this book. To all those people I am eternally grateful. There is no way I can adequately acknowledge or name everyone.

I'd like to thank Mickey first, who has been my soulmate on many levels, and my children, Jessica and Michael, for supporting me over the years in realizing my dreams and fantasies. I hope they've learned through this project that perseverance pays off, and anything is possible. I also thank my sisters Penny Fable and Dorothy Sullivan for their love and support, and my parents who gave me integrity and strength of character.

I extend my graditude and special thanks to Myra Friedman for her insights and creativity, and her unfailing source of words when I could not find ones to fit; Charles Denlinger who has offered emotional and computer support and ideas from before the beginning; my incredible agent and editor Stuart Bernstein—I wouldn't be writing this page if it weren't for his endurance and friendship; Neil Ortenberg for taking the plunge and publishing this book and providing additional editing; Lou Reed for writing the Foreword; Beth Groubert in Lou's office for her diligence and expediency; Ilene D'Arcy in Bowie's camp for her efficiency and kindness; John Russell, Charles Knull and Lowell Kern for acting above and beyond the call of duty; Ritchie Cordell for giving me the gifts of a fax and computer to assist me on my journey, and for his wonderful humor and wit; and Julian Schnabel for his generosity.

The interviews with Mickey are courtesy of Danny Fields and Ryder McClure. Thanks so much for your generosity. The book would not have been complete without Mickey's voice.

I'd also like to thank Cherry Vanilla for her creativity and assistance in writing the back room Warhol chapter with me; Leee Black Childers for all his marvelous contributions; Anton Perich for his fabulous array of photos, along with all the other photographers; Larry Rivers for the use of the *Cedar Bar Menu 1*; Scott Cohen for the Larry Rivers interview and his contribution to the early stages of the project; Bruce Kurtz for the historial aspects of the era; Dick Nusser for working on the beginning stages of the proposal with me; art critic Paul Taylor for his collaboration on the

# acknowledgments

*Fame* magazine article; Dan Pinchback and Gail Love for their permission to use some of the additional quotes from phone interviews conducted for the *Fame* article; Kent Wallace for collaborating with me on my first Max's article—he has been one of my strongest supporters, with his special way of cheering me on with his "Go Girl" attitude; and Jeremiah Newton for contributing his interview with Donald Lyons.

I wish to extend special thanks and graditude to: Debbie Ross, Raamy Brown, Pam Arend, Maggie Carver, Bob Guilmartin, William Thurston, Jeffrey Nickora, Jeff Lieber, Jeffrey Lew, Peter Creswell, Steve Manos, Lynn Shultz, Clay Knowles, Jerry Ordover, Alan Bomser, Robert Fish, Peter Eisenberg, Rick Speciale, Pamela Gia, Ron and Jenny Landfield, Jeff Goldberg and Susan Cooper, Caroline Marshall, Julia Markus, Catherine Hazzard, Monica Behan, Sara Goldstein, Sandy Davey, Denise Mourges, Mitchell Rose, Michael Gross, Tad Richards, Bob Rolontz, Peter Yurkowski, Steve Gaines, Bob Fass, Alice Brinkerhoff, Carol Fonde, Steve Massarsky, Stanley Mieses, Doug Breitbart, Jules Fieler, Holly George Warren, Carol Wilbourne, Holly Lam, Barry Feinstein, Marie Morreale, George DuBose, Jennifer Belle, Marc Kraznow, Jim LaLumia, Frederic Vigneron, Vieri, Mike Sovik, Anthony Olszewski, Lonnie Hoberman, Don Greenholz, Spencer Drate, Victor Bockris, Bruce Ehrmann; to Larry Gagosian and Rick Kaufmann for offering their art galleries for the 30th Anniversary of Max's Kansas City's silent auction and party, as well as all the artists who contributed works in Mickey's memory and everyone who helped on the 30th Anniversary Max's project; to Mark Frisk who worked his tail off to try and sell this book, Howard Buck, Michael Carlisle, Dan Levy, Pauline Neuwirth and Eileen DeWald of Neuwirth & Associates, and Dan O'Connor at Thunder's Mouth Press.

To my interns, transcribers, and researchers: Crystal Waters first and foremost for conducting the interview with William Burroughs when I was unavailable, and doing whatever needed to be done in the beginning stages of the project; and Annie Gifell, Hollie Sobray, Alison Mazer, Josh Taggart, and Denise McNicholl.

I want to acknowledge my respect for Victoria, Jessica's and Michael's half-sister, Sharon, Mickey's first wife, and Kathy, Mickey's widow, and to express my sadness over the loss of Nina, Jessica's and Michael's other half-sister.

I am gratified to have found my son, Gerry Botch, whom I placed with an adoption agency when I was young, and his stepsister Luanne, who have become part of my extended family. I wish to extend my appreciation and thanks to Gerry's adoptive parents Frank and Lucille. Sadly his adoptive mother passed on in 1996.

Lithograph of Max's back room by Richard Bernstein, with overlay of Max's floor plan (courtesy of Richard Bernstein)

# FIRST FLOOR PLAN

SCALE 1/8" = 1'0"

EATING & DRINKING PLACE - U.G. 6

## PROPOSED CONDITIONS

SEATING CAPACITY

TABLES ---- 147 SEATS

BAR ---- 17 STOOLS

159 SEATS

EMPLOYEES ---- 25

TOTAL ---- 184

NOTE: S&B APPROVAL UNDER P.A. 666-63 AS AMENDED
JULY 19, 1965 FOR 184 PERSONS TOTAL

---

# SECOND FLOOR PLAN

SCALE W=1'

EATING & DRINKING PLACE WITH CABARET AS PER SECT. B 32-296.0 PAR-3 ADM. CODE.

USE GROUP-12

NOTE - ALL PROVISIONS OF THE BOARD'S RESOLUTION UNDER CAL 699-66-BZ
GRANTED NOV. 22, 1966 WILL BE COMPLIED WITH

## PROPOSED CONDITIONS

SEATING CAPACITY = 142

EMPLOYEES = 13

TOTAL = 155

When you're young and eager and looking to conquer this city of dreams, you want
to be somewhere. Fit in somewhere. That somewhere usually turns out to be a saloon.
It ain't only a place to get loaded or even to score. It's also your home away from
home, your answering service and maybe even your bank. For myself and many of
my contemporaries, for almost a decade that someplace was Max's Kansas City.

—Joel Oppenheimer

**i**t was the summer of '67, I was twenty-one years of age and free. I had just
graduated from the University of Connecticut. *"No more pencils...."* I was ready
to spread my wings and fly, but literally never having flown, I had a burning
desire to experience the ultimate freedom—to get on an airplane and go! I wanted to
go to the center of everything, to an event, and at that particular moment the event
was Haight-Ashbury in San Francisco. I wanted to be a flower child. San Francisco
was the tie-dyed epicenter—peace marches, flower power, psychedelics, and be-ins at
Golden Gate Park's "hippy hill." Haight-Ashbury was the site of an historical event,
when all kinds of barriers crashed down. Bohemian counterculture became fashionable, avant-garde art mingled with popular culture, social classes mixed, and the
birth-control pill ushered in free love. I arrived at a time of experimentation and
exploration—pot, amphetamines, and LSD—all set against the backdrop of the
Vietnam War, the Manson killings, and rock and roll. Things were happening.

At Haight-Ashbury, I was smack-dab in the middle of it—a-once-in-a-lifetime opportunity. Golden Gate Park was a very magical place, full of breathtaking flower gardens (and flower children), animals of all sizes and shapes, and music. Hanging out on Haight Street, with all its little craft shops, was also one of my favorite ways of passing time. I mingled with like-minded people, conversed with shop owners, acidheads, potheads, intellectuals—everyone but panhandlers. The Grateful Dead performed on the back of a truck, which drove up and down the streets. Janis Joplin was playing at the Avalon. But after a few months, I had depleted my financial reserves and, like all great romances, this one had to end. When my short stint as a flower child was over, I packed my bags, made a sign with three huge letters that read NYC and headed east on Route 66. With Lady Luck on my side, I arrived safely in New York City a few days later.

I decided it was time to start a new chapter in my life, beginning with a waitressing job that could provide enough savings to finance a trip to Europe. Trekking from one restaurant to the next, I discovered that most advertised positions were at real dives, where topless or bottomless was the dress code. I was discouraged and my savings were dwindling. So I decided to pay a visit to one of my high-school buddies, James Hamilton, a noted photographer with the most unforgettable eyes, who was attending Pratt Institute and had already been living in the city for a few years. He told me about a place called Max's Kansas City, where waitresses were treated like stars and made lots of money—definitely my kind of place! He told me that another high-school acquaintance, Patsy Cummings, was waitressing there. "Just call and mention her name," he said. "See if you can get an interview."

"Come between three and five tomorrow," came the voice over the phone. That's encouraging, I thought. Desperate for a job, I made up my mind that this was it. This was the place I had to be. So I spent the better part of the next morning preparing myself—getting psyched. I dressed in a sexy leopard-print dress that was slightly provocative and showed off my legs.

●　●　●

I remember it was a perfect September day in the city—crystal clear, warm, low humidity, and a slight breeze that seemed to blow away the pollution. I walked from the apartment I shared with my sister on West Twentieth Street across town and down Park Avenue to Max's. I loved feeling grown-up at last and being in New York City. I felt anxious, but also self-assured and pretty gutsy. As I crossed at a light, I could hear the Beatles blaring from the radio of a black Porsche convertible. This was a good omen. It made me feel lighter. It gave me confidence.

I arrived at Max's fifteen minutes early. From outside, it was a distinctive place with its huge black marquee jutting out from the front that said in white lower case letters:

## max's kansas city
### steak lobster chick peas

Peering inside, it was the afternoon crowd, so I didn't get much of a sense of hip right off, but I got the sense of BIG. This was BIG. I had no idea what was really "in" for New York. In college days, we'd come in for a night to see Dylan, or to hang out at the Dugout on Bleecker Street. We'd see a transvestite and think that was really outrageous. We'd go home and tell everybody, "You should see what we saw!"

I had a little time to kill and I was about to go scope out the area, when suddenly I saw this guy walking briskly in my direction. He had on a suit jacket and an oversized flowered tie blew in the breeze as he walked. His pants were black—a little short in the leg—and I couldn't help but notice his bright red socks. His face was tan and his nose was long. Shiny jet-black hair hung over his left eye. I liked his look. So I kept watching him. He brushed his hair to one side, picking up speed as though he were in a hurry. Something about his mysterious little-boy look reminded me of a distinguished Ichabod Crane. I followed his movements with my eyes until he disappeared into the Chemical Bank on the corner. There was something about him. I couldn't pinpoint it. A magnetic field.

I checked my watch, looked myself over, took a few deep breaths and entered Max's Kansas City for the very first time. There were several guys at the bar and only a few people sat in the booths along the wall. The interior was not well lit, and the space was long—very long!—and dotted with red tablecloths. The cashier directed me back out the door and up three flights of stairs. I stepped into a dingy, loftlike area with shelves stacked with liquor, boxes, and other restaurant supplies. A caged area off to the right looked almost like a jail cell and contained several desks where people were busy working. Instructed to wait until I was called, I sat down next to a couple of other young, pretty hopefuls.

Finally, my name was called. I walked in to the small cluttered office, looked around, then looked at the man sitting at the desk. There he was! Ichabod Crane! I was taken aback; my face became flushed and my palms became sweaty. "Have a seat," he said, as he looked me over to the point of staring. His dark eyes were penetrating my being. I was beginning to feel uncomfortable. I fidgeted slightly in my seat, adjusting my dress. "So, what do you want to be when you grow up?"

What kind of question is that? I'm thinking to myself.

The conversation went on for a very long time and we began getting more and more

rebellion

enamored with each other. We were sparking some serious electrical charges. I had no idea he was Mickey Ruskin, the man who owned the place. But an eerie feeling began to come over me. An intuitive sense that this man and I were destined to meet. He felt it too. I knew very strongly.

He paused for a minute, then said he didn't want to hire me, that I appeared too scattered, too flighty to be a waitress. "That's really not the case," I said boldly, "I'm just high-spirited so I appear to be scattered, but I'm very focused. Just give me the chance to prove it." "Well, I like you too much," he responded, "and I've found that it's not a good policy to hire someone I'm attracted to. That's why I hire Jewish girls. I can't stand most Jewish girls." Without thinking, I said, "Well, you could always hire me as your personal secretary." Mickey's deep dark eyes stared at me intently for a few minutes, causing shivers to go right through me. I worried that he could hear my heart pounding.

"All right," he finally said, "come in tomorrow and train. You'll be assigned a waitress to trail. You train for two nights without pay. Let's see how you do."

"You won't be sorry," I told him.

It felt like I had just conquered the universe. On my way home, I wondered what it was about this man that blew my dress in the air. Maybe it was his dark eyes or the simple fact that we looked alike. I could have passed as his younger sister, even though he appeared to be much more serious and darker in nature than me. It didn't much matter, though; I was seriously relieved just to have found a job. I ran home to tell my sister.

"I got it, Penny! I got it!" I kept yelling as I raced through the door, completely out of breath. "I got it! I can't believe it. And you know, it's not just any job. It's the hottest spot in all of New York. And I know you're gonna think I'm crazy, but I just met the man who's going to be the father of my children!" Penny was skeptical. But it was no coincidence that I ended up at Max's Kansas City. Mickey and I have two great kids that prove it.

—Yvonne Sewall-Ruskin

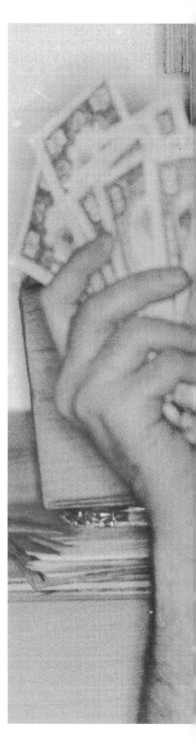

max's
kansas city
steak lobster chick peas

777 7870

**John Chamberlain,** *Ultra Yahoo,* **1967. Galvanized steel, 59 1/4 x 36 1/2 x 16 1/4. Private collection, San Francisco. Displayed at Max's in 1967.** Photo by Sarah Harper Gifford, courtesy Pace Wildenstein. © John Chamberlain

My places have always been my living room and every night I throw a party. But at Max's it went from being just an ordinary little salon and turned into Magic!

—Mickey Ruskin,
owner and proprietor, Max's Kansas City

e veryone who was anyone was there. Max's Kansas City was the place to be. It quickly became the new drug of the late sixties and early seventies counterculture scene and its effects were lasting. The legendary restaurant/bar opened its doors in December of 1965 at 213 Park Avenue South, between Seventeenth and Eighteenth Streets off Union Square, just as popular culture was poised on the brink of a remarkable shift. The mere mention of Max's conjures up images of chic and outrageousness. There never was a place like it and there never will be again.

The key to the energy of Max's was the explosive chemistry among the participants. A veritable who's who of the famous and infamous adorned the place: Mick Jagger, Jane Fonda, Peter Fonda, Roger Vadim, Faye Dunaway, Bruce Springsteen, Allen Ginsberg, Jim Morrison, Lou Reed, Betsey Johnson, Bobby Neuwirth, Timothy Leary, Dennis Hopper, Abbie Hoffman, Patti Smith and Robert Mapplethorpe are a sampling. Debbie Harry or Emmylou Harris may have served your dinner before each got her big break. The quality of the mix led to such meetings as Andy Warhol and

**underground melting pot**

Valerie Solanas; Candy Darling and Divine; Abbie Hoffman and Janis Joplin; Robert Smithson and Tuesday Weld; and David Bowie, Iggy Pop and Lou Reed. David Bowie remembers: "Me, Iggy, and Lou Reed at one table with absolutely nothing to say to each other, just looking at each other's makeup." Where else but at Max's could you find the brilliant feminist Germaine Greer wondering who had surreptitiously unsnapped her bra while at another table transvestite Jackie Curtis shared makeup tips with Kennedy family member Sargent Shriver. Or the elegantly dressed Duke and Duchess of Windsor decked out in their couturier duds perusing menus within earshot of leather-jacketed Patti Smith and Sam Shepard, Max's couple of the month. Up front, artist Robert Smithson might be sitting in a booth with Brice Marden, Dorothea Rockburne, and Carl Andre arguing over his theories of conceptual art, too intent to notice Cary Grant and his party, sitting in a booth across the way.

● ● ●

Max's Kansas City was the nexus of underground culture where anything could happen, and did. People from all walks of life became addicted to the scene. To enter Max's was to confront a heady mix of faces and personalities. To enter the notorious back room was an act of bravery. It was the longest-running party in history and the home away from home

**Center aisle at Max's** (photo by Marilyn Krauss)

high on

for an influential group of artists, filmmakers, musicians, writers, poets, photographers, models, movie stars, and socialites. Young people clamored to get into the joint. The raucous mix led to revolution in every facet of the arts. The action was always shifting and intense. In many ways Max's exemplified instant gratification: drugs, sex, music, exhibitionism and voyeurism—which is not to say that Max's was lacking in intelligent conversation. Everything and everyone became homogenized in the extraordinary, psychedelic, multimedia atmosphere. Journalist Dick Nusser described it as "a coming together of generations whose time had come." It brought the twenties, thirties, forties, and fifties into the sixties, and was the one place where anyone felt safe to let their hair down. Perhaps Jimi Hendrix said it best: "Max's Kansas City was where you could let your freak flag fly."

Max's owed its incredible success to the late Mickey Ruskin, its owner and founder. The name Mickey Ruskin is synonymous with Max's. Mickey was happiest in the company of painters and sculptors; his freewheeling attitude and generosity nurtured the budding careers of now-renowned abstract expressionists including Robert Rauschenberg, Larry Rivers, Brice Marden, Sol Lewitt, and Carl Andre, and Pop Art Superstars like Roy Lichtenstein and Andy Warhol. Ruskin gained his loyal following with a string of artist-oriented bistros, previously having owned the Tenth Street Coffeehouse, Cafe Deux Megots, the Ninth Circle, and the Annex. Mickey Ruskin nurtured the development of the New York underground scene from before the beginning. But Max's Kansas City was his crowning achievement.

His transformation from nice, straitlaced Jewish boy with a Cornell law degree into ultra-hip restaurateur and unofficial rabbi of the demimonde, mirrored the transformation of so many others on the cutting edge of this provocative period who fled safe, middle-class backgrounds, pushing hard at the boundaries in search of adventure, artistic and otherwise.

Mickey Ruskin provided a libertine atmosphere in which the unconventional could flourish. Drugs and sex were definitely a major part of the mix at Max's. In the years before the Stonewall Rebellion, Max's was one of the few places of its kind where drag queens were accepted and, notwithstanding some good-natured ribbing from the macho artists at the bar, gay and straight reveled in each other's company. Blurred sexual identity and sexual preferences contributed to the charged atmosphere. Beautiful young people exhibiting their flesh in black leather and miniskirts fueled the fire. Speed, LSD, pot, downs, heroin, and of course alcohol, all in plentiful supply, removed inhibitions. Photographer Derek Callender recalls, "There were enough drugs in the back room to cause genetic defects."

*Showtime*, a nightly back-room event, often involved a striptease by Warhol Superstar Andrea "Warhola Whips" Feldman that was part performance art and part drug-induced psychosis. Danny Fields said, "It's no cover, no minimum, for the greatest show in town." As far as Mickey was concerned, "If I liked somebody, they had an absolute right to do whatever they wanted." And they wanted a lot. Enter the ladies' or men's room and you might catch a glimpse of blond-haired, blue-eyed Eric Emerson (awarded the prize for the most sexual encounters) getting it on, or getting it up, with Jane Fonda, while her husband Roger Vadim watched. The age of consent in the back room was the age at which one could say yes. After all, this was the sixties and Max's was the place where you could not only confront the values of the next generation—you could go to bed with them.

William Burroughs said, "Max's Kansas City was at the intersection of everything." And what a crowded intersection it was! It was also the wildest party that ever raged. The nightly events at Max's Kansas City have permeated nearly every aspect of modern life, from the way we dress and behave, to our notions of freedom and liberty. Many of today's biggest stars and creative talents had the best times of their lives at Max's. It was where they came of age. Rock icons like Jim Morrison, Alice Cooper, and David Bowie got an eyeful at Max's and then translated it for their mass audiences. Punk was born at Max's. Both Abbie Hoffman and Jerry Rubin used the crowd at Max's as a sounding board for ideas. Politicians and socialites rubbed elbows with radicals and hustlers. Uptown met downtown.

**LEO CASTELLI, ART DEALER:** Max's was the Cedar Bar of its era. The atmosphere was different because times changed so much between the abstract-expressionist period and the period of conceptual and minimal art. There was a great difference in the individuals because art hung on the walls of Max's—beautiful Flavins, Judds, and many others.

**ULTRA VIOLET, WARHOL SUPERSTAR:** Max's wasn't just for painters. It was the melting pot of the sixties. You could be with a senator, a patron of the arts, a dancer, and a hippy. There were uptowners, like Ahmet Ertegun, the Sculls. The place was so in and so wild. Before, that never happened. Then they'd only mingle among themselves. Max's was crucial in setting the tone for the sixties.

**MYRA FRIEDMAN, PUBLICIST/AUTHOR, *BURIED ALIVE*, A BIOGRAPHY OF JANIS JOPLIN:** Max's was a lot more than a magnet for sex games and drugs. It was an earthy, invigorating hangout and the people who Mickey let stay there for hours and hours were definitely a breed apart, when being "apart" had real meaning in the world. I remember it for lots of conversation with lots of people who had lots and lots to say, and looking back on it now, the hum of the place strikes me as sort of the last hurrah of a genuine American bohemia. Like a great piece of writing, it was airborne from the minute it opened. It had beautiful wings; it soared.

**MEL BROOKS, DIRECTOR/ACTOR:** Billy Wilder used to tell me about the coffeehouses in Vienna, and Max's was like that for me. I never knew any other place you could talk with writers, performers, various wandering gypsies, and bullshit about the ways of the world.

**GREG BROWN, FILMMAKER:** It was the first place I ever saw a man walk around in high heels and a body stocking, with monkey fur wrapped around his neck. Once you gained entry, you were accepted no matter what you did, where you were from, if you were a freak, if you were straight. It was that connection that made the place brilliant.

**IVAN KARP, ART DEALER:** This puts me in a kind of existential quandary because I never liked Max's. It was the noise—the din—the din and the lighting were contrary to my sensibility. I'm very sensitive in that regard. Dining and drinking are rituals on a very high order for me—I have no other religious beliefs, and Max's didn't fulfill my conditions for those activities.

**BILL GRAHAM, PROMOTER, OWNED THE FILLMORE EAST:** The word "grungy" comes to mind.

**ABBIE HOFFMAN, POLITICAL ACTIVIST:** Max's was allowable. All the worlds could meet there, and I guess you were kind of gooop [gossip] proof....Whatever happened there was off the record so there was a certain amount of protection.

**RICK KAUFMAN, ART DEALER:** A lot of people were just like nuts and bolts on a listing ship that had fallen out and gotten lost in the waves, and Max's was always gathering them up and keeping them safe and sound and giving them a little cushion against reality.

**DAVID JOHANSEN, ROCK MUSICIAN:** It was so decadent. You didn't have to learn how to do this place because you had already been doing it in high school for four years at the soda-pop shop. I was kind of like a rock and roll mascot to the artists. I used to dance a lot at the discotheque. Max's had the first hip discotheque in New York. I went when Patti Smith had a party in the afternoon. I went to everything. It was like the administration building.

**DANNY FIELDS, WRITER/PUBLICIST:** Max's was a part of everyone's nightly routine, so I was there. Whoever I was with or entertaining I would go with, and it was very easy to bring famous people there because they would never be the only famous people there and there would always be other ones so they wouldn't feel as if you took them someplace where they were exposed. Although they were, but in the kind of way that they wanted to be. The tone seemed to be set at a certain level of lunacy as a base, so that people who were performers immediately felt at home.

rebellion

People always kept the level where they wanted it to be, so you could make an entrance or not make an entrance, and it was sort of tacit agreement between the people coming in, and the people already there. Everybody together regulated the tone so that it was always a show. It was a show being directed by the participants...very theater.

**MARY WORONOV, ACTRESS/ARTIST:** Max's was where everybody met and hooked up with each other. It wasn't very intellectual. In fact, it was hideous to be intellectual. We certainly did enough cutting up of other people. Everybody talked about doing things all the time, but nobody did anything really. The nights were very long, very boring—we were just sitting there. It wasn't even about table-hopping or working the room. It was all about nothing. Sometimes, people would freak out and have fits. I remember Ondine once getting furious in the middle of making a salad and throwing the salad stuff everywhere. It was the place to go but it was very juvenile—nobody introduced anyone, nobody talked to anyone—it was very chic to be like that.

**TERRY O'CONNOR, BARTENDER:** Fellini came in and people were all over the place going crazy, and he came up and spoke to me. Max's was like a Fellini movie, so for him to come there it was like the godhead coming. He came up to me and asked me something...and people came up to me and said, "What did he say?" I said, "He asked me for a book of matches."

**JIM SIGNORELLI, FILMMAKER/PRODUCER:** People expected immersion. They expected to walk in the door and be enveloped by a visual, auditory experience that did not require contact with another human being. Max's was not like that. Max's required contact with other human beings, physical if you were lucky. You had to know how to talk to another person. You had to know how to relate. We were at a table one night and some guy who passed himself off as some aficionado came over and started to razz Poons about his paintings, saying he was washed up. The guy was just ranting on and on. Somebody came up behind him and just took the tail of his suit coat and split it right up the back and walked off. His coat was flapping and that was that.

**RICHARD GOLUB, CELEBRITY ATTORNEY:** I met my first client at Max's—Marjoe Gortner. My secretary at the time was Laurie Sebastian—she married John Sebastian from the Lovin' Spoonful—and she and I used to go there together. You'd see everybody at Max's, from West Village hippies like Laurie to people like Pilar Crespi, who in those days would appear regularly on the cover of some magazine. Everyone from the slick to the mysterious would be at Max's. In those days I was a rock and roll lawyer. I represented Richard Hell and the Voidoids, the New York Dolls, and more transvestites than any other lawyer.

**Mary Woronov**
(photo by Anton Perich)

high on

**PAMELA KRAFT, WAITRESS:** That first time I walked into Max's it was like a strange dream of the most wonderful people that you loved in the art world all sitting in the same restaurant. It was a dream come to life. You had a sense of the absurd given to you in material form. It was a phenomenal sensation, because I think it was more like a great piece of art, framed memories. A great club is that kind of life. Impressions are not linear, they're hallucinogenic, and the great uniqueness of it was that Mickey really loved all of these people. It was this great love affair. He took care of everybody....The sense of being cared for...that's why it could exist.

**BRICE MARDEN, ARTIST:** I remember the night Cary Grant came in, and the night Dylan came. That was the only time anything ever stopped the place. Ten minutes later Mick Jagger and Brian Jones came in and nobody noticed. I remember meeting Hendrix. He had just done Monterey....Years later, it turned into a punk club and my son went there all the time while he was in his Sid Vicious phase.

**TOM O'DONNELL, BALLOON VENDOR:** Mickey and Robin, the manager were standing up near the door bragging about the fact that Cary Grant had been coming in for dinner quite regularly. Everyone was charmed by him. I'm standing there eavesdropping, and I say, "Guys, you know I can get Cary Grant to talk to me." Mickey just looks at me and walks away. A few nights later, I'm standing at the bar and Mickey walks over. "Okay Tom, there's Cary Grant in the alcove eating dinner, I'll wager a little bet with you." So I walked over to the alcove area, and I saw there was a guy that I sort of knew sitting in a booth across from Cary Grant, a guy named Don Buxbaum. He used to make slasher movies in Canada. I walked up to him with my back to Cary Grant, and I started talking to this guy Buxbaum, who didn't particularly like me. I said, "Hey Don, did you hear the news?" He looked up at me like, What the hell is this guy talking about? There's four guys in the booth eating steaks, and probably talking shop. I said, "The Dodgers traded Don Drysdale," the big pitcher at the time, to the Giants, who were the hated enemy of the Dodgers. And then I threw in some double-talk. All of a sudden I felt this tap on my shoulder, and there he was. It was all his real hair too. This was 1967, he was about sixty-two. And he says, "Who did you say they traded Don Drysdale to the Giants for?" And I said, "Are you talking to me?" He says, "Yes, yes, I'm talking to you." I looked over at Mickey and Robin who were standing back near the bus station, and I said, "See that, he's talking to me," and I walked away. I knew Cary Grant was a baseball fanatic.

**JOE EARLY, POET/WRITER:** What happened was that my crowd, mostly writers and the abstract expressionists, for various reasons, it seemed, were not social anymore. The death of the old Cedar was the death of that crowd. It never re-formed again around that place. So when Mickey opened Max's, it became the harbinger of the newer artists who came on the scene. Since I lived right across the street, as soon as it opened, I became a regular. I was living in this loft complex and

rebellion

I brought some friends from the complex over there, including Fielding Dawson. A small group of regular drinkers formed at the bar. There was about ten or twelve of us. Warren Finnerty, who acted in the movie *Cool Hand Luke* and several other movies, became part of our group.

**AL PACINO, ACTOR:** Warren Finnerty took me to Max's for my first time. That was before I had the money to hang out there.

**LYNN HARRITON, WAITRESS AT MAX'S:** The place had a pervasive sexual atmosphere. The minute I walked in, I would look my best. If I was a frazzled girl walking down the street, the instant I walked into that place, the energy had me. The atmosphere was completely tinged. I couldn't wait to get there. I hated leaving. You just couldn't get enough. I remember feeling how lucky I was. I felt like I was on top of the world. It was like a vacuum cleaner.

**JOHN FORD, FASHION PHOTOGRAPHER:** I lived at Max's once I discovered it. No place else in the world existed for me. It had something that doesn't happen now. I ultimately had to move closer to Max's. At the time I was paying $105 a month rent on Sixth Avenue. I was a photographer. I guess I was making fifty grand in about six months. I was really cooking, and I moved from $105 a month to $500 a month and spent $30,000 building this studio on Sixteenth Street so I could be in Max's every night of my life.

I would go to Europe for two weeks, shoot a campaign, come back from the airport, and stop at Max's before I went to my studio. There would be bomb scares, the police would show up and nobody would leave. A fire— the minute the firemen were gone, we'd come back in, straighten up and sit down with smoke and shit all over the place.

I used to cash checks in Max's for $3,000 or $4,000 like that. I mean cash! That's how much money was running around that place. A friend of mine, John Johnson, from Channel Seven, and I were in there one night getting totally ripped, and he said, "Why don't we go to Scandinavia for Christmas?" He had a Diner's Club card and I had a check for $1,500 in my pocket. So I cashed the check, we went to Kennedy, got on a plane, and went to Copenhagen. We got back on a Tuesday, four days later, and I went to the studio, not having slept or anything, shot a job, and went straight back to Max's.

Max's was one of the reasons I didn't like to leave New York. You didn't have to call anybody. It was like being in a living room. You just went there. And if you went there long enough, you had your own table. When I had my wolfhounds, I moved to the big round table in the front, but before that I used to be in the last table in the corner, just before the kitchen. In the course of the evening, fifty people would go by my table.

Michael Caine used to come in all the time and sit way back in the Warhol room, and Richard

★ **MAX'S KANSAS CITY**
213 Park Avenue South    CA 8-2080
(between 17th and 18th Streets)
     This is one of the most switched-on restaurants in Manhattan. There are waitresses in miniskirts and waiters with beards. Max's is a large, angular, two-level restaurant. At the moment it is wildly popular, and consequently there is at times a wait for tables. The service is a bit disorganized, but the simply grilled steaks and lobsters are good. The dishes are à la carte with luncheon entrees from about $1.10 for hamburger on a seeded roll to $3.25 for broiled filet mignon; dinner dishes from about $2.50 for broiled swordfish steak to $4.95 for boneless sirloin. *Cocktails, wines. The house wine ($2) served in a pichet, or pitcher, is dreadful. On Saturday and Sunday dinner is served from* 1 p.m.
AE  CB  DC

From Craig Claiborne, *The New York Times Guide to Dining Out in New York* (New York: Atheneum, 1968).

Harris used to come in and get shitfaced. Every director in the world used to come there. I used to be there all the time with models. I was a pretty bad boy at the time. That was the good old days when you could do stuff like that and get away with it, pre-AIDS, pre-herpes, pre-marriage.

**ED KOCH, FORMER MAYOR OF NEW YORK:** People who came there came from every walk of life, from college kids to punks to the literati and the idle rich, as well as some politicians like myself. In fact, Mickey offered to open my campaign for Congress in an unused space above the restaurant. I was delighted to accept the offer. And indeed the cheap rent combined with a good and inexpensive place for the campaign workers to have dinner, as well as to listen to occasional good music, probably contributed to the success of my campaign.

**HALSTON, FASHION DESIGNER:** Max's brought life into the neighborhood. It was a constant

rebellion

happening. Everybody used to get all dressed up and do mad things. We would go once every few weeks, looking like rich hippies, and take our corner banquette.

**PILAR CRESPI, FORMER MODEL/FASHION EDITOR:** I remember very clearly sitting down one night and thinking about Fellini—that Max's was Fellini, American Style.

**LAWRENCE WEINER, SCULPTOR:** Max's was the only place you could go and find out how you really stood in the world, because at any given moment there were people there from all over.

**LYNN EDELSON, MUSICIAN:** At Max's I got turned on to every sexual perversion that anybody could ever be into, every strange drug.

**IRA COHEN, POET/PHOTOGRAPHER:** Mickey was the captain of the *Good Ship Lollipop* of New York.

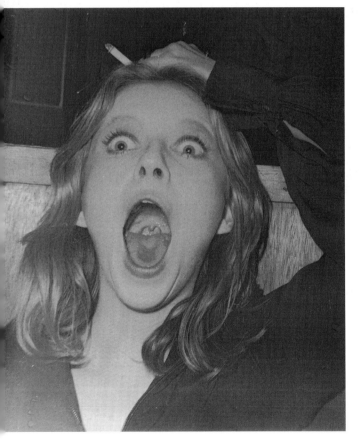

**Bebe Buell**
(photo by Anton Perich)

**OLIVIERO TOSCANI, FASHION PHOTOGRAPHER:** I was twenty when I won a Pan American photographic competition, and they flew me here. Max's was New York at the time. It was to me like an abstract painting, a place where you mix dreams and reality. It was so much an event. All the time Bob Dylan on the jukebox, "Knockin' on Heaven's Door." That song was very much Max's Kansas City.

I used to go there a lot with Antonio Lopez. My fifteen-year-old son saw some of the pictures and was very intrigued. He thought we were living in heaven. Paradise. Very difficult for people—the straight people—to understand that. They want to live a normal life. I wish my children had a place to go like that. Then, fashion was made; now fashion is followed.

**JOHN CHAMBERLAIN, SCULPTOR/PAINTER:** Everyone who went there had their own peculiarities, by just being there. It was a time and a place number, and a clubhouse hangout. It wasn't like restaurants and bars as we know them.

I had some great love affairs there, starting with Ultra Violet. Americans don't meet many people like her, very French. She wasn't very difficult to look at, either. I sort of liked all those Factory people of Andy's. Theirs was always the right shade of craziness. Like Viva, she tore the shirt off my back, because I wasn't paying enough attention to

high on

Oliviero Toscani and Donna Jordan (photo by Anton Perich)

her, or the right kind of attention. Andy would let all those people just hang out at the Factory, and Max's for a lot of people was like a bigger Factory.

**ROBERT POVLICH, PAINTER:** Mickey pulled together a scene that was the closest thing to what you could call a salon. It wasn't like walking into a bar for a shot. It was like a living room where you didn't know who you would see. That was the atmosphere he gave it. You got artists and

rebellion

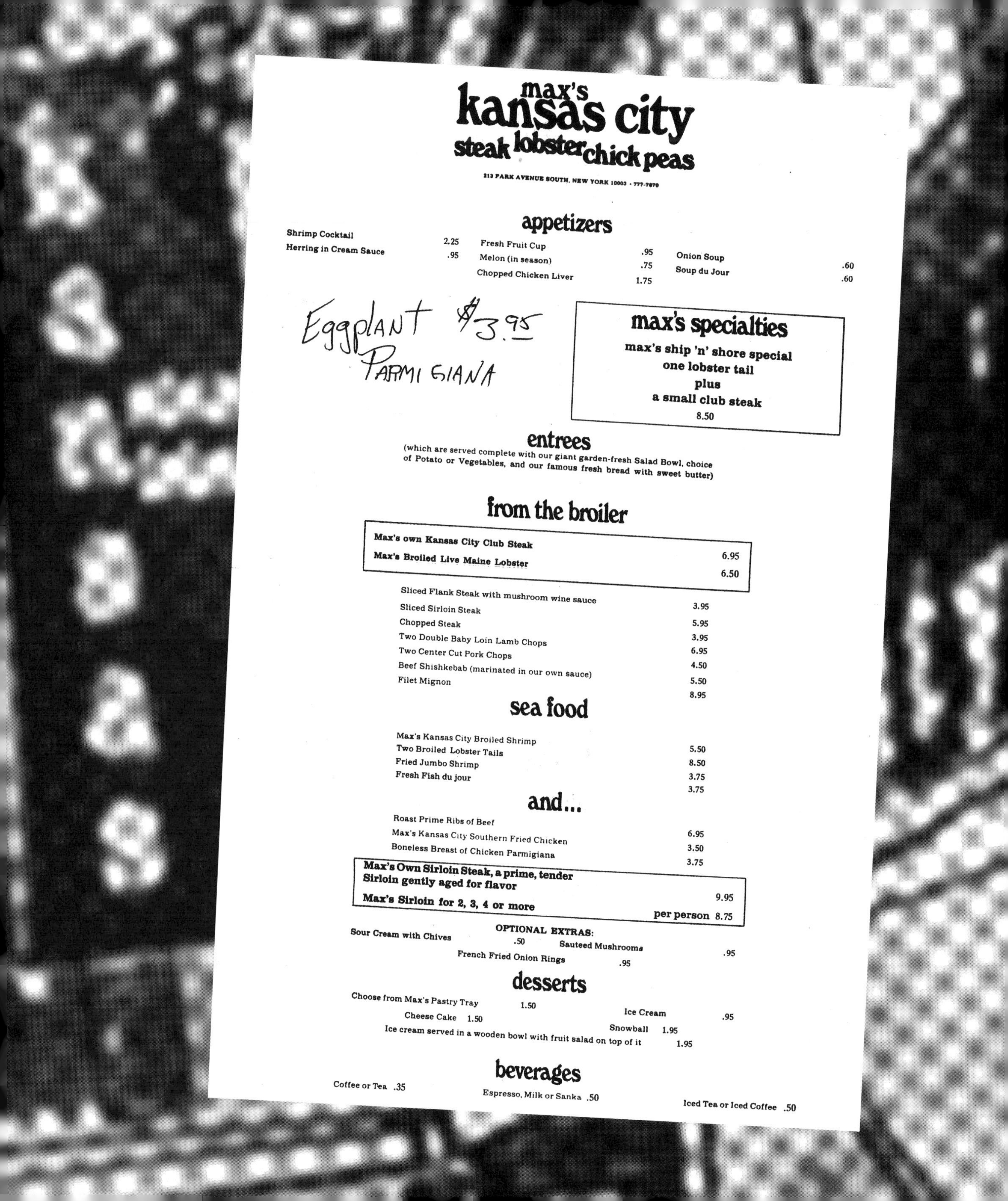

# max's
# kansas city
### steak lobster chick peas

213 PARK AVENUE SOUTH, NEW YORK 10003 · 777-7870

## appetizers

| | | | | | | |
|---|---|---|---|---|---|---|
| Shrimp Cocktail | 2.25 | Fresh Fruit Cup | | Onion Soup | | |
| Herring in Cream Sauce | .95 | Melon (in season) | .95 | Soup du Jour | | .60 |
| | | Chopped Chicken Liver | .75 | | | .60 |
| | | | 1.75 | | | |

*Eggplant $3.95 Parmigiana* (handwritten)

---

### max's specialties
**max's ship 'n' shore special**
one lobster tail
plus
a small club steak
8.50

---

## entrees
(which are served complete with our giant garden-fresh Salad Bowl, choice
of Potato or Vegetables, and our famous fresh bread with sweet butter)

## from the broiler

| | |
|---|---|
| **Max's own Kansas City Club Steak** | 6.95 |
| **Max's Broiled Live Maine Lobster** | 6.50 |

| | |
|---|---|
| Sliced Flank Steak with mushroom wine sauce | 3.95 |
| Sliced Sirloin Steak | 5.95 |
| Chopped Steak | 3.95 |
| Two Double Baby Loin Lamb Chops | 6.95 |
| Two Center Cut Pork Chops | 4.50 |
| Beef Shishkebab (marinated in our own sauce) | 5.50 |
| Filet Mignon | 8.95 |

## sea food

| | |
|---|---|
| Max's Kansas City Broiled Shrimp | 5.50 |
| Two Broiled Lobster Tails | 8.50 |
| Fried Jumbo Shrimp | 3.75 |
| Fresh Fish du jour | 3.75 |

## and...

| | |
|---|---|
| Roast Prime Ribs of Beef | 6.95 |
| Max's Kansas City Southern Fried Chicken | 3.50 |
| Boneless Breast of Chicken Parmigiana | 3.75 |

| | |
|---|---|
| **Max's Own Sirloin Steak, a prime, tender Sirloin gently aged for flavor** | 9.95 |
| **Max's Sirloin for 2, 3, 4 or more** | per person 8.75 |

**OPTIONAL EXTRAS:**

| | | | |
|---|---|---|---|
| Sour Cream with Chives | .50 | Sauteed Mushrooms | .95 |
| | French Fried Onion Rings | .95 | |

## desserts

| | | | |
|---|---|---|---|
| Choose from Max's Pastry Tray | 1.50 | Ice Cream | .95 |
| Cheese Cake | 1.50 | Snowball | 1.95 |
| Ice cream served in a wooden bowl with fruit salad on top of it | | | 1.95 |

## beverages

| | | |
|---|---|---|
| Coffee or Tea  .35 | Espresso, Milk or Sanka  .50 | Iced Tea or Iced Coffee  .50 |

# max's
# kansas city
## steak lobster chick peas

KANSAS CITY consists of 121,901 people in Kansas, and 475,539 people in Missouri. It is famous as a way-station when jazz was traveling up the river, and, earlier, as a way-station when cows were traveling into beef. Geographically it is located quite near the center of the United States, and is part of the Mid-West. Sociologically it is part of the Bible-Belt. It is probably not a very good place to eat (the steaks went to New York), or listen (the music went to Chicago), or live (the people went to ... MAX'S KANSAS CITY is named ... metropolis, and here, in sorrow ... in spend in the ... evening a ...

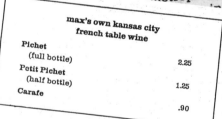

| max's own kansas city french table wine | |
|---|---|
| Pichet (full bottle) | 2.25 |
| Petit Pichet (half bottle) | 1.25 |
| Carafe | .90 |

## red

| BORDEAUX | Half Bottle | Bottle |
|---|---|---|
| **1. Medoc** Pierre Cartier et Fils | 1.75 | 3.25 |
| **2. St. Emilion** Pierre Cartier et Fils | 2.00 | 3.75 |

| BURGUNDY | | |
|---|---|---|
| **3. Beaujolais** Piat Pere et Fils | 1.75 | 3.00 |
| **4. Pommard** Piat Pere et Fils | 2.50 | 5.00 |

| RHONE | | |
|---|---|---|
| **5. Chateauneuf du Pape** Piat Pere et Fils | 2.25 | 4.00 |

| rosé | Half Bottle | Bottle |
|---|---|---|
| **6. Anjou Rosé** Domaine Emil Blanchard | 1.75 | 3.00 |

## white

| BURGUNDY | | |
|---|---|---|
| **7. Chablis** Piat Pere et Fils | 2.00 | 3.75 |
| **8. Pouilly Fuissé** Piat Pere et Fils | 2.00 | 3.75 |

| ALSACE | | |
|---|---|---|
| **9. Reisling** Domaine Henri | 1.50 | 3.00 |

## champagne

| | Half Bottle | Bottle |
|---|---|---|
| Pierre Cartier Brut N.V. | 4.00 | 8.00 |
| Taittinger Brut N.V. | 6.00 | 12.00 |

all of max's kansas city's wines are appellation contrôlée

**Alice Cooper** (photo by Anton Perich)

writers, and poets, a bunch of bohemians, sitting around bull-shitting, exchanging this and that, and you got some guy like Mel Brooks standing right behind them, and all of a sudden, you start attracting people from 57th Street, because that's now the place to be seen, because these people follow the artists. That's what happened.

**LARRY RIVERS, PAINTER/MUSICIAN:** One night I was in there and Jimmy Baldwin, who I knew from Paris centuries ago, was sitting at a table, and he's Jimmy Baldwin now. He's not some black guy in Europe, some gay who's trying to find his way and slowly his writing trickles into consciousness. He was now Jimmy Baldwin, a black spokesman practically, an older man, and he says, "Hi, Larry, sit down," acting gracious and friendly, and when I saw that, I thought, This is some kind of reincarnation of something that, maybe as a young artist, I dreamt what the Deux Magots in Paris was.

**BEBE BUELL, MODEL:** If I was upset or depressed I could always go to Max's to my family. Lou Reed was like Dad and Alice Cooper was like Dad. I don't know who Mom was.

**ALICE COOPER, ROCK MUSICIAN:** I was like a social vampire. I'd get up around seven P.M., watch TV, leave at around midnight and stay at Max's until the sun came up. I probably lived on chick peas and Black Russians. We were pretty much established at the time. I liked it there because all of my friends were there. Iggy was there, Bowie was there, and the Dolls. We were all in the same place so that was the place to be. Mickey used to always treat us right. He would make sure we had the right table, not that we knew what the right table was, but it was the great part about Max's.

**STUART LICHTENSTEIN, MANAGER OF MAX'S:** It was just a marvelous place to be in terms of being a single male at the time. It was the sixties, when everyone was wide open. It was a real major turning point in the United States for freedom, for abortion, for the pill, for ending the war in

high on

Vietnam. There were tremendous things at stake, and people were really squaring off. Everyone was always a fringe group everywhere else they went, but at Max's, the fringe group was the straights. Mickey had singlehandedly created a whole new underground counterculture scene. It changed the lives of just about everyone who gained entry. It was Mickey's topsy-turvy, upside-down world. The mainstays were the alternative-lifestyle people.

The lines were clearly drawn between "us" and "them" in the sixties, between the "freaks" and the "straights." Members of the counterculture usually were pretty identifiable to each other by the way they dressed and behaved. Men who wore long hair were clearly freaks. Other gender-bending effects like jewelry around the neck, earrings, bracelets, and flamboyant clothes, like blousy flowered shirts, sashes, embroidered bell-bottoms, velvet tunics, and colored sunglasses further differentiated the freaks from the straights, along with marijuana, LSD, speed, and other drugs.

By the early seventies, sportscasters, athletes, and other hardcore macho types were wearing long hair, so it no longer meant what it did in the sixties. Homogenization had taken place.

rebellion

Stella, Irregular Polygons, *Moutonboro II*, 1965

To understand Max's you gotta understand Mickey. Mickey was a nice Jewish boy from New Jersey who took his Cornell law degree and went into the restaurant business. He went from superstraight to ultra-hip, bartering food and booze for art with artists who weren't really known yet. His personal flight from the middle class reflects the essence of what happened in the sixties.

—Ronald Sukenick, author/educator

**MICKEY RUSKIN, OWNER AND PROPRIETOR:** I was practicing law and living uptown with Sharon, who later became my first wife. I read an article in the *Village Voice* that said, "Rent or Own Coffee Shop," and I made Sharon answer the ad. We ended up renting this coffee shop on East Tenth Street between Third and Fourth, next to all these little galleries. I was running the coffee shop at night and working during the day. At the time I had given up practicing law and was on the road to becoming a doctor. After a year of taking the pre-med courses and realizing I could get into medical school if I really wanted to, I turned around and decided that it was too ridiculous. I knew it wasn't going to solve my problems, so I went back to facing the reality of working at my father's law firm in New Jersey. In those days, you had to do what they call "clerk" for ten months before becoming a member of the bar. I had become a member of the bar in New York, but in New Jersey you had ten months of clerkship, so I had to work there during the day and run the business at night.

After about three months, I discovered that I was making enough to live on from the coffee shop, so I immediately gave up law. And from that point on, though I didn't consider myself a restaurateur,

in the beginning was mickey

I was in the business and wanted to stay. The first time I started communicating with the public was at the coffee shop, which was not much larger than my kitchen—really small, maybe ten by twenty feet—but it was like coming home. We called it, the Tenth Street Coffeehouse. I was the cook, pot washer, dishwasher, waiter, porter, everything, but it was fun. That was something I wasn't used to—I had never had fun before. And I wasn't thinking at the time that I wanted a big place or this or that.

I think the whole reason I had done this coffee shop was because I had wanted to go to Greenwich Village; I had never been there. I really think that I had wanted to be a part of the Village, and that was the only way I could do it. I had actually been to the Village maybe three times before that, but I had no conception of what it was all about. I just wanted to be involved with creative people, and I knew that I had to change my environment somehow. Most people go to the Village and just get lost, just drift into the Village and start hanging out. Well, whether it was shyness or whatever, I'd just never been able to do that. So I was just hanging uptown with all the rising young lawyers and advertising execs until I owned the coffee shop. Then the poets started having their poetry readings there and that clicked.

Within three months after we got the readings going, the place became really too small for the crowds. Howard brought around another guy who was interested in opening a coffeehouse, so together, we opened a coffeehouse on East Seventh Street called Les Deux Megots. *Megots* means "cigarette butts" in French. I liked the humor in the meaning by changing a letter in the word and not copying Les Deux Magots in Paris. The Paradox restaurant opened in the same spot much later on. Allan and Don Katzman were two of the people who read there, and Allan founded the *East Village Other*. People like Edward Gorham, who lived out in Arizona, and LeRoi Jones. I don't know if LeRoi ever read there, but he used to come around. Denise Levertov, Red Barrett, Louis Zakowski, and Jerry Rothenberg, who's become known as a translator, he translated *The Deputy* from German—all read there. Almost all of the New York Poets, with the possible exception of Allen Ginsberg, read at the coffeehouse.

**LAWRENCE WEINER, ARTIST/SCULPTOR:** Les Deux Megots was strictly a coffee shop, less MacDougal Street, more grungy. It was a combination of the Figaro and Slugs, a coffee shop with a bar mentality. Those were the days when you would walk to the bar and have a couple of drinks, and go to a coffee shop and sit around for a while and then go to the Figaro and have another cup of coffee and make it from the San Remo all the way over to Avenue B. That was your evening out, it was almost your duty.

A lot of the best people were around. All the people around Ginsberg and all the people around Burroughs. Plus, the poetry people and a lot of political people, and the Al Goldstein types from *Screw* magazine, and people like that.

**NAT FINKELSTEIN, PHOTOGRAPHER:** I used to go to the Deux Megots. A film photographer named Mario Joran and I used to hang out. His brother was Mickey's partner in the joint. It wasn't as much an artist hangout as it was poets and hustlers. Those were the early days of grass dealing, and hash dealing, and that was where we went to meet.

**MICKEY RUSKIN:** The first or second waitress that I had hired there was a little girl from San Francisco. One day she brought around her boyfriend and said, "Mickey can you cash this check from the Gaslight for him, he can't cash it anywhere. This is my boyfriend, Bob Dylan, he's going to be a great singer someday." Her name was Averil Weber. They later drove cross-country on his motorcycle, and they got about halfway there when he split from her or she split from him. Then at Deux Megots one of my waitresses used to bring her boyfriend Terry around and told me what a great singer he was going to be, and I thought he was just a nice Jewish boy from Brooklyn. It never occurred to me that he would make it. That was Jesse Colin Young.

The business was going well, but I didn't get along with my partner at all. We had many differences. We got into a fight over who would buy who out, and fortunately he wound up finding somebody to buy me out. I probably would have died there otherwise. Meanwhile, this other guy who I had known from my hometown started popping up. His parents had written to him from Chicago where they were living at that time: "Too bad about poor Mickey Ruskin being a beatnik in Greenwich Village." Their son Bobby figured he had always been the black sheep of the family and thought he should look me up. He started talking to me about opening a jazz club because he was really into jazz. We went looking for a space together, and found an available space in a good location, and we opened the Ninth Circle at 139 West Tenth Street.

**BOB KRIVITT, MICKEY'S PARTNER IN THE NINTH CIRCLE AND THE ANNEX:** Mickey and I eventually opened the Annex on the Lower East Side for the overflow of business. Plus our friends and customers had a place to hang out both in the East Village and the West Village.

**MICKEY RUSKIN:** We ran the Annex for about three months when I sold out both the Annex and the Circle to Bob for a very, very reasonable price, much less than he expected. It was all very friendly and I took off to Europe for a year. I gave him a no-competition clause in the Village, which meant that I could not open another place in the Village for two years. The Village was defined very simply by the Sixth Precinct. When I came back a year later, I asked Bobby if I could buy my way out of the clause. He said no, so I had to look for another space.

A space was available at 213 Park Avenue South between Seventeenth and Eighteenth. It had been run by two old men. The guy who owned it was kind of amazing....He opened the place as a pharmacy and immediately saw that it should be a restaurant. So he made it into a restaurant called The Southern. He eventually sold it to someone who subsequently went broke and he was asked to take it back. He was getting old and didn't want the responsibility, so I got it for practically no cash down, and a very-long-term, very reasonable lease.

I had brought my artist friend Neil Williams over, to ask his opinion. Neil felt it was a natural.

**Neil Williams** (photo by Anton Perich)

He was sort of my guru, so that was the clincher. I took the space. I took over on December 6, 1965. The day I got my license, I just took over his business, which was strictly daytime, though we would stay open till eight or nine at night. Later at night we'd work on reconstructing it, getting it into the shape we wanted.

It was two floors that had limitless possibilities, but I was dubious of the location. As a matter of fact, I was afraid it would fail. I couldn't imagine having a place anywhere but the Village. As we were working on getting it into shape, Neil would drop in, along with several other artists I knew: Larry Bell, Larry Poons, Larry Zox, who lived across the street, Donald Judd, and Frosty Myers, who was one of my close friends.

**FROSTY MYERS, SCULPTOR:** Neil basically designed the layout of Max's on a napkin. He could just sit down, and within moments say the obvious: The bar goes here, the mirror goes there, let's make the booths red, let's paint this color.

**ROBERT POVLICH, PAINTER:** I used to go to the Cedar Bar before Max's opened. So I'm sitting at the bar talking to Tex, who used to hang around the Ninth Circle. He introduces this guy to me as Mickey Ruskin. This Mickey guy buys us both a beer.... Tex says to me, "Look, Povlich, this guy's opening a bar up the street." And Mickey says, "I've heard about you, and I'd appreciate your dropping by." Now, I've never had a bar owner ask me to drop by his bar. If anything, I was being thrown out most of the time....So I go up to this guy Mickey's place on Park Avenue South. Mickey sees me, comes over and says to me, "Well, what do you think?" I look at him and I say, "The men's room is too small. See where the urinal is? You can hardly get your shoulders in there, because the shithouse is there, and here's the urinal, and here's the partition, and you're not going to make it unless you move it." And do you know what that son of a bitch did? Damned if he didn't move it.

**JOEL OPPENHEIMER, WRITER:** I knew Mickey back in his coffeehouse days, when he had the Tenth Street Coffeehouse, and the Deux Megots, but it wasn't till the Cedar Bar closed temporarily, and drove us all out into the street, that I began drinking at the Ninth Circle, and found

high on

Mickey as a friend. Then he left there and we stayed friends. So it was a year or so later that he called me up, and asked me over to his house for dinner, along with Neil Williams. We had steak, salad, potato, and bread. After dinner, he asked us what we thought of the steak, the salad, the potato, and the bread. We said it was great. He tells me he is opening a new joint, and this is what he is planning to serve, and asked did I have any ideas for a name. When I was a kid, all the steak-houses had Kansas City on the menu because the best steak was Kansas City–cut, so I thought it should be "something Kansas City."

A lot of people thought that Max's came to mind because of Max Finstein, a musician/poet from Boston, who met me through my contemporary, Robert Creeley, and we ran together. He became my first wife's second husband. So people say that after me and my first wife broke up, she and Max got together and ran off to Mexico, that I was paying homage to Max, but that's not so. If you're looking for an M name and you want a restaurant kind of thing, Max's comes to mind. Wouldn't you eat at a place called Max's? The next day, Mickey called and said, "Look, Joel, I looked through the telephone book, and there's a Max's this and a Max's that." And I said, "Mickey, believe me, it's Max's Kansas City." Two days later, he called back again and said, "I don't know why, but I mentioned the name to some people, and they all loved it."

So despite Mickey's misgivings about my choice, Max's Kansas City was born. Then he said, "Gee, it would be nice if we had some gimmick I could serve at the bar, like the peanuts at the Ninth Circle." And I said, "Chick peas," thinking of the *bupkes* that my mother served that were soaked and boiled. Mickey didn't know from *bupkes*, which is also an idiom that means "nothing," so not knowing from *bupkes*, he bought the chick peas, and put them out dry. What do the goyim know? They thought it was wonderful, breaking their teeth on them. I mentioned it to Mickey, but he said, "Fuck 'em, if they can't take a joke, fuck 'em!"

**LARRY ZOX, PAINTER:** While Max's was being renovated, I was going over and testing the steaks. We were aging the steaks and drinking our brains out. Putting meat downstairs in a cooler and letting it age, trying different cuts. Some of it was terrible....All the activity from construction, which usually would bother most customers, was great, because everybody had so many ideas about what to do while Mickey was constructing it. We were part of its creation....Mickey talked to me about putting a piece of my art up. I said, "Well, are you buying it?"

Mickey issued "Max's charge cards" to his artist friends and allowed them (many unknown at the time) to barter artworks for food and drink. This enabled them to wine and dine the art dealers and critics in style when often they "didn't have a pot to pee in." Max's served as an art gallery as well as a meeting place. It became an extension of the art market. Mickey cashed checks, loaned money, and offered advice. He even drove people home in the Max's van, and put them to bed when they downed a few too many of who-knows-what. There were notoriously ridiculous bar tabs that reached into the tens of thousands of dollars. One of the bartenders, Joe Bird, recalls, "Mickey told all the bartenders not to cash this one son of a bitch's checks, because they always bounced. So the guy comes in one afternoon, walks up to the bar, hands me a check initialed by Mickey and says, "Mickey says to cash this." I look at it, go over to Mickey and say, "Hey, you told us not to cash this guy's checks and you initialed it, what's up?" Mickey looks up, looks over at the guy, and says, "Yeah, well, it's okay, he told me it would bounce this time."

**LAWRENCE WEINER:** Mickey was this lawyer who was looking for an alternative lifestyle. He was like someone on one of those *Hill Street Blues* shows. One half of him is trying to be Michael and the other half is trying to be Mickey Ruskin. He was a very straight guy. He didn't drink, didn't do any drugs. He was totally perplexed by people doing drugs around him. He had this middle-class Jewish thing about being fascinated by the sort of idiot-savant mentality which comes from drinking, when confronted by somebody like John Chamberlain or Neil Williams, who literally were drinkers, and so were all these other people from Dillons and the Cedar Bar days. He was astounded. This to him was some sort of nirvana. He was able to be around people spouting things that in the world he had come from, they would never say out loud, they would never voice. Remember, there was a celebratory aspect. It was against society, this whole network. And that's what attracted Mickey. It was basically celebratory, because it was a carryover from the abstract expressionists, where all that self-reflection, that angst, was a celebration, because it was the first time that American males were being allowed to deal with that part of their psyche that Europeans were always able to do, and that's what fascinated Mickey. That's what makes the Beats so interesting. That's what makes Ginsberg such an interesting poet. It was the first time these people could deal with the fact that they had insecurities, that they really didn't understand their psyche.

**MICKEY RUSKIN:** The major thing that I did was build the alcove area. I put in new air conditioning, but that came later. Neil came up with the idea for Formica panels behind the bar. They were built by Gil Henderson. Then Neil made arrangements to give me pieces from Donald Judd, Larry Zox, Dan Flavin, and John Chamberlain, all in trade for tabs. Putting the art on the wall was Neil's idea; trading it was about the only way I could afford it. It was not part of the grand plan, but it turned out to be one of those fantastic coincidences. It was potentially meant to bring in business, but I mainly put up the art because I liked the artists. I never judged art by anything except my feeling for the artist.

**JOHN CHAMBERLAIN:** I gave a sculpture to Mickey, sort of in exchange for my tab. At first he put it about mid-bar, by the alcove, so the waitresses had to go around it. I remember all the waitresses used to snag their stockings on it so Mickey had to move it. Then I started working in another medium—foam rubber. He had other people's art on the walls. It wasn't a matter of having an exhibition or anything; it was just a room with this stuff in it. It was a hangout.

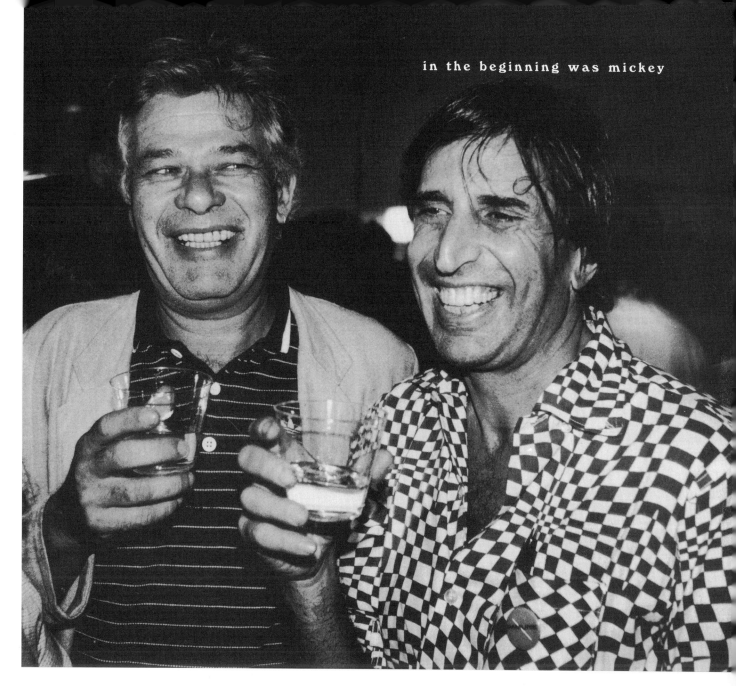

Neil Williams, Frosty Myers, and myself were the first freebies at Max's. It wasn't really free, it was a tab. I included the tip and Mickey said, "No, you have to tip yourself." At the time I wasn't making any money...I made about $500 a month in those days, and anything I could scrounge up in a freebie at the bar, which isn't bad income. But when there is that much whiskey and all you have to do is sign for it—well, it certainly isn't good for your health.

**John Chamberlain and Mickey Ruskin**
(photo courtesy of Ten Coconut Photo, Inc.)

•

rebellion

**GERALD LAING, ARTIST:** I had also met Mickey at the Ninth Circle, and I was one of the handful of artists who Mickey invited to trade works of art for food, even before work on Max's was completed and the restaurant opened. In all, I gave him two pieces, and for that I received $8,000 in credit, a very large sum to spend in a restaurant in 1966. Consequently, my diet there was luxurious—lobster and champagne was the norm. It also made it extremely difficult to eat at any other restaurant in New York, and if we did, the result was inevitably disappointing, for no other place had the drama, excitement, and sense of purpose that Max's did.

**LARRY POONS, PAINTER:** The night that Max's opened in December of 1965, only a few people showed up. John Chamberlain and Neil Williams asked me to come with them to the opening of Max's, which was a huge place whose size was emphasized by the fact that nobody had shown up. We got there at about four-thirty in the afternoon and by seven Mickey was pacing back and forth. When he gets nervous, he really gets nervous, and he was walking around like a slow-motion skiing accident. Finally we hit on the idea for the three of us to go from booth to booth, ordering a drink at each one—we'd already had quite a bit to drink by then—to give Mickey the illusion of one hundred glowing afterimages at all of his tables.

**LAWRENCE WEINER:** One of the keys to success in running a restaurant or bar is to attract two people: artists, because artists drink, usually right to their income whether they're poor or rich, and fashion models. Along with the fashion models you have to put up with the photographers, who have lots and lots of money. And they spend money on the stuff that a bar makes money on.

**ROBERT POVLICH:** Mickey was the first guy to give artists credit. He'd give the artists tabs and they would give Mickey art. He was also the first to buy from the artists. He had one of the best art collections: Stella, Warhol, Carl Andre, Flavin, Chamberlain—he had them all—and Neil Williams was the most important one in steering him to the ones to buy. Mickey said, "Look, I'm going to give you credit here and you can have dinner." Once you attract those people, all the other people come because they want to be seen sitting with all these famous artists. Then he got the actor crowd, the writers—it was so fast. A whole group of young artists had broken away from the abstract expressionists. Hard-edge had come in and all of a sudden a lot of young artists were making a hell of a lot of money. And there were a lot of young people making a hell of a lot of money on the stock market and they wanted to be socially acceptable, so they got involved in the art scene and they started buying paintings.

**MICKEY RUSKIN:** What I didn't know when I opened Max's was that almost every major fashion photographer in New York had a studio within five blocks of the place. Tex, my carpenter who was building for me at night, was working for a photographer named Jimmy Moore during the day. Jimmy, at the time, was one of the hottest photographers. I'll never forget that one day, this group of what looked like thirteen-year-olds walked in and I was really nervous. I had no idea who they were. They all looked so young I was ready to go over and card them. Then Tex walks in behind them and calls me over and says, "Mickey, I want you to meet Jimmy Moore." After Jimmy, Jerry Schatzberg and Faye Dunaway started coming in, then Jerry Czemberg, Jerry Salvati, Chris von Wagenheim, just a whole bunch of them....Meanwhile, the night business started growing even before I had the grand-opening party on January 15, 1966. I don't remember sending out invitations to Max's big opening. I kind of recall handing out invitations, and the rest was word of mouth. I must have had 1,500 to 2,000 people come through the place. From that night on, it just took off like a shot.

**TOM O'DONNELL:** I walked into the grand opening on January 15, looked around, and said, "This will never last." The scene was always from the San Remo, to the Cedar, to Dillon's, to the Ninth Circle, to the new Cedar, which never really caught on.

**RON LANDFIELD, PAINTER:** A lot of people I knew were at the opening: Michael Steiner; Peter Weinberg, who was a poet and an old friend from Berkeley; Teddy Bernstein, who introduced me to Brice Marden and Bobby Neuwirth, both of whom Teddy knew from Boston; Tex Wray; Peter Young, the painter, who Michael Steiner introduced me to and who was the ex of Twyla Tharp. The opening was the most incredible party of hip, wild, and really artistic people who were famous or about to become famous, who were about to explode and create the sixties.

**JOHN CHAMBERLAIN:** It seems that if you need something, it's supposed to show up—and that's what Mickey did: he opened a need and everybody showed. Mickey was a Toots Shor of this particular audience at the time when the audience needed a Toots Shor. He was an eccentric himself, whether it was the way he dressed or the way his hair was combed. He was one of the first people to stand at the door and cast his own audience. It was his living room and he had in who he wanted. From the opening on, Max's was always packed, except maybe around eleven in the morning, which was always a good time for cognac and coffee.

(photo by Fred Lombardi)

rebellion

Marisol, *Dinner Date*, 1963. Photo by John D. Schiff

# the door

One of the things that made Max's unique, was that once you gained entry you were free to do your own thing. It was similar to a clubhouse where there were not a lot of rules. Mickey, who looked like someone a club owner might want to kick out, determined customer's fates. He sensed the "right" people intuitively, and eighty percent of the time he was right on the money. And, of course, there was that twenty percent. A rule of thumb was that he would turn away the straightest-looking people, while giving the nod to questionable sorts.

● ● ●

**JULIAN SCHNABEL, PAINTER:** Mickey would stand at the door picking his nose and the people he let in. He had great style. A broken silver tooth added to his mystique. I admired him.

●

**Mickey Ruskin in cowboy hat**
(photo by Anton Perich)

**PATSY CUMMINGS, WAITRESS:** Of anyone I've ever seen on the door, Mickey had the most uncanny way of judging people who were not particularly famous. He didn't judge for potential. Maybe they didn't look like an artist or something, but he had a way of saying a couple words to them, and making a judgment whether this was an interesting person to come in and socialize or not. And he kept this great mix. He did also let kind of touristy people come in too. The mixture of all kinds of bums, drug dealers, speed freaks, middle-class people, family people, animals, and artists. It was great. It was amazing that with all those crazy people he didn't get punched out or sued a million times. He used to stand up to Tiny of the Hell's Angels. He'd talk them down. It's amazing the people he talked out of that place.

**LARRY RIVERS, PAINTER:** Mickey was one of the first to have a doorman at the place to turn away people. At first he didn't let in gays. He didn't want the place to become a fag bar, I swear it. Certain times, not all the time, he did choose. The ones he knew, yes. But he didn't want it to be a gay pickup bar. He didn't want it to be Eighth Street.

**JOHN FORD:** I used to go to a place called the Limelight on Seventh Avenue South and there was the guy from a radio talk show who started being in there on Saturday nights. So us regulars had no place to go. I had known about Max's, because I had known about Mickey since I was a kid, when he had that joint called Deux Megots. That's when I first started going to the Village, when I was fourteen. I was living in Brooklyn and would commute to the Village—who the hell wanted to live in Bedford-Stuyvesant? Then, Mickey had the Ninth Circle and a lot of people I know used to hang out in there, because it was just around the corner from the Limelight.

One night I decided that if I'm going to lose Saturdays at the Limelight, I'm going to find somewhere new to go, so I went over to Max's. It wasn't that good when I first went, but a couple months later I went back again and the place was transformed. They got the velvet rope and Mickey standing around sayin', You can come in, you can't. Everyone thought the guys at Studio 54 started that shit, but it was Mickey who did. I went in, I don't know how, and man, it was great. Anyway, after I had been there a few nights and there weren't many black people coming to the place, so I was pretty conspicuous, Mickey said something like how he didn't want me ruining his place like I did

high on

the Limelight. He wasn't teasing; it was very strange. I think I told him, "Fuck you," and he never said another word. I was a Max's person.

**MICKEY RUSKIN:** The one thing I've always been good at is control. I can sit outside or on the rail and without moving know when I have control and when I don't, knowing who to watch and who not to watch. When I worked the door it was even easier because I could screen people as they came in. I'm a master at it. Just watching who's where and who's mixing.

Fabrizio, one of the night managers, was working the door and this group was walking down the street. I was standing with Fabrizio outside and he says, "Can I help you?" And this guy slams him in the mouth and they walk on in and sit down at a table. I was standing there stunned for a minute, and someone says to me, "Mickey, that's Peter O'Toole." So I'm standing there like a schmuck and I suddenly realized, "What the fuck difference does it make who this guy is? I mean, this guy just whacked my man and had absolutely no reason to do it, and I'm not going to let him get away with this shit." So I walked over to the table and said, "I'm sorry, I'm not serving you. Mr. O'Toole whacked my employee for no reason at all." They got up and left.

**FABRIZIO, MANAGER, MAX'S/LEVINE'S:** I was up front, and I always had a little camera, because I had been helping rep Izzy Valaris, the French fashion photographer a few hours in the morning. I was taking pictures across the street, and as I was doing that Peter O'Toole and a couple ladies came in and they put their hands on the lens, and we got into a tussle, then Peter O'Toole punched me. The two girls, I guess they were dykes or something, they held me down and he punched me. That really upset Mickey, so he threw them out.

**ROBERT POVLICH:** Jack Lemmon came up to the door one night while Mickey's sitting up front by the cigarette machine, picking his nose as usual. Mickey took one look at Jack Lemmon and says, "Couples only." So Lemmon goes back to his limo which is double-parked and takes off. I say to Mickey, "You know who you turned away? That was Jack Lemmon." Mickey said, "I don't care, he looked like a short Jew to me." And went back to picking his nose.

**MICKEY RUSKIN:** I see this kid come in one night with this black chick, and I immediately give them this little table in the corner somewhere. Then one of the managers comes over to me and says, "Mickey, that's Brian Jones." I wasn't even sure who Brian Jones was.

**HOWARD SMITH, JOURNALIST/FILMMAKER:** Yoko called me from Canada. I had known her from the early days of my column, because I had written her up a lot, before she ever knew what a Beatle was. She didn't trust many people, but she figured she could like me, because I liked her. I didn't like her when I wrote her up, but she called me from Canada and said I could come up and do a long interview with John.

rebellion

I met John, and we did this long interview. We more or less hit it off, and Yoko was instantly trying to control everything. She traded off with me. I could get this interview if I came up there and told John how great New York was. She was trying to convince John to move to New York. John, in his paranoia, was afraid to come to New York, because everybody would think he was nothing. And if he did come, he wanted to be on the art scene.

I did, in fact, think New York was the place for him. So I told him that, and a few months later, I got a call that they were coming. Yoko asked me to set up some things for them to do. So, I went down to Max's to speak to Mickey. He said, "Fine!" as if nothing was special. I had to explain to him that the Beatles were different from normal famous people. People went crazy over the Beatles if not handled well.

I thought that the alcove would be the best section to sit in, because it was raised, yet secluded. They could see, they could be seen, yet it was hard to get to them. So, I set it up with Mickey, and he wasn't to tell anybody. Now, Mickey didn't reserve booths, but this night he actually reserved a booth for us. He was as excited as Mickey gets about a musician. De Kooning would have been a different story, because he didn't regard the artists as a flash in the pan, as he did musicians.

So we come in, and they are really recognizable, but the Max's crowd is fairly cool. It went smoothly, and according to Yoko, this was one of the key factors that convinced John that New York was okay, that he could hang out at the very center of where everything was happening, and everything would be okay.

**DORY WEINER, DISCO DJ/DOOR LADY:** Mickey told us that John Lennon and Yoko Ono were coming for dinner, that they made a reservation, and Frosty and I were with Brigid Berlin. We were sitting across from them, me, Frosty, Brigid, Bob Feiden, and we all crashed their table. They were having a nice quiet dinner. It was like one of their first times there, and we just like barged in. They really didn't want us sitting there, it was very embarrassing.

**GAIL MUTRIX, MAX'S REGULAR, FRIEND OF MICKEY'S:** I was coming into Max's one night with Sharon, Mickey's wife. We were standing behind these two guys at the door. Mickey looked them over and said, "Couples only." They immediately turned to us and said, "We're with them." Mickey let them in just for being clever.

**ED TISCH, CAB DRIVER:** I think the first time I felt I really belonged at Max's is when I was seeing this girl Judy; she was a real hippy. She had given me some beads which I wore religiously. I liked the way hippies dressed. They looked innocent and wholesome. We went out to Max's on a Saturday night, and the line was out the door and up the block. Judy says to me, "I'm too hungry, I don't want to wait." I told her I'd go find out how long the wait will be. So we walk up to the door and Mickey's standing there, took one look at us, his face lit up with a big smile, and he beckoned us into the place.

**MICHAEL POLLARD, ACTOR:** I was out in California working on *Bonnie and Clyde* in 1966, and I heard about Max's. When *Bonnie and Clyde* opened, I went to New York to live. I was going to Max's to meet Warren Beatty. There was a line outside, but my wife and I were let in. We were in there waiting and waiting, but no Warren. We couldn't understand what had happened to him. Finally he shows up. When I asked him what happened he said, "I couldn't get in. I had a suit and tie on." He had to go back to the hotel and change.

**DAN CHRISTENSEN, PAINTER:** There was a time I was sitting with Mickey up on the rail up front next to the cigarette machine and he refused entry to this guy in a tie and a suit. The guy was insulted and says to Mickey, "You're Max? Well, this is outrageous what's going on here?" Mickey just looks at him and burps right in his face. It was awful. That's when I started calling him Mr. Personality.

**STUART LICHTENSTEIN, MAX'S MANAGER:** Max's was pretty strange, because if you had a tie or a jacket on, your odds were pretty good that you wouldn't get in the door. We had a very distinct problem in that area because of the type of place Max's was. It was a hotbed of the sixties and you had a lot of political activists, you had a lot of long hair, and we were right on Union Square where there were a lot of union meetings. You had to be very careful to keep out union members, who would always look for a bar after a meeting. If union members got stuck there too late, there would always be trouble. It was really an alternative-lifestyle place.

**PHILIP LOCASCIO, BUSBOY/FLOOR PERSON:** Mickey didn't want Patti Smith in at first because she looked too grungy. There was still that very affluent clientele that ate in front and along the side, like Visconti, Fellini, Antonioni, and that was a very sophisticated movie crowd. They enjoyed the costumes that everybody wore, but Mickey still didn't want anything scrungy around. He had to appeal to these people's sensibilities. They like to look at it, but they didn't want to be terrorized by it. That also happened the first night Janis Joplin came to the door. Big Brother had just come in, they were staying at the Chelsea. I was standing at the bar with Mickey and Stuart or Robin was behind me, and all Mickey saw was the first door open of double doors, and then when the second door opened, this girl was standing there with straggly hair, ugly as sin, coming in, and Mickey said, "I don't want that person in here, tell her you have to dress or it's reservations only." I got up close to her, and I went back to Mickey and said, "Mickey, that's Janis Joplin." He said, "Then tell her to go home and take a bath." Eventually she did get in that night. She came back later with the band.

**JEFFREY NICKORA, MAX'S CASHIER:** When they were shooting the movie [*April Fools*] with Catherine Deneuve and Myrna Loy, Deneuve came in with two other actresses, and Mickey or Stuart put them upstairs where no one could see them. Deneuve was painted and so-o-o blonde that she looked like a hooker. Mickey thought they were three Park Avenue hookers.

The only time I saw Mickey really impressed by anybody was when Henry Morgan came in, and Mickey flipped out. He was one of Mickey's boyhood heroes, a radio personality.

**TOM O'DONNELL, BALLOON VENDOR:** Mickey would get this sly, secret smile over his face when he would tell real pompous straight people, "I'm sorry, but it's just the bar tonight, there's no room in the back." And they'd get bummed out seeing what looked to them like tramps getting in. A lawyer would be standing there and Eric Emerson or some engaging creation with a ripped shirt and torn dungarees would say, "Hey, Mickey," and Mickey would lift the rope and say, "Go ahead," while the lawyer stood and watched.

**BOB RUSSELL, MAX'S BOUNCER:** I lived in Boston and I knew this girl Ruth Buxton; she was a cashier at Max's. She was a friend of several Boston people, and that was their connection somehow to Lou Reed. I came down to visit, it was 1966, and I was sort of thinking about working in New York. I came in one night to see Ruthie, and I was sitting at the bar near the cashier's booth. I said to Ruthie, "Are there any jobs available here?" "Well, I don't know," she said, "but the owner is around, and he'll talk to you."

So I was sitting waiting for the owner of Max's to show himself. I'm sitting next to this goofy-looking guy with black pants, black shoes, red socks, and it was Mickey. I had been sitting there talking to him, and I didn't even know it was the guy I had been waiting for. Ruthie introduced me, and I told him I was looking for a job, and he said, "Have you ever been in a fight?" And I said, "No, I've never been in a fight in my life." He said, "Good, you're the bouncer." His theory was that people who like to fight, get into fights. Since I spent so much time avoiding them, I'd probably be a good candidate. I think I was the first doorman Mickey hired.

**CAROL WILBOURN, AKA PIXIE, MAX'S REGULAR AND FRIEND OF MICKEY'S:** Bob Russell fit in immediately. We adored him with his Gucci loafers and that preppie look. When he worked the door, my sister Gail and I would sit down and talk to him forever.

**BILLY, AKA FUDGE, MAX'S REGULAR:** When I first met Bob Russell he'd get dressed up in the costumes. For a while he dressed up as a priest.

Anytime there was a full moon Mickey often felt that Bob Russell and Stuart weren't quite big enough or heavy enough, so he would call me to come over to be the bouncer. It always got crazy on the full moon. One time I had to turn away a six-foot-four African gentleman, and that was a little tense.

**ABIGAIL ROSEN, MAX'S FIRST DOOR LADY:** At first Mickey hired me as the coat-check girl, but it was on the second floor and we were schlepping coats from downstairs to upstairs, and taking them back down when the people wanted to leave. It was not a good plan, besides which people would go up and steal coats. So we abandoned the whole idea and I became the door lady with Bob Russell. The embarrassing times were when Mickey asked us to kick somebody out. The philosophy behind it was that no one would beat on or abuse a woman.

I was asked one night to kick Stanley Kubrick out. He was drunk and obnoxious and neither Mickey or I knew who he was. I said, "Sir, I think it's time for you to leave now, you're not going to be happy here." And he left. Then Mickey found out the next day who we had kicked out, and he yelled at me for not recognizing him. "That's why I have you here," he said, "you're supposed to know who these people are."

The Elaine's crowd came on Monday nights from uptown when Elaine's was closed. Then you would get the mixture of uptown and downtown.

**SHARON POWERS, CASHIER/DOOR LADY:** Mickey had this extraordinary ability to suss people out, everybody who walked in. Maybe it was his style. He'd look away, look at the ceiling, but he knew them down to their toenails.

**BOB RUSSELL:** Dorothy Dean started working the door at one point. She started as sort of an assistant when I was working the door upstairs. She went to Radcliffe. I met her in Boston. There were a whole bunch of people that came to New York from Harvard at the same time that Dorothy did. All those people through Andy were hanging out in the back room. Dorothy was very slight with harlequin glasses, and her purse was half the size she was. She had worked for several magazines, but she drank too much and she was incredibly bitchy. Her obsession was with gay men. She had this one man who she was completely in love with. She used to call him the Sugar Plum Fairy. Lou Reed refers to him in his song, "Take a Walk on the Wild Side." She was often found in leather bars in the West Village in pursuit of the Sugar Plum Fairy. That was her love, and then Lou Reed became the focus of her life.

Mickey didn't like black guys at the bar hitting on white women. He wanted to get rid of these two guys, so he sent Dorothy Dean to do the job. After agitating with them for a while, she told them to leave, that they were 86ed. "First of all, my name's not Yo. Secondly, I'm not your sister, and thirdly black is not beautiful, it is pathetic, get out." And they left.

Sugar Plum Fairy, left, with Dorothy Dean (photo by Billy Name)

rebellion

**Dorothy Dean and Jackie Curtis**
(photo by Anton Perich)

**ALICE WEINER, WAITRESS:** There was this little girl named Ronnie that Mickey hired. She was about four feet tall. She started out at the cash register, and then became the bouncer. Mickey thought her height and her sex would deter anybody from messing with her. She'd sit on this high chair at the door and bounce people out.

**DEBBIE ROSS, WAITRESS:** Everybody said, "Mickey, what the fuck are you putting that little girl on the door for, you've got to be crazy." But Mickey psychologically knew people. He said, "No one is going to touch this little girl. No one will give her a hard time. She'll be able to kick people out." She told Lynda Bird Johnson or one of those girls that she had to sit upstairs. And she said, "No, I'm the President's daughter." And Ronnie said, "Well, there are no tables down here, you'll have to sit upstairs."

Another thing Mickey did was to take bar stools away so that people would not be too comfortable. He said, "People should be waiting for a stool at the bar." He would tell the waitresses, "Don't be too nice to the customers." They wanted it like they were in this special place, and they were lucky to be there. And it was amazing because people from the suburbs sat upstairs, Jewish couples who normally do not like to wait and like to be treated like royalty, these people waited, and they

high on

just tolerated it. It was a good meal at a fair price, and they were hoping to see a celebrity or two.

**JACKIE SHERMAN, WAITRESS:** Mickey had those two witches at the door, Dorothy Dean and that other one. Dorothy had a vicious biting tongue. The two of them sitting on the door screening people, and everything was open for combat. "What, your name is Schwartz? We don't allow Jews in here." I remember them saying that one night. "Sorry, it's couples only." Or, "Sorry you can't come in without a jacket." Then they'd go and get a jacket and they'd say, "Sorry, you can't come in with brown shoes."

**PAMELA KRAFT, WAITRESS:** I was working the front room when a guy punched Mickey in the mouth, knocking his tooth out for refusing to let him in. Mickey fell into the big front window, and it cracked.

**LAWRENCE WEINER:** Mickey believed so much in the fantasy of his life that the belief carried over to the bar, and everyone connected with Max's believed in the fantasy of Max's Kansas City. It was like the Figaro in Paris. It became something, but it became something because Mickey really believed it to be. He had fantasies that he was the center of the intellectual cultural world, and for a rather long moment of time, he was.

**Sally Kirkland** (photo by Anton Perich)

rebellion

# Dear Dorothy
## by Robert Creeley

*for Dorothy Dean*

Dear Dorothy,
I thought a lot
of what you said—
*the gentle art of being nice—*

For finks—for you,
"just let me out—
fuck off, you creeps!"
I'd like to get it right

for once, not spend all
fucking life in patience.
I get scared of getting
lost, I hold on hard

to you. Your voice was
instantly familiar. My middle
agéd hippy number
is more words. I like

the tone and place.
I like to drink
and talk to people,
all the lovely faces.

But in the car I'm driving
back to some place on
West Broadway, a man is making
faces at me through the window—

scared, confused at why he
wants to do that. Why the

constant pain. It always
hurts—hence drive away

from him. Or, drinking,
go into the men's room,
then come out to
indescribable horrors, lights,

and people *eating* people,
*awful.* Sounds and noises,
*horror,* scream at
"what's the matter?" *don't*

you *ever* touch me—
wanting love so much.
Can shake for hours with
thinking, scared it's all got lost . . .

"Would you *fuck* that?"
"My God!" Your ineluctable
smile, it falls back in your head,
you *smile* with such a gentle

giving up. I sadly loved
it that you wopped me with your
purse.
"Stupid!" I think of things,
I'm loyal. Narcissist, I want.

From *The Collected Poems of Robert Creeley, 1945-1975,*
University of California Press, 1982

## DOROTHY DEAN

Dorothy Dean, a former editor for The New Yorker and for such publishers as Times Books and Harry N. Abrams, died of cancer Friday at the Hospice of St. John in Denver. She was 54 years old and lived in Boulder, Colo.

Ms. Dean had also held editorial positions at Vogue magazine and at Harper & Row.

From 1963 to 1964, she was a member of The New Yorker's research department — then called the fact-checking department. At her death, she was a proofreader for The Daily Camera newspaper, published in Boulder.

Ms. Dean was born in White Plains. She was a graduate of Radcliffe College, and earned a master's degree in fine arts at Harvard University. She also studied art history on a Fulbright scholarship in Amsterdam.

It says she died of cancer, and I suppose that might be true, but I know she left New York because of a severe problem with alcoholism . . . and was incommunicable during her first year in Colorado.

She was also a dyke, but I don't believe that was common knowledge in the early 60s. I found out because she had an affair with an indescreet woman.

She told me a story about Stefan Brecht who was at Harvard while she was there. Stefan turned in his Ph. D. dissertation on Hegel The committee told him it was too long, had to be cut. He went away and returned at some later time and the dissertation was three times longer.

*Geo. A.*

Dorothea Rockburne, *Extasie*, oil on canvas, 1984

**eat your art out**

**O**nce I started my new waitressing job, I still had no idea who this Mickey
character was. I thought he was just some young guy who was managing the place. I did observe, too, that because we looked alike, customers
often asked me if I was his younger sister.

The place was just unbelievably busy, and there was always fabulous music coming from the jukebox: the Stones, Doors, Cream, the Who, the Beatles, Jackie Wilson,
and Aretha Franklin. At first I worked the upstairs, known to all the employees and
regulars as Siberia, where the bridge-and-tunnel crowd were seated, and the middle
section downstairs, known to the waitresses as sections three, four, and five, near the
kitchen. There would be a mishmosh of celebrities, photographers, filmmakers, writers, and assorted others. Mickey would never put you in the back room right away,
'cause it would probably come close to destroying you. The people back there were just
too much to handle. But a few of the staff members did make sure to fill me in on
Mickey right away, especially one of the male staff members. He told me in no uncer-
tain terms that Mickey did not like women, that he could be very sadistic, but he liked
it if you stood up to him. He definitely had his favorites. It was obvious that Max's was

a very male-oriented place. The women were there for the men, or so it seemed. A waitress was the lowest person on the totem pole. Everyone wanted to work at Max's.

Before the back room became notorious as the nightly home of a certain group of Pop Superstars, the front room and the bar, particularly at cocktail hour, were populated by the macho abstract-expressionist and conceptual artists, businessmen, drag queens, art dealers, collectors, photographers, models, stockbrokers, and the ragged denizens of the underground who came for the free hors d'oeuvres (known as "the trough") and the acceptance that they received nowhere else. At night, celebrities from all over the world flocked to Max's.

The front room in the booths across from the bar, and seated at the bar, is where you'd find your heavy-hitters: the painters, sculptors, writers, and poets. They were the first "regulars." They were the "heteroholics," the abstract-expressionist heterosexual alcoholic types who kept the joint lively. The bottom line at Max's was if you didn't belong, you felt it. The bar scene was equivalent to an episode from *Cheers*. Every afternoon starting at around cocktail hour you could find the likes of John Chamberlain, Neil Williams, Larry Rivers, Joel Oppenheimer, Larry Zox, Michael Steiner, Larry Poons, Frosty Myers, Dan Christensen, Robert Povlich, Fielding Dawson, Joe Early, Bob Pauls, Donald Burns, Don Phelps, and many other unsavory characters sitting in their self-designated seats. There was also an influx of younger-generation artists from the art institutes and Ivy League colleges who came on the scene to mingle with and learn from their heroes: Brice Marden, Ron Landfield, Tex Wray, Peter Reginato, Peter Forakis, John Clem Clarke, Dan Graham, Joseph Kosuth, and on occasion Julian Schnabel, but they usually drifted in later in the evening. Women artists who frequented "the store" as Mickey called it, were few and far between. Feminism was just starting to gain some attention, and it prevailed as did the women artists who chose to join the contingency of male painters and sculptors at the tables up front, and make themselves known: Dorothea Rockburne, Nancy Smithson, who was married to Robert Smithson, Ruth Kligman, Carolee Schneemann, Rosemarie Castora (who was married to Carl Andre), Marisol, Lee Lozano, Helen Harrington (who later married Brice Marden), Barbara Kruger and Colette, Francine Tint (who was a stylist at the time and later became an artist in her own right), and Jeannie Blake (who worked for both Jasper Johns and Richard Bellamy) usually sat at the bar. "It was great when Max's opened," recalls Ronnie Landfield, "because I didn't know what to expect, but when I got there, all the artists I knew from downtown like Tex, Neil, Frosty, John, all of them were there. I was eighteen at the time,

**Marisol at right, sitting in front room of Max's**
(photo by Marilyn Krauss)

de Kooning (photo by Anton Perich)

Bar patrons, including Warren Finnerty (photo by Anton Perich)

Brice was twenty-six. I kind of grew up at Max's. I always used to flirt with the waitresses. The bar permitted an intense choreography of flirtation. There was definitely a lot of pickup action going down, and legendary sexual encounters." "The artists were always cruising to see who their next victims would be," recalls Gisella, one of Max's regulars. "Max's was the place to pick people up."

The painters attracted the art dealers, the collectors, art critics, and art groupies— young, pretty girls there for the taking. Both the front and the back rooms had a groupie contingency, but Mickey felt that they blended in nicely and added to the flavor. Then photographers like Richard Davis, John Ford, Bill Salano, Benno Friedman, Izzy Valaris, Steve Steigman, and Jimmy Moore often came with the models of the moment: Twiggy, Veruschka, Jean Shrimpton, Benedetta Barzini, Andrea de Portago, Penelope Tree, Pilar Crespi, and Lauren Hutton, who often came in with her investor boyfriend, Bob Williamson. It was like a mix of the most beautiful, the most elegant, and the not so elegant, birds and colors.

## anyone for cocktails?

**FIELDING DAWSON, POET/WRITER:** People didn't consciously come to Max's; they were drawn to it. It was magnetic, and it was definitely hypnotic. The world just disappeared. I was at the old Cedar Tavern, when Pollock and de Kooning hung out there, the same thing happened. It's totally decentralized today. There's just no one place anymore where there are a lot of creative people, I mean a lot of creative people. We're not just talking about Sunday painters; I mean, when de Kooning and Barney Newman were at Max's, they could absolutely relax. It was cool. Bob Smithson, he wasn't my cup of tea, but he was a good guy, and he was an honest, kind, gentle man, and it was a deep shame that he died so young, and when you have a whole bar full of people like that, I mean, man, a different shape takes place.

**JIMMY MOORE, FASHION PHOTOGRAPHER:** We used to hang out at cocktail hour when it wasn't so crazy. I would go there with Frank Simon. He was a cameraman at the time, and then he became a director. He made a film called *Queen*. My circle was Frank, Rod McDonald, John Filler....We would go there and the Beatles would come up and park their car in the middle of Park Avenue and just come in. People would come in just to see the Piranha being fed.

It was the kind of thing where somebody would be having a party upstairs and we would go up check it out, and then come back downstairs. There were so many things happening. Mainly sitting around and talking about life. We were all creating. Everyone was doing something. It wasn't like now when everyone talks about money. In those days nobody talked about money. We were very serious in those days.

**ROBERT HEIDE, PERFORMER/WRITER:** Materialism and money was not what people thought about. It was a kind of anti-materialism and reactionary kind of thinking. Off-Off-Broadway meant that we didn't want to have anything to do with established theater…the counterculture. Of course, this was not true but there was this little thing happening like when we did *The Bed* at the Cafe Chino, there were two men in a bed so the FBI came down, thinking they were having sex in bed. There was this real counterculture within the establishment. The Living Theater was at the center of that. There was a sense of wildness in the air, or "Fuck you!" That was the atmosphere around Max's which was, Do your own thing. I mark the shootings at Kent State, 1972, as the point at which Nixon and the fear of the counterculture went on.

**JOE EARLY, POET/WRITER:** At first a little group of ten or twelve of us regular drinkers, Chamberlain, Williams, Warren Finnerty, Bob Povlich, Frosty Myers, me, and some others would drift into Max's around cocktail hour, late afternoon. Mickey was very generous. He would spring for cocktails, and let us write checks. And then some of the fun started, like the piranha. Mickey decided that he needed a gimmick to draw more people so he brought in the piranha, two tanks, one on each side of the bar. He let it be known when the feeding times were. Sure enough, cabs would start pulling up and people would jump out and sort of elbow us away from the bar and sit around the piranha tanks. And we would fume. Then Mickey would bring out the goldfish and drop them in, and everyone would sit around and watch the piranhas do their thing. This went on for a few months. These people were kind of getting in our way. Then they'd all leave. They'd have a drink, maybe two, then split.  At first we berated Mickey. Then one day, we knew we had to take some action. The next day Mickey came in and there was a third of a piranha floating around, half of a piranha floating around. He didn't know what the hell happened. There was all sorts of speculation, but the true story is that Povlich, who hated the piranha with a passion, went in there one night, and when the bartender was gone, pin-pricked himself and put blood into the piranhas' water and the piranha proceeded to duke it out. Mickey did think of bringing them back, but he never did.

**DEREK CALLENDER, PHOTOGRAPHER:** There was something weird about drinking a drink and looking at a piranha eating a goldfish at the same time. It's just bloody unsettling. You began to wonder, What the hell is in this drink?

**ABBIE HOFFMAN:** I would come in at happy hour between five and seven. I would come to eat, and occasionally meet people that I didn't want to take where I was living, like reporters. I often had my afternoon business meetings there and ate the hors d'oeuvres and flirted with the waitresses. I spent a lot of time in the phone booths because I had to use the phone a lot and all the phones worked.  I used to sit up front in the booth in front of the jukebox. Janis Joplin liked that booth too. If you came early to cocktail hour you would meet people….The one meeting I remember was quite

(photo by Anton Perich)

45

rebellion

astonishing. I mention it in *Woodstock Nation* written in 1969. It happened late 1968; hippies were being discovered by the corporate world as a coming fad. The clothes were marketable, the beads, the music, etc. So all these major corporations—AT&T, IBM, the U.S. Army—were there at this big dinner at Max's hosted by Stan Freeman, one of the owners of the Electric Circus. He was kind of the go-between. They had packets with love beads, protest buttons, and incense on all the tables. It was about $100 per person. I think Jim Fouratt participated—explained the world of the Lower East Side and the hippies to corporate America. I walked out.

**STEVE CANNON, POET/WRITER:** I met Joel Oppenheimer at the St. Mark's Poetry Project. Joel was running a poetry workshop, and he hung out at Max's. Fe [Feilding] Dawson was around. Joel and I became fast friends. He would go around all the time with that beard he had, saying, "I'm the one who named Max's Kansas City."

**MICKEY RUSKIN:** The mix at Max's had already started to take shape when the photographers, models, artists, and Warhol got there. Art was the hot commodity back then, so other people started coming in, because the artists and photographers were there, plus, I made them feel at home. Intuitively I took to these people. It was never conscious on my part. Max's became Max's because of the key figures like Neil Williams, John Chamberlain, Warhol, and Danny Fields, who brought in the people. Danny was involved in the music world. He started coming in, because he lived a couple blocks away, and he liked the atmosphere. So he brought in musicians and music-industry people.

**RON SUKENICK, WRITER:** One night, Dominick Izzo, who runs the disco upstairs, is sitting downstairs at the bar with Frosty after the disco closes at two A.M. Dominic is a sculptor who used to run the Waverly Gallery, but with his large bulk and deep voice he comes on more like a mafia street torpedo. Frosty goes to the phone booth to make a call and he comes back and says someone is sitting in the phone booth and won't get out. So Dominick walks back and asks the guy, "Hey, do us a favor, we want to use the phone."

"Because the phones are always jammed," says Dominick. "Everybody's calling their connections, their bookmakers, or whoever the fuck they were calling. So the guy gives me the finger. I wait awhile, I didn't say nothing because Mickey didn't like violence. I don't blame him, I don't like it myself. So finally I go to the phone booth, I says, "Listen, I work here, come on, get outta there." The guy is sittin' in there and he's steamin'. I say, "Get outta the fuckin' phone booth." He says, "Whatta you think, you're a tough guy?" I says, "Yeah. Get outta the fuckin' booth, or I'm goin' to drag you, one or the other." He says, "Oh yeah." He gets up and yanks the door open. I back off a little. He says, "Hey you! Come 'ere!" I say, "Who you tellin' to 'Come 'ere'?" And in slow motion, he starts to knee me in the balls. I hit 'em a fuckin' crack as I knock 'em across Max's floor, right? So everybody jumped in, some little fuckin' rat grabs my arms.

So I walk away from it, I go in the back room and here's Mickey. Mickey comes back with the long face and the nose. He says, "You know who you hit?" I says, "Wait a minute, you know he tried to knee me in the balls?" He says, "That was Rip Torn, the distinguished actor." Then the next night Torn comes in with a bottle of champagne for Dominick and apologizes. But after four drinks he's trying to start a fight again. I say, "Hey Rip, forget about it, it's all over." He does that for two nights, he brings a bottle of champagne, then after that they become good friends.

**ALFA-BETTY OLSON:** I had a friend who was working for MGM at the time they were making *Zabriskie Point* [1970] and the FBI had targeted that movie. They just kind of dropped in and chatted with the people who were friends with Michelangelo Antonioni. It was this bizarre intimidation that was going on.

**MARSHALL EFRON:** I was home when President [Lyndon] Johnson came on and said he was not going to run for [the presidency]. So I called Bob Fass at WBAI and said, "I'll meet you at Max's." Then we met Abbie Hoffman, Jerry Rubin, and Paul Krassner, and we all sat at Max's celebrating the fact that Johnson, the war president, was no longer going to be our president.

**JILL JOHNSTON, FEMINIST CRITIC:** I was writing for the *Voice*. It was noisy and fun and smoky and exciting. I saw Frosty all the time at the bar. It was a meeting place. I walked out of Max's with one of my most important lovers. She had been in there and I had been in there and we met right outside on the street. October of 1968. She came home with me right that evening.

**PAUL EDEN, MAÎTRE D':** In those days, one did not really need to work to live. You could live off the chicken wings and chili at cocktail hour and pick up jobs here and there. So many of those people had a very casual attitude about the work world.

**RITA FECHER, ARTIST:** When I came to New York, I was a divorcee with three kids, in my early thirties, and I used to go to Max's. I would take the kids with me, because we didn't have a lot of money and I couldn't dump my kids anyplace. They were about ten, eleven, fourteen. I made them all blue velvet suits with bell bottoms and capes. We would go to Max's for happy hour so we could get the free food. They were so beautiful with their long hair and their velvet suits, and their little Beatle jackets, that they got a lot of attention.

**BOB PAULS, FINANCIAL CONSULTANT:** Mickey came in from the bank and was bitchin' and moanin' that he had a phony $100 bill and the bank was going to confiscate it. Povlich says, "I'll give you twenty bucks for it." Mickey says, "Okay." Povlich says, "Well just take it off my tab." So he didn't even give Mickey the $20. Mickey goes upstairs, he's running the business. Povlich goes to Frank at the bar and says, "Buy the guys a round of drinks." The tab comes to about $7.50 or something and Povlich gives Frank the phony hundred and takes the change.

**NILE RODGERS, PRODUCER/MUSICIAN:** We used to go for cocktail hour, my friends and I, from the School of Visual Arts. We'd go because they had good-looking girls, and if we bought one drink we could get the free food. That's how I ate every day. We were really poor; we had no money.

**BETSEY JOHNSON, FASHION DESIGNER:** I used to have my business people meet me at Max's cocktail hour, which was really a riot. These were straight businesses like Braniff. I'd usually meet them at six o'clock after work. I would never bring them there at night. I didn't want to get that close. Now I know about the power of territory. Then it seemed very natural that if they wanted to see me they should come to my environment. They weren't dummies, they knew something was going on. That's what kept things going in that period, that there was enough heavy-duty establishment money people seriously attracted to this situation. The fashion industry didn't like it. They read it as "youth," and they weren't young. You could be young and rich, and fitting, but you couldn't be over thirty.

**DONALD PHELPS, POET/FILE CLERK:** I did become acquainted with the singer Bobby Darin. He'd come in early Sunday afternoons. He talked about his art collection a lot. I asked him if he saw George Burns, who was his patron. He said that he did. He told me once I was the best straight man he met at Max's.

**DEREK CALLENDER:** Mickey had begun to attract local businessmen. These guys who sold insurance for a living would filter down and hang out at the front of the bar near where the buffet was. They would usually clear out about seven-thirty to catch the trains back to the suburbs. But more than once they would stay a little later and some of the Warhol entourage would show up. Pat Ast was a somewhat heavyset woman who would occasionally show up with very bizarre makeup and silver paint in her hair. The contrast between these people with the silver hair and the makeup and these insurance guys in business suits...all you had to do was stand back and watch the chemistry. They were driven mad by it every time. You thought immediately of Bob Dylan's song, "Ballad of a Thin Man": *"Something is happening, but you don't know what it is, do you, Mr. Jones?"*

**MICKEY RUSKIN:** To me, the insurance men and company executives that came in for lunch and cocktail hour were every bit as important as everybody else. I fired a guy right off the floor one time because he insulted one of the insurance-company executives. I took him right off the floor. They didn't account for a large part of my business, but they were just as important to me.

**ED KANE, ATTORNEY FOR GUARDIAN LIFE INSURANCE:** The day Max's opened I said, "Let's go in." It was before lunch. I walked in and sat at the bar with a friend of mine—I was this straight guy working in the law department at Guardian Life—and I saw this guy in a fringe shirt and a beard and he kept looking at me. He walks over and he throws his arms around me and says, "Eddie, it's me, Joel Oppenheimer." I went to high school with Joel. I hadn't seen him since high school. As a matter of fact, Joel even in high school was a revolutionary kind of guy. He was always in trouble and he went to Black Mountain College and eventually ended up at the *Village Voice*. Since I was sort of the ringleader for all of the guys at Guardian, I got them to go next door for lunch and then at four-thirty. Once we got out of work, we were down there drinking until they went home and commuted. Of course, I didn't commute; I just drank. I was probably the only guy in New York that could walk into that place anytime at night with a tie and a suit on, because I knew Mickey so well and I knew all the bartenders. I was the token conservative. I'd sit there till all hours of the night getting drunk, arguing with Abbie Hoffman, and Allen Ginsberg and the whole bunch of them....The president of Guardian Life always thought that Max's was not a place that should be next to a big sort of old-time, old-line life-insurance company. And of course, I'd say, "We don't have any legal grounds to do anything about it, chief." I didn't want him closing down the only place I liked to drink in.

**FRANK DI BENEDETTO, BARTENDER:** This one woman came in the place every afternoon for lunch, very reserved, stuffed-shirt type. One time she came in the evening by accident; she had to come down to the city for something and stopped in. She came in and thought she was in the wrong place. She came in the next day and said, "Oh my God, Frank, do you know what goes on in this place at night?"

**Frank Di Benedetto, bartender at Max's, and Allegra Perhaes, day manager**

• • •

**JEFFREY BRENNAN, UPSTAIRS MANAGER:** Divine showed up at cocktail hour when all the businessmen were there. She'd come sashaying in with her 250 pounds and five guys would drop their drinks. It was quite a show when the late-night people showed up in the afternoon for free hors d'oeuvres. They lived off the free food, and if they came for afternoon freebies, usually they were there until closing.

Frank was the only bartender to remain from the inception of "The Southern" until the closing of Max's in 1981.

rebellion

**MICKEY RUSKIN:** I never had any idea that I was feeding a small population. It was really unconscious. Every once in a while, in the years after Max's closed, someone would say to me, "My God, I lived off you for years." You basically bought a beer and then you went and ate all you wanted. A lot of places put out something for cocktail hour. It wasn't really an original idea. It just so happens that the people whom I was basically supporting couldn't get in anywhere else. This was not done by design or out of any intention of charity. It was done to enhance the business.

**HOLLY WOODLAWN, WARHOL SUPERSTAR:** When I started going to Max's regularly, we'd go for the afternoon brunch that Mickey put out because we needed a place to eat. We swore those chicken wings were pigeons they killed that day. We lived on them and the chili for months.

**CYRINDA FOXE, ACTRESS:** I never went for cocktail hour until Jackie Curtis dragged me in there for the free chicken wings. Actually, one afternoon I went to the Factory and we came with Jackie and some other people to cocktail hour. I was sitting at the table talking to someone. It was up front right up close to the bar. Gregory Corso came over and sat down and he's sitting there and staring at me. He's talking gibberish and crazy. Then he says, "You know, I have a present for you." He takes his hand out from under the table and he's jerked off under the table. And he's blown his wad. I was like, "Eeeeewwww you're so disgusting." Mickey just blew. "That's it for Corso." He said, "You're out of here."

**JEFFREY NICKORA, MAX'S CASHIER:** I remember seeing Connie Stevens in the daylight coming to Max's on an afternoon, with all that makeup. Steve Lawrence and Edie Gorme showed up one afternoon. They didn't bother to come at night.

**ALFA-BETTY OLSON:** I brought Mel Brooks to Max's. We were doing *The Producers,* which we were shooting during the day. Then at the end of the day we'd see the dailies and we'd go have dinner at Max's. We went almost every night. It was Mel, me, David Millerpat, sometimes the cameraman, and the producer, Sidney Glazer. Once we took the comic Dick Shawn there. He hated it. He was very reactionary. He couldn't understand all these longhairs. He suspected many were against the war. He sat there and looked around and it was some of the most important people in the world, and he sat there and said, "These guys should get a job."

**LI-LIAN OH, ACUPUNCTURIST:** I had a boyfriend at that time and he was looking for a table. I was standing there talking with Jackie the waitress, and she says, "There's someone here who would like to meet you, this is Mel Brooks." I didn't know who Mel Brooks was. He says to me, "Hello, would you like a drink?" I wasn't paying much attention, I say, "No thanks." I was very rude. And he says, "I'd like to have dinner with you sometime." I thought, Why is this man pestering me? I said, "No, no, no—no thanks." So he said, "Don't you know who I am?" I said, "Yeah, she just introduced me, your name is Mel." He said, "You don't know who Mel Brooks is? I'm a very famous person." And I said,

"That's your problem." And he laughed and said, "Can I use that line?" I lived on Charles Street, and the next day I went to this pancake house on Greenwich Avenue with my girlfriend for breakfast, and there is Mel Brooks and Anne Bancroft. He just hung his head down like he didn't notice me.

**BOB RUSSELL, BOUNCER:** We were sitting around waiting very patiently one afternoon for those horrible chicken wings that everyone thought Mickey was reprocessing down in the basement. For many of us that was dinner. The chicken wings would arrive and there would always be this mad dash….On this particular afternoon there was some dame giving me the elbow. She was trying to get in before me so there was this elbow fight at the chicken-wing trough, and it was Janis Joplin elbowing me out of her way.

**LAURA KRONENBERG, ARTIST:** John Chamberlain was my big hero. I was doing sculpture and I was welding away, and Jim Jacobs was working for Leo Castelli, and I went to the gallery and he said, "Oh, I have a surprise for you"—and that evening he took me to Max's and introduced me to John. And John had this big credit because of the sculpture he gave to Mickey, so he bought us all dinner. John invited me to go to a party at Claes Oldenburg's, and it was a great party, and that was my first time in Max's.

**KERRY RIORDAN, MODEL:** Laurel Delp had keys to Max's because she would pass out there so many nights. She came to Max's from Bennington with her Porsche and hit a garbage truck outside with her enthusiasm to get into the bar. And thousands of bagels went all over her. She completely destroyed the little red Porsche.

**ED LEFFINGWELL, DESIGNER:** Louise Nevelson would be sitting at the bar with her false eyelashes. She was probably the most distinctive-looking person who would come there. The hands, the jewels, the eyelashes, the hats…

**ALAN MIDGETTE, ACTOR:** I was sitting by myself at Max's lost in thought, and suddenly someone came up and touched me on the forehead. I looked up and it was Pierre Clemente. He was in *Belle de Jour*. I couldn't speak French and he couldn't speak English, but we both decided to leave. We both thought we were going to the other person's place. We got in the cab and just looked at each other, so we got out, and went back into Max's. Nico came in a few minutes later and she spoke French, so we could communicate.

**MANOLO:** I was busing tables at Max's, and Linda Eastman came in right after she had spent the day with the Beatles. She was showing everybody all the incredible pictures she had taken.

● ● ●

rebellion

**GERALD LAING:** In the sixties, we all believed in the romance of the bar. We had abandoned the set-piece situation of dinner parties and even cocktail parties. The bar was better, where anything could happen or any encounter was possible. Not any old bar of course, but a place like Max's where everyone went and encounters were interesting. Mickey was the first person to give a restaurant a distinct identity and pull people from all over town. Plus it was the only place in town where artists were treated like human beings. It was our place, and the only place I knew of where the uptown people and the jet set were second-rate. The hierarchy was reversed.

**JOHN CHAMBERLAIN:** I'd see some wench sitting at the bar, wondering what to do with herself, so I'd get in collusion with the waitress and give her a list of say, eight drinks that were different, and tell her to serve that girl this drink, and in eight minutes this drink, and in eight minutes the next drink, and on and on, and in forty-five minutes she'd be too drunk for me to have anything to do with her. She'd be just looking around trying to figure out who was doing this to her. But she'd drink them. They'd literally have to pour her into a taxi.

**DEREK CALLENDER:** About halfway between the front and the back on the right-hand side of the aisle that led to the back, were kitchen doors. Max's was odd in that respect because the kitchen was more or less in the center of the joint and it got hot as hell in there. Then there was an old-fashioned telephone booth that sat next to the doors that led into the kitchen. In that telephone booth there were a number of men who had company, because the booth had side panels so when you closed the door, you couldn't see anybody kneeling in the booth so it was a very popular phone booth. Then at the bar there was what's called "playing hand puppets." You'd stand at the bar and you'd notice some guy who's directing some woman like a hand puppet. But the telephone booth was sticky as a result.

**FRANCINE TINT:** Everybody fucked everybody. It was like a drink of water. I don't even know who I went home with.

**DEREK CALLENDER:** I met this woman who was a Scientologist. So we're sitting in a booth along the wall and we are doing something absolutely bizarre. We are actually playing footsie. I have taken my shoe off, my sock off, and I am stroking this woman's vulva with my toes. It was dark on that side and I got my foot on her snatch and she's playing with my dick with her toes and we're pretending to eat our salad at the same time. It was a wonder I didn't pass out. I'm sitting there with this monstrous erection and the waitress is asking, "Can I get you anything?" Meanwhile we're discussing Scientology over salad. I think we finally wound up fucking in a garage.

**SUSAN DALTON, WRITER:** David [Dalton] and I split up and that's when I started hanging out at Max's all the time, and my drinking really escalated. Max's became my bedroom, my living room, and my kitchen—my everything. I screwed Neuwirth in the dressing room upstairs one night. That

high on

was 1973. Then I started seeing this drummer. You know when you have friends that you fuck—well, you know where the jukebox was across from the bar. I'm in the booth going into the alcove, I'm facing the jukebox. I'm sitting there and I'm bragging, "Well, I can give head and drink Jack Daniel's at the same time, what's the big deal?" All the guys in the band are sitting there egging me on, going, "Nah, you can't do that." "Sure, I can." So one of them says, "Prove it." He was smiling. I said, "Sure." And not under the table. I just leaned over; he was sitting next to me. That was Max's.

**FIELDING DAWSON:** The sex scenes at Max's were much more bold than at other places. Much more up-front. I mean, it was hardly subtle. A lot of kinds of women went there. And a lot of kinds of men. Therefore, a lot of women hated Max's. Not because it was a macho place. But it was clear that it was a male-dominated place, with Mickey at the top, and Mickey was not macho, he just did not like women, so there were a lot of guys there who did not like women. Women aren't fooled by that scene. What woman would be fooled by that? And the singles scene back then, especially in New York, permeated night and day. You go up the strip, right up to Elaine's, and it was like singles bars, and God, they were terrible places. And women went there for one reason—not to meet somebody you might *like*, but to meet somebody who you might like to fuck. And at Max's she might meet somebody intelligent to fuck. Or a woman who was possibly in rebellion against the feminist theology. I mean, Max's was poison to the feminists.

**TOM PUNZIO, BARTENDER:** Wayne was tending bar—this big, Beach Boy, lovable guy with his Hawaiian shirt—and his wife just happened to come back early from having been away for a few days. So it's Saturday night about eight-thirty, and there were a few people at the bar and some people having dinner, and he's upstairs when someone goes up and tells him his wife's downstairs looking for him....Wayne came down and she held up their bedroom sheets, which obviously didn't just come out of the Laundromat. He had obviously been doing his homework, but not with her, and she says, "These are our fuckin' sheets and who have you been fucking in our bed?"

**KEN VAN SICKLE, PHOTOGRAPHER:** Dominic and Louie were always picking up ladies. They were great ones for the ladies. They were standing at the bar one night with a couple of ladies. It was pretty crowded and they're laughing and drinking and at some point this guy who is walking kind of fast goes by Dominic and bumps his shoulder by mistake. Dominic jumped back because he was always ready for a fight, and yelled and raised his fist so everybody kind of moved out of the way. He happened to expose Louie who was getting a hand job at the bar but it didn't seem to affect anybody. They went back to drinking as usual. They played under the table a lot with the ladies. Dominic's foreplay was when he snapped his fingers: "Hey, get ovuh here!"

**FRANCINE TINT:** The very rich and the arts have always been kinky—artists because they are experimental, and the very rich because they are into power.

rebellion

**FIELDING DAWSON:** This girl came in and she was really cute and she had on a really beautiful dress. And she would take guys into the telephone and blow them for five bucks. She could make a couple hundred dollars a night and come back the next night. Well, she was wearing the same dress and after the fourth or fifth night she was looking pretty ragged. Then apparently she bought herself a new dress and then she came in and the same scene went on for about ten days. She'd come in relatively early, when the businessmen were there. Mickey 86ed her, finally. It finally got through that slab of concrete up there, that something was going on that was really not kosher.

I was sitting next to Larry Hellenberg at the end of the bar one night and I look over and I see this hand come up and stroke Larry's leg. Larry looks that way and there's a chick there and she wanted to blow him.

Eric Emerson would blow guys at the service end of the bar. It's a shame that he died.

**DEBBIE ROSS, WAITRESS:** The girl who gave the blow jobs, she was not attractive at all. She would come in and she would be on her knees going up and down the bar giving these guys blow jobs. It was the weirdest thing I ever saw. She wasn't even interesting. She was dirty. She didn't even do it for money. She just liked the idea of giving blow jobs to famous artists. Mickey could put up with a lot of things but he didn't like dirty people, and they had to be interesting. He finally 86ed her.

**MICKEY RUSKIN:** I wish I had a nickel for everyone who got fucked in my phone booths.

**CORY TIPPIN, STYLIST FOR THE FACTORY:** One afternoon Geraldine [Smith], Patti D'Arbanville and I were sitting in a booth. It was a real funny time and we had missed free food. We were not sitting in the back room, because at that time the back room was completely empty. We were sitting in the middle section across from the kitchen in a booth toward the back stairway. We were having like a Coke or something and these two secretaries, very conservative secretaries, came in and sat down in the table right next to us. There was a whole crowd of serious diners that came from maybe six o'clock until around ten P.M. Advertising and insurance people. Immediately Geraldine and Patti are affixed on these two girls. They're like sitting and they are not paying much attention to me. They are looking at these two girls and making comments like, "Patti, look at her. Look what she's got on!" Getting louder and louder. These two girls are kind of oblivious but they are feeling the pressure of Patti and Geraldine. They get up and Patti sticks her arm out and of course the secretary bumps Patti's arm.

It was as if a keg of dynamite went off under our table. Patti jumps up and pushes the girl, pushes the table over with all the food on it. Geraldine jumps up and they just literally attack these girls. Fights were something that girls did in those days. They really fought, they really brawled, they really hit. The two secretaries fought back. The upshot of it was, Ritty, or whoever was working the floor, came over and tried to separate them. It ended up that the two secretaries got thrown out instead of

Geraldine and Patti. They started their act and were crying, "We weren't to blame, she knocked my arm. She started it, didn't she, Cory?" I'm sitting there: "Oh Patti please leave me out of this." So Patti and Geraldine go back to sipping their Cokes.

**GERALDINE SMITH, WARHOL SUPERSTAR:** We were wild and crazy. We were on acid a lot. Everything was a trip. I would go home once in a while to get money from my mother. I'd even attend classes once in a while at Washington Irving. We grew up on the streets. We would take downs and ups and drink, mostly pills. We didn't take LSD as much in the seventies, because we had taken so much of it in the sixties. We were more into pills....

These two girls started in with Patti and I, and I turned around and started arguing with them and Patti threw the girl off the chair, turned the table over and started beating these girls up. I think it was we felt like we owned the place.

**IRA SCHNEIDER, FILMMAKER:** One time I was with some friends of mine at the bar and they had some THC, and I said, "Great, I love THC," and so I took the pill, but instead it was PCP. So within twenty minutes, I found I couldn't see my feet, I couldn't walk. I was still at the bar. My friends had gone in the back room, so I thought maybe I'd better crawl out of the bar, and go up the stairs and turn myself in. I couldn't see where anybody was. So I crawled up the stairs and asked some-one to get Mickey. One of the waitresses gets Mickey and I say, "Mickey, I can't see my feet. Someone gave me some kind of drug. I can't walk. I'm perfectly fine inside, I just can't walk." Mickey looks at me and says, "Ira, you shouldn't have done that." But he got my friends, and they put me in a cab, and took me to a party. I felt like a slug. I knew I was in there somewhere. I warned every-body about PCP after that.

**JACQUES, MAX'S REGULAR:** An old friend of mine had just flown in from South America. He rang me up and we agreed to meet at Max's. He said he had some refreshments: "So be ready to party, my man!" The place was jumpin' and so were we. We sat in the alcove area facing the door so that we could see who was coming in and possibly pick up some chicks. We ordered something to eat and were shootin' the shit when he hands me a bag under the table. "Why don't you take a trip to the john and test the goods, my man?" Going to the shithouse at Max's was always a trip. You never knew what sex would be in there and in what position. The graffiti on the walls and in the stalls made up the decor and defused your attention from the otherwise bleak atmosphere and lack of space. I entered one of the stalls, took a piss and went for that little brown bag hidden in my pock-et. Flake upon flake of the prettiest cocaine I had seen in a long time sparkled in the dim light and there was plenty of it. I knew the night was just beginning so I made up a little package for myself. We snorted and drank and partied. Two women friends joined us and we sat there until closing and continued to party into the next day.

This went on for a few days. Each night we'd arrive at Max's around ten or eleven and start again. I was so high by the fourth day that I started sneaking lines on the table when the waitress wasn't looking. At one point I took out the top of my ballpoint pen and used it as a straw. My nose was totally numb by now. The next night I had to take a break and get some sleep. I woke up in the middle of the night with this sneezing spell. It felt like I was literally blown away. I just kept blowing my nose and sneezing. There was blood dripping from my nose. And I looked in the hanky at one point and there was the spring from my ballpoint pen. I was so goddamn high I snorted the spring right up my nose!

**JERRY HOUK:** I remember the night Rauschenberg was in there and it's four in the morning and Mickey says, "Okay, we're closing, get this guy outta here." He didn't know at that time what Rauschenberg looked like. I grabbed Mickey and I said, "You know who that is, don't you?" And he said, "No. I don't know who it is. We're closed. It's time to go." I said, "Mickey, that's Robert Rauschenberg." He says, "Oh!" And a week later you'd think they had been friends for years.

**DEREK CALLENDER:** The woman who was the animal trainer showed up at Max's with a baby elephant. We are standing down near the end of the bar and sure enough there's a goddamn elephant, about four feet tall at the shoulder, is walking past. It went into the back room because that's where they were taking him. Then the problem was they couldn't get him out. The elephant must of liked the chick peas or something. So there was a bunch of us went back, naturally we followed the circus, and I'm wondering what Mickey's going to do if this animal shits on the floor, 'cause it's an elephant, for christ's sake. This ain't somebody's poodle. There were about eight of us back there trying to get this elephant to move. You have no idea how strong an elephant is. There is just no way. And on top of that you had to be afraid of the thing. It's not the teeth, but if it puts its head against your chest and crushes you against the wall, you can lose your life. Finally the elephant got bored and turned around and walked out. That was the great thing about Max's, you never knew whether it was going to be an elephant, Antonioni, or Jim Morrison. It was very unique in that way. The people were just like Ping-Pong balls just bouncing about and striking sparks.

**WILLIAM THURSTON, TEACHER:** I was just standing at the bar and in walked a group of people. With them was an orangutan and an elephant. I sat down and we had dinner and drinks with the orangutan and the elephant. The orangutan was eating off my plate and the elephant came over and leaned on me and knocked me off my chair.

**LARRY ZOX:** There I am sitting near the front and I reach for something and this girl says to me, "I wouldn't reach too fast." I said, "What?" And I look over at her and here's this tiger sitting with this woman. This huge fucking tiger with teeth this big. That same night someone came in with a baby elephant. I said, "I don't fuckin' believe this, next it will be grasshoppers."

**Baby elephant**
(photo by Anton Perich)

**J.Fred Muggs (from the Today Show)**
(photo by Anton Perich)

max's
kansas city
steak lobster chick peas

● ● ●

**FIELDING DAWSON:** The painters used to show up around cocktail hour. That was about the time Mickey would turn off WNCN, which played classical music, and the jukebox would come on. Then, later on, people would come in from everywhere….I liked sitting at the bar because you could see who was coming in the door. The actor Michael Pollard was there all the time, always friendly. There were a lot of writers, actors, movie people. Warren Finnerty came in every afternoon; he was in *Cool Hand Luke*. One night he introduced me to Sidney Kingsley. He was sitting over in a booth. He was a playwright. He wrote a play called *Dead End*. And the movie that had Lillian Hellman and Bogart in it. He wrote the screenplay that was the birth of the Dead End Kids. He was a contemporary of John Steinbeck. Meeting him for me, it was like literally meeting a piece of history. Then a year or so later I met Antonioni. I was standing up front and one of the waitresses came up to me and said, "Fe, Max's Kansas City is not the world." But once you walked through the door and the scene got going, it sure felt like it. I mean what other world was there, unless you were at your typewriter or in front of your canvas?

Later in the evening, starting at around eleven P.M., the heady, argumentative crowd would drift in, artists like Carl Andre, and earthworks sculptor Robert Smithson. A slew of other artists like Richard Serra, Mel Bochner, and art historian Ted Castle would drop by the table for some drink and often-heated art discussions. There were certain regulars who were notorious for table-hopping, Michael Pollard being one of them, which was a convenient way of escaping the tab, because by the time it came, someone else at the table would invariably pick it up. By midnight the bar was hopping and the joint was packed. The energy around this time was pulsating. The artists who usually sat at Smithson's table became disruptive, loud, raucous, and on many more than one occasion, obnoxious. It was not on most waitresses' list of preferences as a table to wait on.

**LYNN HARRITON, WAITRESS:** I used to follow Michael Pollard all around Max's keeping track of his tab. He was usually drunk and he'd join everybody's table long enough to order a drink, get his drink, drink part of it, and move on—leaving them with the tab. This got to be a regular complaint. People were paying for his drinks and he wasn't sticking around. I'd have to take it off other people's, and put it on his own. God knows how it ever got paid for, because I never got any money from him. I'd just hand it in at the end of the night and say, "This is Michael Pollard's tab."

**CATHY DREW, WAITRESS:** I didn't judge people by their art, I judged them as people, and Smithson was always difficult to wait on, never left a decent tip, and was usually morose. Helen Marden's main problem was that she did not want to be seen as just Brice Marden's wife.

Gregory Corso and Michael J. Pollard, face to face
(photo by Anton Perich)

**PHILIP GLASS, COMPOSER:** The places in New York were much more intense and interesting than the cafes in Paris. The cafes in Paris were basically social, and very middle class. The thing about the art bars, they were really art bars. There were very few people in those bars that had no business being there. People talked about art. They threw each other through windows because they disagreed about art. It was intense. People would have a few drinks, and sometimes they would start swinging. The Cedar was famous for that. For the bars of the seventies, Max's was the prototype of that. They were very intense places. Very polemical. Very ideological. The discussions were passionate. You got the feeling that these were life-and-death issues that were going on. These were not dilettante conversations, either. These were people unwinding after a day in the studio and they sometimes came on pretty heavy. Smithson was famous for inciting those passionate arguments at his table. The talks could be about conceptual art, for example. There would be a lot of discussion about the process. The relationship between the work to, let's say, Duchamp, and John Cage. To what extent the visual content was the real content, or whether the ideas were the content—this is what people went through windows for, and the big front window at Max's seemed to be broken at least twice a year. I once saw a guy go through it.

**GERALD LAING:** Many of the artists were raucous because it stems from that tradition. It stems from Pollock and the Cedar Bar, very macho, very heterosexual, very aggressive–type attitude. Neil Williams' face getting progressively more scarred as he got older; he sort of relished it. He reveled in those scars. And Larry Poons turning up with a pile of paint on each toecap of his shoes, really on purpose. At that time it was okay. Now it would be really corny to do that, because you'd be proclaiming you're an artist, and everybody's had artists up to their eyeballs. In those days it was sort of a revolutionary thing.

**HOWARD SMITH, WRITER/JOURNALIST:** The painters stood at the bar, but almost never hung out in the back room. If you were a painter and you hung out in the back room, it meant you were breathing too hard, that you wanted to be like Warhol. I did not like the back room. I know that was the *in*-est of the ins. I didn't care for that because I wanted to be in a spot where I could see who was with who and what was going on.

**RONNIE CUTRONE, PAINTER:** The front room were the drinkers, and I didn't drink in those days so it was not for me, and they fought verbally and physically about art. They would fight and challenge each other to fist fights on the street. I

rebellion

59

**Malcolm Morley**
(photo by Anton Perich)

worked with Andy on *Popism* and there's a part where he says, "You know it was so weird, those expressionists artists. Could you imagine me and Roy Lichtenstein saying, 'My art's better than yours, Roy, and if you don't think so let's go out on the street and slug it out.'" That was the difference in mentality. I was in the Pop scene which was cool and aloof. The front of Max's was hot and drunk so I never really fit in. I was a druggie so I was with Andy and the amphetamine crowd. The artists that talked about art bored me. I was from the Andy school— we don't talk about art; we'd shut up and go to the studio. At times I would drift into the middle room to see what tourists I could have sex with....

I remember the "baldies" when everybody shaved their head. It was Tony Shafrazi when he was an artist, Larry Bell, Larry Poons, Malcolm Morley, and Robert Smithson. The baldies were the hardcore artists, and they'd fight all the time. One night they were all fighting, and Malcolm was very drunk and said, "You want to see art? Let me show you art." And they all said, "Fuck you, Malcolm, but we'll go anyway." And they go over to his house, and Julian Schnabel, who was there that particular night, follows along. Malcolm in his drunken stupor throws down a board, squeezes some glue, breaks plates, throws the plates on, paints them over, and, the story goes, that's where Julian got the idea for his broken-plates pieces.

**JIM SIGNORELLI:** The first conversation I had with John Chamberlain in the place, in the window around the summer of 1966, John had a piece that was a galvanized made from a piece that Judd had given him: some rejected piece that was somehow imperfect. And John and I were sitting there and he was complaining as usual that everybody liked his art but nobody liked the process and nobody understood how things got made. And out of nowhere I said, "Well sure, it's like that piece there, if you look at that it is perfectly clear that it was a cube at one point." And John said, "Really?" I said, "Look right there, you see those three lines? That's clearly the corner of a cube." Now this had never occurred to John. It was only something that I projected, but he was so amused by that idea. It was almost as though people who were making stuff got a direct and immediate reaction. Some of it a little prejudiced and some of it informed by a chemical stimulation. It was a very fertile area.

**LAWRENCE WEINER:** John [Chamberlain] and Neil [Williams] were famous for their fights,

high on

which were about love. Two rams banging their heads against each other. It was a psychosexual relationship. The fights between them went on forever.

**WENDY YUJUICO, WAITRESS:** Johanna Lawrenson, Neil, and John were always sitting up front. Neil and John would usually end up having some fight and Johanna would end up picking glass out of her knee, and Neil would be passed out at the table. It would come time to pay the bill

**John Chamberlain and Jim Signorelli** (photo by Gerald Malanga)

rebellion

and she'd take his hand and make a big *X*, or try to sign his name. I would say to myself, I wonder if it's okay with Mickey that there's just this big *X* on the check?

Then John was always telling the waitresses how semen was good for the complexion.

**JOE BIRD, BARTENDER:** Neil got whatever he wanted. He always had a bottle on his table. He was always demanding something of the waitress. "Get me my sour cream." Margaret, my wife, was waiting on him, I met her at Max's. One night he's drunk and he screams, really ragging her, "I want that sour cream now!" Margo hustles to get him his sour cream, puts it down in front of him, and he passes out right in it. He could have died from suffocation. She left him there. She said, "The hell with you."

**ALAN SHIELDS, BUSBOY/ARTIST:** Neil and John would get in these fights, and since I was one of the biggest busboys, I was required to not hurt them but stop them if I could, to grab them. Neil was part Mohawk Indian and when he drank he had to fight. They would pound on each other but it was like a physical thing that they had to do. With John, I actually rode on John's back. I had ahold of him and he went running toward the front like a bull, he stumbled and fell and went right through the plate-glass window. That window was broken a number of times.

**TONY GOULD, MANAGER:** John Chamberlain was sitting at the last table across from the bar, before the jukebox, and he was raising hell and throwing things. He suddenly falls back over the jukebox which is on wheels so it slides out, and he falls behind it and he's tangled in all these wires, and they're all dirty as hell with cobwebs and crud and it takes about an hour to get John untangled. Then he just got himself up and sat down. Neil didn't have much of a sense of humor when he got loaded. He got tough.

**JIM JACOBS, ARTIST/ART DEALER:** Neil and John used to fight a lot. I mean not just argue—fist-fight. I think one night Neil had gone out with Susan Hoffman, aka Viva, before John did. He said something disparaging about Susan and John just punched him square in the face. Then they were down on the floor. It was an absolute brawl. Susan just loved it. She thought it was great, but Mickey actually got both of them to leave and they weren't allowed to come back for about a month. Then John gave Mickey another sculpture and everything was okay.

**VIVA, WARHOL SUPERSTAR:** Neil was an extremely violent character when he drank. He pushed Janis Joplin under a table at Max's, and he beat me up once. He gave me some acid, and took me home. I went on this acid trip where I decided that he didn't want to be a painter anymore, and he just wanted to watch TV. So I tried to wreck his paintings, and he picked up that I wasn't making any progress, so he picked up the brass bedpost that I had been using, threw it across the room, and it went through another painting. So he dragged me across this splintery floor, and this just went on and on. When I came off this acid I said, "I hope this was all a hallucination." I was afraid to look in the mirror. I looked in the mirror and I was black, blue, and yellow. He was so apologetic. He said he was never going to touch a woman again. He fed me, he took care of me, he took me to Max's with sunglasses on, and took care of me for three days.

**JOHN CHAMBERLAIN:** People talk about the fights between me and Neil, but I don't remember them. That's why you drank—to forget.

**WILLIAM WEGMAN, ARTIST/PHOTOGRAPHER:** I remember a big argument with Conrad Fisher and Rauschenberg there. Fischer just told Rauschenberg that he was passé and no one really took him seriously. I guess Rauschenberg made a little rebound in 1973 or '72.

**JOSEPH KOSUTH, PAINTER:** I had art fights with Smithson and Serra. We were all sitting at a table one night, Dennis Hopper was there. He and I were both sort of interested in the same woman, and it was like getting toward closing time, and she couldn't quite make up her mind. Dennis says to her, "You know, honey, James Dean knocked me out in *Giant*." And she looked at me and said, "That does it, let's go."

**JEFFREY LEW, ARTIST:** I always sat in the front section. I hung out with Mickey a lot. People always said to me, Mickey didn't talk, but that was insane, because Mickey talked to me constantly about everything. I really came to Max's to see him. Robert Smithson gave me a hard time, but he respected me a great deal. Right before he died he called me up and he told me to come to Max's, and he told me he was sorry he had treated me so poorly, and he thought I was in the art world to stay. I always felt [like I was] on the outside to be honest, but Mickey made me feel important. One time I came in, and I told Mickey I had no money, and Mickey said, "Give him anything he wants."

Fashion photographer John Ford held court at the round table across from the bar, in the front window. John was very tall, lanky, sexy, loquacious, and incredibly handsome, with light black skin and tinted glasses. Unlike some of the other regulars, he was already successful. People would always drop by his table, especially since there was usually an assortment of stunning, ethnic models. John liked this table because he could view everyone who was coming through the door. Then he got those two monstrous wolfhounds that took up half of the front floor. They were laid out like Persian rugs. I believe they are the largest dog known to man. One of them was seven feet long from nose to ass. They ate a wall in his house.

**JULIE NEUFIELD, ART DIRECTOR:** John made a wager one night with this guy at the bar to see whose name was more famous, not knowing who the guy was. It turned out the guy was Claude

Picasso, Picasso's son. John thought he would win, because his last name was Ford. I don't know who won the wager in the end.

**JIM JACOBS:** John Chamberlain and I would watch all the models come in. My best friend Phil Bleeth is still married to a model he met at Max's. His daughter is on *Baywatch*. I got him a job at Castelli and one night we're coming into Max's around ten-thirty, eleven, and we see these two girls—very, very beautiful women. One is about six feet, her name was Nadesh, and the other was Corinna. Somehow we got talking to them and we sat down and had dinner with them. I ended up spending about two or three months as Nadesh's boyfriend, but Phil married Corinna at twenty-one and had this daughter, Yasmin.

**ALAN SHIELDS:** There was a South American sculptor from Brazil maybe, and he was a big guy. He came in and started yelling at Andy. Andy had for some reason sat in the middle section, not in the back. The guy started throwing things at Andy in the middle of the main room, making this real big scene. It was prior to [Andy] being shot. Andy crawled under the table. The poor guy was so scared. There was a lot of stuff thrown and Andy was cowering underneath the table....

Mark di Suvero had a big show somewhere, but he was really excited and really high and really going....He came over to me and I was working the back room and he handed me one of those splits of champagne and a $50 bill, and he said, "I want you to pour this on that guy's head over there." I turned around and I looked at him and I knew who it was, and I said, "You think this is enough?" because it was Henry Geldzahler. I don't know whether it was a bad review or just exuberance. I said, "I don't know if this is enough. I'll probably get fired for this." And he gave me another $50. So I went over there and I told Henry, "How much you going to pay me not to pour this on your head?" Finally he said, "Ah, for that, pour it on me." So I poured a little on his head and we split the rest.

**HENRY GELDZAHLER, WRITER/ART CRITIC:** I was in charge of the National Endowment for the Arts back then, and I was actually scared by artists a few times in Max's—I remember one confronting me by the phone booths: "Where's my money?" they would ask, or, "How do I get a grant?"

**IGGY POP, ROCK MUSICIAN:** I used to go there in the afternoons a lot when nobody was there, with Nico. That was our little place to go have a private lunch.

**FROSTY MYERS:** There were about two hundred really cooking artists when I came to New York from San Francisco in 1961. Now, there are two hundred thousand artists in the city and they don't all know each other. In the sixties, artists could find housing for low rents.

**LARRY ZOX:** I was twenty years old when I came to New York. As an artist then, no one had anything on their mind about making money. That was like, You gotta be kidding! You did it and you

Robert Rauschenberg (photo by Brigid Berlin)

Jason Holiday and Mickey Ruskin
(photo by Brigid Berlin)

Roy Lichtenstein (photo by Brigid Berlin)

Julian Beck (photo by Brigid Berlin)

Todd Rundgren and Patti Smith
(photo by Brigid Berlin)

Brice Marden (photo by Brigid Berlin)

were really passionate about doing it. You didn't care where you lived as long as you could do your art. And because Max's brought so many different groups of people together, it is possibly the first time that the arts came together. That busted the whole cultural thing wide open. It was the beginning of all our careers at that time, from Stella for abstract painting to Lichtenstein or Warhol in the Pop world. We were all there. Someone would come over to your studio and you'd hook up and go over to Max's and have a late lunch, and you'd make deals.

**RYDER MCCLURE:** I brought this publisher I was working with in one night and he was a pretty straight guy. I don't think he ever got over it. He was just blown away that all the artists would all just bunch up there in one spot and hang out like plain people.

**LARRY RIVERS, ARTIST/MUSICIAN:** Larry Poons hung out there, but I didn't like him. Although we were friendly, from my point of view he was weird. He'd laugh at things that I didn't know why he was laughing and he'd be angry at things that I couldn't understand why he'd get angry. His conversation was never witty. I didn't mind his work; at that time he was doing these dots....

Rauschenberg would come to Max's sometimes, although he would never go to the Cedar. He wasn't exactly a closet queen, but he was busy proving somehow that he's not gay, exactly. He got married, he had a child, and the Cedar was definitely a heterosexually-oriented place, unless it was friends like Frank O'Hara, who had a large circle of friends in a mixed bag. Rauschenberg and I came into our own just about the same time, and Jasper Johns too, though they were a year or two younger than me. Overall, the tendency in all the areas of Max's was toward cliques, and the competition for a pecking order and hierarchies was fierce....When a new young artist attempted to emerge as a part of Max's inner circle, his work was almost always challenged and scrutinized before he was accepted as part of the establishment. If it was a woman artist, forget it.

**VALERIE PORR, FASHION DESIGNER:** I think the women artists were twenty times more competitive, more racist—barracudas, impossibly competitive with one another. I found the women artists to be totally impossible, and I did not find that with the men.

**COLETTE, ARTIST:** Something really wonderful happened with Smithson. I was painting the streets at the time and I had this southern girlfriend. You know the typical southern belle with this southern accent. She was helping me paint. She could appear to be naive and so could I, but actually we were very bright. We were talking to Smithson at Max's one night—he was really drunk. I was explaining to him how my street works related to his earth works. So we all decided to go to my place at the end of the night so he could see my work. I think all the way in the taxi, Smithson had some strange vision of this wild orgy that he might have with us and that's not what we were into at all. We knew that's what he was thinking and we were playing with him.

I lived in what was really a created environment and when Smithson first entered my place, I think he

**Earl McGrath and
Larry Rivers**
(photo by Anton Perich)

felt completely in outer space like, Where am I? Am I dreaming? Although he was convinced that I was up to something that was quite different from his works, he acknowledged my work as being valid. We played music for him, drank coffee, and actually had some very nice conversations about art. I think he was kind of taken with it all. Then we sent him on his way. From then on I felt he respected my art because he would introduce me to the other artists at Max's. It became more serious—instead of, "This is Colette who is trying to pick up a famous artist or whatever," it was like, "This is Colette. She is a serious sculptor, you should see what she's doing." And it was not a time when men were especially respectful of women artists, or women in general.

**TED CASTLE, WRITER/ART HISTORIAN:** The battles among the young sculptors were ferocious. Carl Andre, Robert Smithson, Richard Serra, and John Chamberlain all had completely different ideas about what to do. But they were all in the same boat and respected each other a little bit. These arguments have long since gone up in smoke.

**TONY SHAFRAZI, ARTIST/ART DEALER:** Carl [Andre] influenced my life in a big way because he was a teacher and a very brilliant talker. He had a very dry, poetic delivery, loud statements. Smithson was an influence because his range of discussion went from cinema to literature to European art, and between the two artists there was a tremendous respect back and forth. A great thing to learn and watch. It was like being at an open university that went on till the wee hours of the morning.

**ELAINE GROVE, ARTIST:** I went out with Tony Shafrazi. I met him at Max's. The afternoon that the tragic, fatal...the famous afternoon that he went up to the Modern and sprayed Picasso's *Guernica*—at that time I was working at Peter Max's uptown—and he called and said he was going up to the Modern, did I want to come up with him? I said, "No, I'm at work, I can't leave." And I get home and I turn on the TV, and he's being arrested; he had just defaced the *Guernica*...and I couldn't believe for what reason. He told me that it had to do with artwork being revered and becoming icons when in fact it's a work in progress is what it should be, and it shouldn't then be idolized as something other. He said he knew that the lacquers and stuff were protecting it. He knew what he sprayed on could be taken off. It must have been 1970, '71.

**JOSEPH KOSUTH:** I think a lot of very important conversations that constructed the discourse of the art that was to have a major effect in the next thirty years, really took place in Max's—the big battles, the great intellectual struggles. Nobody takes into account those kinds of institutions in which real human life goes on, and you know it's this kind of interface between one's other aesthetic battles, that is, between your eating, your drinking, and your sexuality that goes along with your ideas, and the rest of the thing.

high on

It's really the full human picture of those points in which that sort of human struggle goes on. It was really that point at which all these different people involved in various kinds of cultural activities, and also even disagreements within each one of those, all worked together and there was this incredible interchange.

**DOROTHEA ROCKBURNE, PAINTER:** I was beginning to exhibit, and I was getting an enormous amount of attention. It was making these guys nervous because I don't think a woman had really done that before. At least not a woman they knew; Eva Hesse had done it. They started taking shots at me. They took shots at anybody who made one step forward, and they took shots at each other. But Smithson devoted this evening to taking shots at me. He said that the days of studio art were over, and ahhh "give up your studio." The old ideas of a studio were as over as the easel had been for Jackson Pollock. And I said, "Well, that's really too bad because I'm always going to have a studio. I'm a hands-on kind of artist." Smithson, you know, as rude as he could be, could be equally sensitive. By the time the evening was over, I started playing with him. I said, "I think you should work in the studio too. I know that your work doesn't require a studio, but when you go out and do things in the desert, you do photograph it and bring it back, and how nice to have a place to pin the photographs up." In fact what I was saying was, "You are full of baloney, because no matter what you say, you still seem to haul back a lot of stuff." The discussion went on ferociously for a long time.

Then one time Carl attacked me, because I was going to South America to have a show in Argentina. He said I was being co-opted by their government. I started to laugh. "You think the Argentinean government is co-opting me?" I was thirty-two at the time and it seemed to me to be hysterically funny. He said, "Oh, they're going to use your name in publicity," and he went on and on. I went down and did the show and I was telling the director about our conversation, and he mentioned that he had a letter from Carl Andre suggesting a project that he wanted to do.

**DAVID PRENTICE:** I found Dorothea to be mean-spirited. Marisol was interesting. She was like being with a handful of mist or fog. She was so ethereal. I thought she was very sexy. Colette was always so flouncy and cute.

•

eat your art out

**Ronnie Cutrone and Tony Shafrazi**
(photo by Anton Perich)

rebellion

**JACKIE SHERMAN, WAITRESS:** Who else but Mickey would let Carl Andre in wearing his paint-splattered overalls, looking like a bum? He was so sympathetic to anyone who was struggling. He had an astonishing ability to get people together, to make them want to come there. He was rude, but he had something people were drawn to. The artists, he just couldn't do enough for them. He was supporting half the artists in New York before they made it big. He was buying everybody's work. They weren't paying; they were running up bills. The art scene was basically remnants of the Lion's Head and the Cedar from the fifties. There wasn't any kind of art scene yet in the sixties. Artists weren't celebrities then like they are now.

**JEFFREY LEW:** I never understood how, intellectually, you could get into an argument so fiercely about these issues. Helen and Brice [Marden] used to fight about who was better.

Brice would come up to me and say, "Sit down. You know something? you're the worst artist in the whole world." And I'd say, "Well, thank you." Then he'd call me up the next day, and start screaming at me that he was the worst artist in the world.

**ED TISCH, MAX'S CAB DRIVER/ARTIST:** I went to Brice's studio and saw his "black drip" paintings. I looked at it, and it was all black and drippy down the bottom, and I'm thinking to myself, I hope the guy has a second job to fall back on.

**BRICE MARDEN, ARTIST:** I went to Max's right from the beginning. I'd see artists there like Frosty Myers, David Novros. I talked to Carl Andre. I learned a lot from him; he was a little bit older than me and had been around a little bit more, and we were both doing minimal work.

Basically whatever happened to me in New York happened through Max's. I met my wife Helen there—that was really the most significant thing. She was working there. The first night I remember seeing her was the night before I was leaving for California, and I was with Bobby Neuwirth who had just returned from touring with Dylan and the Band. He was just reunited with Edie Sedgwick, who was nervous because he was really kind of crazy at the time, so there was a lot of tension in the air. Bobby was great at hanging out. He was a laughing man—you know, people who keep everything relaxed and gets along with everyone—he was Dylan's "Laughing Man."

**MARJORIE STRIDER, ARTIST:** All the guys had tabs. Mickey wouldn't trade with me. I guess I wasn't famous enough. He wouldn't trade with any women, it was a very sexist place. However, he did let me run a tab, and if there was a crowd outside, he did bring me in.

**ELIZABETH DESALES, ARTIST/ILLUSTRATOR:** I came to the U.S. in 1972. I had been trained as an artist in France. I married artist David Budd in 1973. My English was not strong so I was listening and observing the scene. Everybody at our table drank a lot, even David, he drank too much, and I'd be sitting there with my orange juice. Larry Poons would talk about his work, and con-

high on

versations were a lot about the work of the artists. Sometimes I'd leave because everybody got so drunk and I didn't drink. I was not always able to communicate with John Chamberlain, because his manner was abrupt. At the same time I made allowances for this kind of behavior, because I had been trained in art school, and there was traditional certain character of rough behavior on the part of men toward women, somewhat abusive, very surly. Maybe I was such a wallflower they were nice to me.

**PHILIP GLASS:** I don't know if Mickey was swapping food and drinks for art with women. I imagine that he did. I don't know if he took a political position about women artists, but I don't think men in the art world were very comfortable with the subject. It was obvious the galleries were run for men and by men. There are women who became very well known, but it was basically a male society.

**COLETTE:** I had this crush on Larry Poons and I finally picked him up. I was a kid. The danger of a woman at that time who was young and attractive, and wanting to be an artist, was not to be a groupie. I had to be careful not to become that because I was very ambitious from the beginning and I knew what I wanted. I wanted these men to take me as an equal, not a groupie.

Larry respected the girls that looked like guys and painted like him. Then he could have a rapport with them. With me he was completely confused, because I wasn't supposed to look like a woman if I was going to be a serious artist, and I wasn't quite a groupie.

**JOE BIRD:** Rauschenberg is at the bar one night. I'm bartending. Finally I say, "Listen, Bob, you've got to pay your tab; put up or shut up." Bob takes his cock out, puts it on the bar, and says, "This is all I got tonight." So that's when I got the idea for Brigid [Berlin]. It was the invention of the Plaster Casters and the tit prints. It all started with these cock prints and it was Bob Rauschenberg who started it by putting his cock on the bar.

**JASON CROY, HAIRDRESSER:** I met Peter Fonda one night at Max's, and he put his cock on a stamp pad for Brigid for her cock book. I think Dennis Hopper was in it, too.

**PENNY ARCADE, ACTRESS/PERFORMANCE ARTIST:** I remember when Brigid was doing all the cock prints and asshole prints of the boys in the back room, and here it is two or three years ago and I'm reading in the society column of the newspaper and it says, "Brigid Berlin, the daughter of Happy and Richard Berlin, is exciting everyone with her needlework." I couldn't believe it. This woman was always shooting up, and now she was exciting everyone with her "needlework," and matrons are forming lines around the block at Martha's on Park Avenue to buy up her one-of-a-kind sweaters.

Several of the front-room regulars like John Ford, Neil Williams, and Robert Smithson, and back-room regulars—Warhol and his entourage, Danny Fields, Donald Lyons,

rebellion

and Terry Noel—would be seen sitting at the same table night after night. It became their designated table. If they weren't there, you were surprised or thought they were sick, or something happened to them. Mickey recalled, "The thing about Max's was that certain areas became certain people's spots." All the factions were very territorial, but when push came to shove, and the comforts of their "home away from home" became threatened by an intruder, a fire or whatnot, the Max's territories became one. That's when the family came together, and fought to protect their territory.

**JOHN CHAMBERLAIN:** When you think of a major fire in a crowded place, you think of people running, but everyone pitched in. People were taking down the paintings from the walls and bringing them to safety; no one fled. The waitresses and the bartenders were mopping the floors. Everyone else stood quietly out on the sidewalk for hours and watched and hoped. Paths opened for the firefighters. No one interfered with what had to be done.

**ED TISCH:** The fire engines are outside. Smoke in the place. The inside door from upstairs, here come all these people dancing down the stairs, some of them singing, *"We're having a fire."* I remember taking the cab in and coming back and grabbing a mop. I'm mopping. Next to me, Rauschenberg is mopping. Everybody came. I'd never seen anything like that in my life.

**PHILIP LOCASCIO:** It was crowded, and the band was going on. It was around eleven P.M., the Velvet Underground were setting up. It was just before the release of the *Banana* album. The smoke started bellowing upstairs, and the electricity started to go because the wires were melting. There was a lack of light. We got the customers on the street, but we didn't know what to do about the artwork and the money upstairs. My first reaction was, I had the waitresses out on the street collecting the customers' checks in between the firetrucks. Here they were with their little bohemian black miniskirts, trying to collect the checks. We got upstairs, and we got the *Soup Can* paintings off the walls, and Stuart got up to the third floor, and got the money, but it was such a frantic frenzy, because the walls were part of our lives, and we were very concerned about the artwork.

**JILL LUMPKIN, WAITRESS:** It was scary. Like that fear of losing your home and family.

## baseball max's kansas city style

At the bar, on any given night, was poet Donald Phelps, often showing off his vocal impersonation of the Indy 500. His drinking buddies at some of these impromptu performances included Donald Burns, Gregory Corso, Fielding Dawson, Bob Povlich, Diane Wakoski, Robert Creeley, Joe Early, and other distinguished writers and poets. Toward the middle, all the photographers would hang out, including Izzy, the French photographer, and his friends, who were nightly fixtures. Sordid members of Max's legendary baseball team sat at the other end of the bar, trading stories with the bartenders, who were unquestionably part of the show, as well as the team. The Max's team, financed by Mickey, once challenged the guys from Los Angeles' Cafe Figaro, owned by New York's Tom Ziegler. Unquestionably, more bull than balls got tossed, and the Max's team struck out in more ways than one. They didn't make many home runs, but they broke their own record for making whoever and whatever else was within their reach. Mickey was not a happy camper.

**Max's baseball team**
(photo by Barbara E. Jaffe)

73

**JOE EARLY:** At first Mickey was sour on the idea because we didn't have a very good team. His interest started coming alive when other bars started getting into it and we started winning. Then we became very good. We got an infusion of youngsters which is what we needed, and we were winning all the time. Now Mickey would come to the games and he got into it insofar as he was really a sports owner. He owned a team in the nicest possible way. He arranged for us to go to Florida and he arranged for us to go to California. Tom Ziegler, who owned the Figaro, had moved to California. He and Mickey were in touch. He was in New York one night at Max's and he laid down a wager to Mickey.

Now, it turned out that Mickey had made a very large bet with Tom Ziegler. The Sunday before we were scheduled to go out, we were due for a practice. We were all at Mickey's at ten in the morning in a snowstorm, which took care of the practice. We did practice drinking but we didn't practice softball. Tom Punzio didn't, and I didn't want to travel with a bunch of maniacs, so he and I went out ahead of time. Everybody else left the next day, and as I understand it, the plane trip was a riot.

**BOB PAULS:** Stan Kurzon, myself, Fe Dawson, and Larry Hellenberg were the start of the softball team. We'd all meet at six for drinks, eat a couple chicken wings and bad chili. We became friendly and then John Clarke used to hang around with Dan Christensen and Ken Shoal. We all decided to get together and have a catch. We met down at Second Avenue and Twentieth Street, at the old schoolyard. We'd start having catch, and we'd have choose-up games. Then we'd play with some of the kids that were hanging out there. Essentially this was just a bunch of barfly drunks, some of who had no ability, some of whom had limited ability, and a couple actually had some ability. It was not a team per se, it just snowballed.

**Robert Povlich, left, and Tom Punzio**

"It is my belief that the Max's Kansas City baseball team actually started the bar league in NYC."
—Billy Hoffman

high on

# baseball max's kansas city–style

## by kent wallace

**b**ASEBALL. A bet. Mickey Ruskin's Max's Kansas City versus Figaro's. (Backed by Bill Cosby, Tom Ziegler had moved Figaro's, his popular McDougal Street night spot out west.) New York versus Los Angeles. Sabotage. Sacking. A one-run game.

The action started with the uniforms. Continued on board the flight to LAX. Carried over onto the baseball diamond. Wound up as scandal south of the border—baseball Max's Kansas City–style.

The uniforms: Joe Early (manager and sometime player) went to Paragon Sporting Goods on Eighteenth and Broadway. He brought with him a Max's Kansas City matchbook (for logo purposes). Joe's first managerial decision was to unite his team by having them all wear the same number. He settled on 4. Each of the black jerseys with the white sleeves bore on its back the number 4.

Early told the Paragon people that he wanted their jersey logo to look exactly like it was on the matchbook. The jerseys arrived with "Max's Kansas City—Steak, Lobster, Chick Peas" across the front and "Close Cover Before Striking" along the bottom. Baseball Max's Kansas City–style.

The flight: Povlich boarded the plane wearing a cowboy hat and a western-style jacket with a sheriff's badge pinned to his chest. He sat next to Blackie and Babbo. A stewardess asked him if he was on official business. Povlich informed her that he was extraditing the two Mexicans (referring to Blackie and Babbo, who were in fact from Puerto Rico) back to California. The stewardess asked if there was anything she could do to help. Povlich requested that his "prisoners" be given no booze or sharp objects. Blackie and Babbo wound up being served plastic utensils with their meal and finding nothing more than Coca-Cola in their Cuba Libres. Baseball Max's Kansas City–style.

The game: Mickey had wagered a sizable sum on a side bet with Ziegler. The Max's team (which consisted of Povlich, Mike Shapiro, Joe Early, Larry Hellenberg, Dick Wells, Tommy Punzio, Fielding Dawson, Blackie, Babbo, Dick Evans, Evans Webb, Steve Miller, Warren Finnerty, and John Chamberlain, who went along for the ride) was coming off big wins against the Taurus Bar and Restaurant in Florida and the *Phoenix*, a popular print rag from Boston.

Unbeknownst to Mickey, Ziegler had loaded his team with ringers (a couple of semipro ball players). What was obvious was Ziegler's generosity. He plied the boys with booze and food (which he supplied at no charge). Ziegler's girls keep the team up late—very—the night before the game.

The game was close. Max's lost a tight one. 10–9. Lost in the last inning. A home run by one of the ringers. Mickey lost the big bet. Povlich lost a bundle on a side trip to Vegas  But in the end it was the Max's crew that had the last laugh.

While the celebration was going full-steam and the skulking Ziegler was cherishing his chicanery, Blackie wound up running off with Ziegler's wife, his car, and his vaunted pet sea otter—turning up in Mexico (of all places) and that, my friend, is baseball Max's Kansas City–style....

rebellion

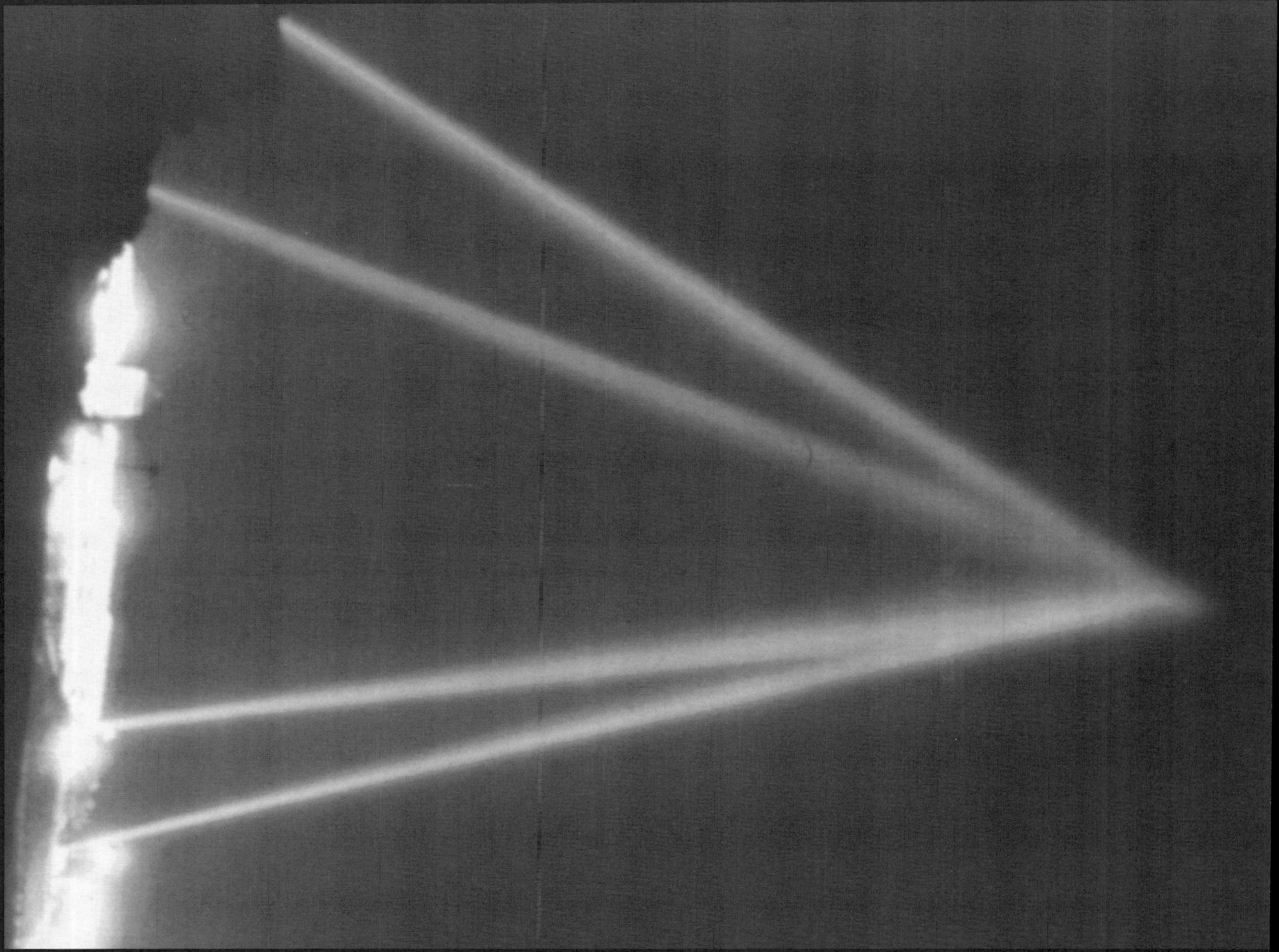

**Forrest Myers, *Search Light Sculpture*, 1966. Max's party in Union Square, 1969.** Courtesy of Artet Industrie.

# the laser beam

**OLIVIERO TOSCANI:** I remember the laser beam. It was the laser beam that got me interested. Going down Park Avenue and then the angle into Max's, it was like following a star.

**FROSTY MYERS:** The piece was actually designed on paper years before it was done. I knew I wanted to do this piece, but this was before private people could get their hands on lasers or I didn't know that one of my buddies, Bobby Neuwirth, had gone up to this electronics show at the New York Coliseum and saw this laser demonstration. He struck up a conversation with the laser salesman that worked for the company, Electra Physics, and invited him down to Max's after the show. So when the salesman got there he was in a suit and tie, and of course at that hour, was probably the only one at Max's wearing one. We got him to take off his tie, got him extremely drunk, got him a girl that he fell madly in love with, and we kept getting him drunker and drunker. Finally he gave us his demonstrator. He actually gave us a laser and that was the laser that I used to go from my studio on Nineteenth Street across the street and down one block to Max's.

## the laser beam

I cut a hole in my window so that the laser wouldn't hit the glass. It went through the window across the street and hit this small mirror that was affixed to the outside of the building of Max's. And then the mirror directed the beam inside the big plate-glass window, the front window of Max's, and straight down over the bar about three feet above everybody's head, right down the bar, and into the back room where it hit the wall. There was so much smoke in Max's at the bar that the beam showed up sometimes like a hot wire. Other times it would disappear and go through different atmospheric changes depending on how much moisture was in the air, like humidity, snow, rain. It would interrupt the beam. Or when you got outside, you would see the beam sparkling. It looked real pretty when it snowed.  At the time it just seemed so natural, because it was something that I thought about so much, that when I finally did it, it wasn't that it was anticlimactic—it was very exciting—but it just seemed sort of natural. It was on a timer so it would go on at eight o'clock at night and it would go off at four-thirty, five in the morning. A lot of people didn't know what it was, they would just discover it.

When the beam finally hits something it has a 3-D like quality to it. Sometimes I'd take the laser off the stand and I would work it out on the street. I would get people standing in front of Max's waiting to get in, and I could split the people up. They would think it was something from outer space. They would absolutely freak. Some people would freeze and, of course, some people knew what it was.  I remember a couple that was going into Max's. She was all dressed up. I guess they were from New Jersey. She had on what looked like a white ermine coat. Well she saw the little red speck and she dropped the coat and started to run up the street. The husband, I split him off and got him going in the other direction. Anyway it was his job to go and get the coat, so I would let him get almost up to the coat and I would take the beam and back him off again. It was like an adult water-gun. It was just fun and games. In the end, it was a work of art!

rebellion

*Divine, Courtesy of Richard Bernstein*

I've done a lot of things, but
I ain't never been no waitress.
—Candy Darling

**i** really basked in the glory of being a waitress at Max's. It was one of the most desirable and sought-after positions on the restaurant circuit in New York. It was like being a Rockette at Radio City Music Hall, or becoming a member of the hippest, in-est of in, private clubs. It was glamorous, excessive, spontaneous, the money was exceptionally good, and the people who came there were extraordinarily interesting. Jill Lumpkin said, "A lot of the waitresses went to Europe for their four days off, they made so much money," and Mickey would let certain waitresses go for several months and come back and pick up where they left off.

Newcomers to Max's often found the job to be either distasteful or downright demeaning. It definitely had its stress factors. There were probably very few of us who didn't break into tears at some point while working there. But there was the undisputable fact that we were also a major part of the attraction in our little black miniskirts and black tops. "The waitresses were more appetizing than the food,"

# letting it all hang loose

recalled Dennis Hopper, who frequented Max's while promoting Peter Fonda's movie *Easy Rider*. Several of the preferred customers made it their policy to take a waitress home for an after-dinner nightcap. Max's was the only restaurant/club where waitresses were treated like celebrities instead of indentured servants.

Like all new waitresses, in the beginning, I got the shitty shifts and stations: the front room (the bar and the booths across from the bar), the back room, and the upstairs, better known as Siberia, where the tourists were seated. Once I got the system down, I served my tables with a fresh-as-flowers country attitude and a happy-go-lucky smile, yet I'd still get comments from some of the regulars like, "It's obvious you haven't been working here long with a smile like that—just give it a little time."

**JILL LUMPKIN:** It was 1967 and I was working at the Figaro. One of my best friends, Marsha Harris, was friends with Helen Harrington. They were both working at Max's, so we used to go there. One night we were sitting there and I said, "Gee, I'd really like to work here." And they said, "So would everybody." But I was just drunk enough that I wasn't afraid. I went over to Mickey and I said, "Can I work here?" He said, "If you can prove you are twenty-one, you've got the job." So I went back to the table and I said, "I've got the job." They didn't believe it. I did tell Mickey I was friends with Marsha and Helen. Besides, Mickey really liked me....

He used to put Helen and I up front on Thursday nights and all the guys would come in. He would let us dance in the alcove on Thursday. Bob Sigans, Brice Marden, and Bob Neuwirth were all friends. They were three of the funniest guys in the world. They never missed a beat. We'd all sit in the alcove and take acid. We used to give head under the table just to see if we could get away with it.

**SUSAN DOUKAS, WAITRESS/ACTRESS:** This tall waitress, a beautiful light-skinned black girl, said she had Dylan's baby. I think maybe they lived together for a while. Well, she didn't actually have the baby, the rumor was that she had an abortion, and kept the fetus in formaldehyde in a glass bottle.

**JEFFREY BRENNAN:** The first time I ever went to Max's was with my cousin Jill Lumpkin, her friend Helen, and two other women who were six feet tall, and the waitress comes over with champagne for everybody. I'm thinking, These are waitresses and they're getting champagne, that's a switch.

**JILL LUMPKIN:** Our uniforms were the hippest. Talk of fashion in the sixties, that is part of what made Max's, Max's. A lot of the girls had been to England, and we all wore miniskirts that didn't cover our ass. There were great-looking waitresses, and we had skirts that when you leaned over the table your bum showed.

**RUSSELL RYAN, ILLUSTRATOR:** Christine Lombard was the French waitress. She was pretty tall and when she sat down the guys were always trying to see under her little skirt. Christine would say, "Ah, you want to see my black pussy," and she'd pick up her skirt, but she'd have tights on.

**JOHN FORD:** The waitresses used to wear those miniskirts, and this one waitress wore her skirt so short that the fuckin' string on her Tampax was always hanging out, and nobody bothered to tell her.

**LARRY ZOX:** I thought Mickey was running some kind of service up on the third floor. When he was interviewing waitresses they would come in waves. There would be these beauties, I mean beauties, lined up waiting for an interview. I said to Mickey, "I think I'm going to have to come up there with you." So I would listen in on a few of them. The questions were perverse. "Do you carry any Vaseline?" But he sure hired stunning waitresses.

**FIELDING DAWSON:** God knows, the businessmen were there because of the waitresses. And for myself to be alive meant to be at the bar at around four-thirty, five o'clock in the morning, and the waitresses would sit in the back and do their tallies and talk. This was classic Du Maupausant–Chekhov country, when the working class gets off work and starts telling stories about what happened during the night. And the language! My hair used to curl when some of them started going, talking about the customers.

Then just being there and watching Mickey and the way he treated the waitresses, it would be easy to say that man hates women. That he absolutely hates women.

**BOB PAULS:** Everybody hit on all the waitresses. There was one waitress who was very funny. Heather was her name. She had the biggest tits of anybody who worked in that store. She would stop traffic. She was a painter from Ohio. All I remember is that for a while we lived together and she would come home from work and the first words out of her mouth were, "If somebody refers to me as 'Them' again, I'm goin kick them in the nuts." And it was true, every time she'd walk through the store everybody would say, "Hey, look at them."

**PAT SQUIRE, HEAD WAITRESS:** I don't know how I ended up being the head waitress. I think that Mickey knew that I would abuse the waitresses.

**JACKIE SHERMAN:** All the waitresses at first were terrorized by Pat Squire. She was the female half of Mickey, very bossy. She was the den mother. I was fortunate because Patsy Cummings took me under her wing. It was Patsy and Cathy Drew. There was a very tight clique. Then there were the glam queens: Jill Lumpkin, Helen Harrington, the big blonde, and Marsha Harris. You couldn't even think to get into that group. Little me, I was the smallest, and I'm not small but compared to them. I

always felt out of place, because I was so small and they were so huge. And they were so black and so white. The glam queens were very involved with rock and roll, you know, Bob Dylan, Jimi Hendrix. Jill was with Tom Rush and I was still with Jeremy Steig.

Then Mickey got perverse and decided to hire all these girls named Jackie all at once. He hired three Jackies, and one looked exactly like me. I said, "Mickey, did you do this on purpose?" And he laughed and walked away....

The conditions a new waitress had to work under there were very strenuous, and Mickey always told us, "I can get a waitress anywhere, they come a dime a dozen."

**ABBIE HOFFMAN:** I flirted with the waitresses lots of times. It was the closest you could come to liking bunnies and get away with it, given the rise of women's liberation. My favorite waitress was

high on

Paula. I followed her from the Paradox, a restaurant in the East Village. We never did anything. It was my fantasy. The ones you strike out on are the ones you think about forever. Patsy Cummings had a lot of fans.

**TOM PUNZIO:** When I first started going to Max's as part of the softball team, the waitresses were like little fantasies to me. I had to stop going in or my marriage would have fallen apart. I was interviewing waitresses on a nightly basis. I didn't make it home sometimes, and even when I was off I wanted to be there.

**HOWARD SMITH:** After all, for a girl, being a waitress at Max's was almost considered like being a rock-and-roll star, so there was this rumor going around that you had to sleep with Mickey to get a waitressing job, but that was ridiculous. What came across as rudeness toward women, was really shyness. Mickey was one of the shyest people I've ever met, about sex especially. He used to tell me over and over again the story of him being a virgin until he was twenty-nine years old.

**LYNN MYERS, WAITRESS:** When I started waitressing at Max's I found that everyone was taking drugs, so I said, "Oh boy." I didn't want to be not hip, and by this time everybody was immediately my best friend. I was very friendly. I took to the amphetamines like a duck takes to water and immediately blew myself completely out to the point where Stuart, the upstairs manager, and I, would work my tables. It was like first he would say, "Lynn, your food is up!" Then he would just deliver it. This went on for a long time and I was just getting nuttier and nuttier, and faster and faster the brain cells were keeling over. I lasted about six weeks. It was glamorous, it was excessive, and it was spontaneous. It was the best party of my youth. I did things in there that I didn't do in the rest of the world, because it wouldn't have been safe for me to do them.

I went to work one night and Robin Cullinen, the manager, comes up to me and says, "You're fired, Lynn!" I said, "Oh!" I didn't even have the nerve to ask why. The fact that I couldn't get a plate to a table had nothing to do with it. It was amazing I lasted as long as I did. I was told to finish out the night and I got the back room. At this point I'm sort of really, really depressed and wasted and strung-out and suicidal, and the only person that I thought I could talk to on the entire planet (I decided) was Leonard Cohen. I had never even seen the guy. It just came into my little drug-abused mind. I had read all his books and had really gotten into his music and I was obsessed with him. I was so despondent that I couldn't even talk to my friends. I only wanted to talk to Leonard Cohen and I was convinced I had to find him. I had no idea what he looked like. I spent the whole night, between serving tables and crying, scrutinizing people to see if it was him. I didn't know if he even came in the place. I was doing one of those manipulations that you do with God: "If there's really a God, you'll let Leonard Cohen save my life."

I would work my way to the bar to pick up my drinks and each time I walked by, I noticed this one man staring at me. I noticed it as I went by again. So I just walked up to him and said, "Are you Leonard Cohen?" He said, "Yes!" I said, "I've been waiting for you," and I sat down with him and started talking. "I really need to talk to you, but I'm working and this is my last night." I go back to working my tables and at one point he comes up to me in the back room and he says, "I'm leaving, leave with me!" I said, "I can't leave now, I have to work until four A.M." This is what the insanity of drugs does. Just because I was fired, that had nothing to do with it, I was responsible. He leaves, and now I really start to cry. Here's the love of my life, God had sent him to me, and I let him get away. Well, he came back at four in the morning and got me. When I was checking out at the end, he came and sat down next to me. We left and we drove around New York and went to a coffee shop and drank coffee and ate breakfast and sang songs and made out until around eleven in the morning. It really was Leonard Cohen.

**JILL LUMPKIN:** Max's in many ways was a great initiation place to drugs and things more exotic like hash. There was no other club in the world that I ever did drugs in. We'd go out and smoke, but where else would all the help be eating hash brownies on New Year's Eve? Even people who didn't know what they were, were eating them. Not everybody took drugs when they started.

**ELLEN GOFEN:** One of the waitresses made a cake with hash in it for New Year's Eve. She gave it out to people. I had a piece; it was very strong. It was like working underwater. I wasn't taking drugs at the time at all. There was a young waitress who was working the upstairs who was very straight and very square. She made a lot of money. She was fast and thin, and she didn't know anything was in the cake. After eating a piece, she became close to hysterical. Peter Berry, the bartender, never took another drug after that. Izzy the cook, I was told, ate a piece, and the manager had to take over and cook for him. Mickey was not at all amused.

**PAT SQUIRE:** Susan Donner freaked out when someone gave her a hash brownie. She was crying and screaming. Someone had to take her to the hospital. I remember the whole restaurant was moving in slow motion. The people were going, "Where's my this, and where's my that?" All the help was on hash.

**ALICE WEINER:** Mickey's favorite waitresses got whatever they wanted. Patsy, actually the two Pats—Patsy Cummings, Pat Squire—and Marsha Harris were favorites. The most peculiar thing that he would do is, he would replace waitresses, after they had been there for a long time, with someone who looked like them. He liked to clone them....

The first night I put drawn butter for the lobster in a plastic shrimp-cocktail-sauce thing. They both looked exactly alike, except one was plastic and the other was glass. And I put the melted butter that was suppose to go in glass into the plastic thing. That was the first time he turned the jukebox all the way up and started to scream at me....

I must have worked at Max's for two years on and off, but it must have been a year and a half before Lawrence Weiner really got drunk with John Chamberlain and fell in love with me. I was living in my VW at the time.

**LAWRENCE WEINER:** It wasn't a bus, either. It was a Beetle. We had an affair in her Volkswagon filled with millions of wire hangers. Mickey read me the riot act the first night I came to pick up Alice: "This is not for you."

**ALICE WEINER:** He told Lawrence that I would just forget him after the next guy came along; I'd just junk it. That I was that kind of girl. I'd turn him over, just like a table. Mickey stood me right in front of the jukebox, turned it all the way up and screamed at me.

**LAWRENCE WEINER:** One of the things Mickey said was, "Hey, listen, you think you got it made, you know you can walk into this place, and you can walk into these other places and you can sort of do whatever you want, you know, like fine. You need somebody with some money and she ain't got it. You need somebody with some education, and she ain't got shit." But Mickey, I must say for all his prudishness, once it was a fait accompli that Alice and I had decided to have some sort of relationship, he made things reasonably comfortable. He'd have his opinions about things, and talk about it and talk about it, but once it was a fait accompli, it was a fait accompli. That was it. If you can't love me, love my dog. But he'd argue completely about the dog first. But once it was obvious that this person was going to schlep the dog into his restaurant all the time, or this person was going to be with this person, he'd just accept it. And then he would try to find something interesting in the other person. But he would still say, "Oh, so-and-so lives with a sleazeball."

One night I was working the back room and there was this gorgeous creature sitting at Danny Fields' table. He looked like a cherub. He had this mass of curly hair and this angelic smile that just lit up the room. I was *so* attracted to him. He had that lost-little-boy look, similar to Mickey's but different. We had this flirtation going on across the room. We kept eyeing each other and I'd make the happy, sad faces, where you run your hand down your face and you frown, then you run it back up and you smile. It wasn't till much later on that I found out he had an album out called *Happy/Sad.* He'd look away for a while and then he'd look up from underneath those blond curls and shine those big brown eyes at me and I'd melt. And he had these beautiful white teeth that went perfectly with his smile. I could tell that he was kind of shy, but I knew he liked me. The room cleared out at four A.M. except for a few diehard barflies. I tallied up my tabs and handed my checks in to the cashier, changed my clothes, and got ready to split. I walked out of Max's and there he was, this sweet thing, just standing there all alone. I knew he was waiting for me. It was such a rush. I felt giddy, like I was back in high school. I didn't know who he was or

Tim Buckley upstairs at Max's
(photo by Anton Perich)

where he came from. I had never seen him at Max's before. He just appeared out of nowhere, a Danny Fields special.

"Where ya goin'?" I asked. "Nowhere in particular." He looked down at the ground, shuffled his foot, and then looked up again. Our eyes met. We both smiled. "Well, where you staying?" "Nowhere in particular." "You can come home with me." I was smitten. I thought he was just about one of the hottest creatures I had ever laid eyes on, and just to think, he was waiting for me. I suddenly remembered the Dylan album cover, *Freewheelin' Bob Dylan*, where he and his girlfriend at the time, Suze Rotollo, are walking arm in arm down the streets of NYC. For that very moment, that was us. I had never been so blatantly seduced by anyone before. It gave me a certain thrill, a certain high like the kind you get on mescaline where everything is dreamy and perfect. This was to be my first Max's Kansas City sexual encounter. He told me his name was Tim Buckley and that he was in New York from L.A. I didn't know at the time who Tim Buckley was, or that he had a record out on Elektra and was already on his way to becoming the new folk/ pop star on the label. All I knew was that he was making me hot. I was so embarrassed when we got to my apartment because I didn't have any of his records. He said he liked that I didn't know who he was, that it made him feel secure. His shyness

**Tim Buckley**
(photo by Lilly Hou)

added to the excitement of the tenderness in the way he made love. I felt like a virgin being deflowered. I had never been out with a musician before or gone home with one, for that matter. But one thing was definite: from that moment on, I knew I liked musicians. I also got the word from Lillian Roxon that Linda Eastman was very jealous.

Shortly after he left for L.A., I was working the upstairs when I felt something trickling down my leg. I was thinking, "What the hell is going on? What is this?" At four A.M. when I was turning in my checks, Marilyn Eiser, the cashier who knew everybody's business, said to me, "I noticed you've been hanging out with Tim Buckley." "Yeah, so what's it to you?" I snapped. "I just thought I'd mention," she jeered with much satisfaction, "that Tim has a girlfriend, Janie, and I heard all the way from L.A. that he just gave her the clap." It wasn't like I was out to be totally promiscuous or anything, I was simply eager for the romance and the sexual adventure that comes with being young and free. I was only twenty-one, working my first job in New York in the most sexually permissive atmosphere I had experienced to date. We were wearing our skirts shorter than anyone had worn them in history, smoking pot, staying out all night, enjoying a renaissance in music, and going home with whomever we wanted, often the same night we met them. But that was nothing compared to the back-room people who were actually giving blow jobs there at the tables and in the bathrooms....

Not all the waitresses were natural beauties but they were unique unto themselves, each with their own style and personality. I remember when Charles Goldstein told me that Tony Gould remarked that I was one of the ugliest waitresses Mickey hired. Several of the waitresses were foreign, and were not fluent in the English language, nor did they always comprehend what the customer was saying. There were even a few "bimbos" added, justifiably so for flavor. This was all part of the ambience. It took a particular type of character to be able to handle the intensity and bizarre insanity that went on night after night—part three-ring circus, part *National Lampoon's* high-school reunion.

**JIM BELL, MAX'S REGULAR:** There was a waitress who had just started working; I think she was from Europe. She was taking our order and someone at the table ordered a Wild Turkey and she asked him if he wanted gravy on his Wild Turkey.

**CHRISTINE LOMBARD:** A guy came over to me one time and said, "Where is the john?" I said, "I don't know where John is." I never heard the bathroom referred to as a john before. I just had not mastered the language.

**JACKIE SHERMAN:** Warren Finnerty, who was in *Easy Rider* and a regular at Max's, came in one night with Warren Beatty and Dennis Hopper, and he introduced me I got friendly with Dennis, and after the movie came out and he got successful, he hung out at Max's a lot. They both came over to me when I was waiting station two one night and hugged me. The other waitress said, "You know them? Is that the kind of people you meet working here?" I said, "Yeah, girls, eat your heart out."

Of all the celebrities that came in, Cary Grant was the only one who had all the waitresses acting like giggly teenagers. (You know we never really made a fuss over anybody.) He was so lovely and charming. He sat in the alcove on station two. He had ordered wine and and he got up from the table and I was standing there. He said, "Well, girls, I had this really good wine and there's a lot left over, so why don't you have it, I'm going to leave it with you." He was just so charming and we were all very impressed.

**PAT SQUIRE:** I thought Cary Grant was a pain in the ass. He would not eat anything to do with charcoal because if he did, it was cancerous. He used to do that whenever he came in. He gave me a big hard time one night because his steak had charcoal on it; he wouldn't eat it.

**JILL LUMPKIN:** I waited on James Coburn; he was with a beautiful woman. Then the Stones came in and they were like little church boys, because they had been warned that no one wanted to wait on them.

**WENDY YUJUICO:** I waited on the Rolling Stones. They were sitting in the middle room. One of them asked me to get a pack of cigarettes. I was sort of floored. I was impressed by Bianca Jagger....

When the model Twiggy came in, everyone gave her a hard time. No one took her seriously. I remember Celeste Holm, and the time Kirk Douglas came in and stood at the bar.

The time Liberace came in, he waltzed through with his entourage and cape. He walked down the runway to the back where the stairs were that overlooked the room. He walked up the stairs, stopped at the top, looked over the room, turned around and came back down. It was like his grand entrance.

**ED TISCH:** There was a night when the waitresses and the busboys and the managers were running up and down the stairs, and they're screaming. "He's here, oh my God!" And I'm saying to myself, Who could this possibly be? I mean, Janis Joplin was probably sitting in the back room with Warhol and his crowd, and you knew Rauschenberg was in the place because you could hear him laughing. So who were they running upstairs to see? Liberace. I learned something at Max's—you don't run to see famous people, it makes no difference.

**ELLEN GOFEN, WAITRESS:** Mel Brooks used to come in all the time. He always talked to me because I spoke Yiddish. I could never get over the fact that Timothy Leary ordered pork chops....

There were these two four-seater tables, and there was a little two-seater table right in the middle, and Bobby Schwartz, a dancer/choreographer, used to sit there. He was sitting at the two-seater facing front, and Keith Richards was at one of the four-seater tables with this woman, and they started talking to each other. Bobby had just choreographed something and they got into this whole discussion about the music he was doing the choreography to, and it turned out that Keith had written the music. Bobby had no idea that he had been talking to Keith Richards, and Keith didn't know it was Bobby who had choreographed his music. It was nice how they met....

**Tinkerbell** (photo by Anton Perich)

91

Ornette Coleman came in very often. I was waiting outside after work one night for a cab and Ornette was also waiting for a cab. I was going to Brooklyn and he was going uptown. I was struck by the fact that he wanted to share a cab because cab drivers wouldn't stop for him but they would stop for me. Here he was, a famous musician, and because he was black he still had trouble getting a cab.

**SUSAN DOUKAS:** Nancy Sinatra was sitting with the Warhol crowd one night, which I thought was interesting. And Peter Allen would come in with Liza Minnelli. And I didn't understand why Janis Joplin was almost always there alone and almost always sad.

**PATSY CUMMINGS:** There was another night I had this guy, a good-looking guy with a beard, and he was in a booth drinking, and he's getting louder and louder. He wasn't really annoying anybody, but the loudness was bothering Mickey. So I go over and I try to get him to leave. Finally I have to say, "Look, you're really loud, and the owner asked me to get you to leave." He says, "No problem." I went to get his check at the cash register, and I notice he's getting up out of the booth, and he moves to the back of the alcove, and he's looking at the picture window and framing it up. Before I could move, he's running and he goes right through the plate-glass window, picked himself up, brushed himself off, and started walking uptown. Mickey didn't even bother to chase him. He said, "Is he hurt? Call the glass company, get another window."

**JEREMIAH NEWTON, SCREENWRITER/FILMMAKER:** Mickey would orchestrate the waitresses, and they went back and forth through that narrow corridor and people would come out of the bathroom and collide with the waitresses, and they were all tough and they didn't take any shit from anybody. Some of them reminded me of Charles Manson's girls.

**TONY GOULD:** Mickey basically hired me to fire everybody, to clean up the place. He had a monster on his hands, and he was used to a smaller store. He could take the heat; he wasn't afraid of anything but the place was so huge, and I had already run huge places. I had been working at Arthur's, and the Limelight before that. He and I couldn't have been two more unalike people. He spent about a month right on my side introducing me to who all the personalities were, and it was time very well spent....

So I'm in the back room seating people, and I'd just put the menus down, and I hear this horrendous noise. I was real quick in those days, and I came out of the back room, and I'm running as fast as I can. The whole aisle was empty all the way around him, and I can't imagine who in the world would jump through the window. I get up there and this guy in a leather jacket is lying there, and it was Bob Clark. He was a black guy, more of a poet, and he was crazy. He had about an eighteen-month cycle, and he'd do something like this. He'd pull some monstrous stunt. I'm looking up at these shards, and I didn't know if he was dead or alive. He started moving, so I grabbed him by the coat, lifted him back up, and he looks right in my face. I've known Bob for years. I say, "Bob, what are you doing?" He says, "I just had to do it." So I say, "Bob, I'll see you in a few months." And he just walked out. It took us all night to clean it up. That front window was cut into three sections. Both of the side sections had been broken and replaced with modern glass, but the biggest section was the original glass from 1919. It was like an inch thick, and it was like steel plate, extremely heavy and very dangerous. It was a real mess.

**JOE BIRD:** Izzy is trying to put the make on this new waitress as usual; she says, "Fuck off." Izzy hops over the steam table, pops her one; she went through the swinging doors, over the middle row, and ends up in this guy's salad. I came from behind the bar to help her out. Here's this guy trying to romance his date, we pull [the waitress] out of the salad bowl. Mickey says to her, "I'm really sorry, but I'm afraid I have to let you go." She says, "Hey, wait a minute, I didn't do a goddamn thing, that fuckin' asshole in there hit me." "I know," Mickey says, "but waitresses are a dime a dozen, and good cooks are hard to find."

**CATHY DREW:** Patsy was the practical joker among the waitresses. It started with the rubber chicken. The kitchen was a zoo, and Izzy the cook was a maniac. He was out of prison on a murder charge and would walk around with that meat cleaver, shaking it at you or threatening you when he got angry, which was more than often. You'd be frightened to death to bring back a steak that was either too well-cooked or not cooked enough. "Oh, Izzy, this is too well-done." Suddenly the largest butcher knife in the place would start slamming against the sheet metal and twenty-three waitresses would freeze. Or he would take out his dick and threaten to pee on the steak. He'd get madder and madder and drunker and drunker as the evening went on, but you knew that waitresses came a dime a dozen and the cook was indispensable. I was in tears a couple of times, but Patsy went about things in a different way. To her it seemed a little bit more obscure. I would come crashing through the kitchen door with eight plates dangling up my arm, and there was Patsy very politely and languidly holding up this rubber chicken to these customers. "Would this be all right?" I couldn't believe my eyes. "When they order chicken," she said, "I write it all down, and then I go into the kitchen and come out with this." She would try to encourage me to do it.

**JEFFREY BRENNAN:** Anton Perich was the world's worst bus boy. The waitresses would always go, "Is this guy working?" I mean it was a joke. Finally someone said, "What's the deal here?" Well, it turned out that Mickey liked his photography and wanted to help him out.

**JEANNIE BLAKE, ARTIST:** Mickey encased Patsy Cummings' apron on the wall when she left Max's.

At the end of 1967 when Max's was just beginning to reach its peak and I was finally feeling at home with the regulars, I left my long-sought-after waitressing position.

rebellion

I was seeing the night manager, Charles Goldstein, who was extremely jealous, accusing me of flirting with the customers and giving out my phone number. Charles got angry with me for some stupid reason and decided not to seat anyone in my section for about two hours. That was the straw that broke the camel's back. I can step in shit but I'm not going to eat it. So just when I had been getting all the better shifts and the best stations for making money (Mickey moved me up in rank because he knew I was good), Charles issued a "Quit, or I'll have you fired" edict. I quit.

I really missed all the excitement of Max's, and most of all, I missed Mickey. I walked into Max's one afternoon around four P.M. and Mickey was standing near the bar. He saw me and immediately came over. He asked me how I had been, and we started talking and I went with him to pick up his daughter Nina. I loved riding in the Max's van with him. He picked up Nina and we continued to talk about this and that. He dropped me off at my apartment, and as I was about to get out, he blurted, "Can I see you again?"

Mickey and I lived together for three years and then on and off for a few more years after that. In many ways it was a storybook romance. We were the perfect complement to each other: he was painfully shy, unknowingly powerful and charismatic, while I was strong, independent, frivolous, daring, and carefree. We both shared an intuitive sense, and often operated strictly on instinct. He was a patron of the artists, and I was sympathetic to the struggling musicians on the scene. He initiated the salonlike atmosphere for his artists' friends; I was instrumental in helping him create "upstairs at Max's" to debut unsigned musicians and bands. He introduced me to a world of art, culture, glitter, and glam, and I taught him to experience the basic pleasures of life.

I didn't like it when Mickey still treated me like a waitress. When I was a waitress it was okay, but when we were living together, and it would carry over into the home, and he'd start giving me orders, I really took offense at that. On the other hand, Mickey was very romantic, something people didn't see in him. He would bring me the most incredible flowers. The most outrageous colors, roses of every color. He loved buying me things. He would say, "So-and-so owes me money, have them design some clothes for you, or go have Larissa measure you for a coat." He was always surprising me with presents. Mickey was very generous in that way. It was his way of showing me that he cared, because he wasn't able to verbalize it. He wasn't the type of person to tell you how much he loved you, so he bought me presents, and took me places, including Europe. We'd go up to the Cloisters, lie in the grass, and listen to chamber music. We took sailing lessons in the moonlight on City Island, then rented a house on Fire Island for the summer, where we'd take long walks on the beach in the evening. We were a real family. We attended the best parties, and he flew me everywhere. Mickey took great pride and pleasure in opening up this new world to me, and I couldn't get enough of it.

Nonetheless, he still felt insecure with me, because I was very aloof and carefree, and much younger than most of his friends. He was always afraid I would run off and leave him. I very clearly asked Mickey if he wanted to have children, as I did, and he said, "Yes, I love having children." So when I became pregnant with Jessica, it became much more serious. Mickey didn't actually get a divorce until right before I delivered. Marriage didn't really appeal to me, I was looking for the right man to have children with, so it didn't matter that we weren't married, but I definitely wanted him to get a divorce. We did sign papers before Jessica was born stating that he was the legal father and willfully abided by that responsibility.

**Outside of Max's**
(photo by Raeanne Rubenstein)

rebellion

**b**y November of 1967 Max's had reached its peak. The crowds were massive. It was three-deep at the bar and there was no relief in sight. So Mickey took a space across the street on the southwest corner of Eighteenth and Park. It was a long space with lots of windows and an alternative hangout for the spillover of Max's regular crowd, an ice cream parlor with liquor and bright lights. There was that fantastic Mark di Suvero swing up front, which added to the glamour.

**FROSTY MYERS:** We called it both Longview Country Club and the Broomstreet Expressway. The Broomstreet Expressway was threatening Soho and that was something that everybody was talking about. The Longview was designed to look like an art gallery; it was completely white and had track lighting, and it had one of the best group shows in town. Frank Stella had a piece, as did Peter Reginato. He had a beautiful sculpture that you could actually sit on; a big yellow U-shaped sculpture in the middle of the room. The booths and the floors were painted gray so it looked like an artist's loft. We put diecrode lights so that the shadows of the people became the opposite color of the light. It was an attempt to make people part of the artworks. It was a conceptual piece.

**MEL BOCHNER, PAINTER:** I have very fond memories of the Longview Country Club. I actually preferred that period, because Max's had gotten overrun at that point. The brilliant thing that Mickey did with that space was turning the lights up, making it bright. That's exactly what the tourists and the crowds didn't want. They wanted the atmosphere of Max's. When you walked across the street there were the big windows and the Mark di Suvero swing, and the menu was mostly hamburgers, ice cream, and alcohol. People intermixed much more there. It was very lively. Rauschenberg spent a lot of time at Longview.

**FROSTY MYERS:** The only problem with the Longview Country Club is that it was competing with the greatest bar in the world which was right across the street and it was the same customers. Levine's became a last-ditch attempt at trying to do something with the place.

**LES LEVINE, CONCEPTUAL ARTIST:** Levine's restaurant was hooked up through John Brockman. Mickey approached me and said, "Do you want to trade a piece for a tab?" And I said, "Well, I'm a conceptual artist, so what can we do in relationship to that?" After a certain amount of time, Mickey came to me and said that the Longview Country Club across the street wasn't making enough money, and we talked over ideas. The video screens were very much ahead of their time. The bartenders would forget to turn them on because they just didn't like the feeling that they were being watched. They felt that "these videos are here so Mickey can watch what we're doing." Plus, they were much more expensive in those days. Levine's was the first restaurant to have monitors. After a short run, it fell apart when Mickey had a fire at Max's and temporarily moved Max's over to Levine's. Levine's never got off the ground.

When he opened the uptown place in 1969, people really didn't like to go uptown. Most people didn't like to go further than where they lived. Mickey got into empire-building and you can't physically be in all places at one time, and even though he had the Max's bus service from uptown to downtown, what you are doing is physically taking people out of one place and moving them to another. The concept doesn't work.

The original concept of Max's Terre Haute, located at 1359 First Avenue, on the southwest corner of Seventy-third, was to attract the hip Upper East Side artsy crowd. Frosty displayed his talent once again by designing a laser beam that went around the restaurant and ended up at the restrooms. So when someone asked the bartender or the waitress where the bathrooms were, they would say, "Just follow the laser beam." Johanna Lawrenson installed a small boutique, the place was painted, and the lighting was changed. But what Mickey found out is that the crowd that the restaurant attracted was not his crowd, and so the initial excitement wore off shortly after it opened and the place just fizzled.

I met Bobby Neuwirth while I was having dinner with Mickey at Max's Terre Haute. Neuwirth hung out everywhere. He was a scenemaker as well as an artist and musician. He was sitting in the balcony area with his girlfriend Tanto, who later married Jackson Browne. I noticed him instantly. He had a very strong presence. They came over and sat at our table. He was in the music world, that was my world, as opposed to the art world, which was Mickey's. Then the next time I ran into him was at a party. Mickey had to work late so I went on ahead. I walked in, it was very crowded. I saw Bobby and immediately gravitated toward him. He appeared to be slightly inebriated. We were definitely flirting; he asked me to take a walk and smoke a joint with him. I asked him if he was aware that I was Mickey's girlfriend. He said he was, so I said, "Let's go."

We got our coats on and walked outside. It was snowing and windy so we ended up sitting on the top stairwell joking and smoking. I was lost in the fantasy of the moment. Then we started necking. I was lying on my fur coat, when all of a sudden we heard someone coming up the stairs. We saw the bright orange down jacket. The coat could not be mistaken, it was Mickey's. My heart was beating like a scared rabbit. It was dark so he was obviously unaware that it was me on the floor under Neuwirth. He said he was looking for the party and Neuwirth told him, "It's on the bottom floor, man." Mickey, who was embarrassed, chuckled and went back down the stairs, and into the party. And, so the story goes, Mickey with his shit-eating grin started announcing to everybody that he just saw Neuwirth upstairs fucking some chick. I didn't know how to get out of this dilemma, so I hightailed it out of there. I heard that Mickey looked around and couldn't find me so he asked someone at the party, "Have you seen Yvonne?" "Yes," was the reply, "I saw her leave about twenty minutes ago with Neuwirth." Remember, we were very very young and the times were cooking....Bobby told me to deny it was me, but I felt too guilty. We weren't fucking, but needless to say, Mickey was very hurt and humiliated. He said he needed a few days to think things over, so I took Jessica and went to my sister's.

I called Bobby the next day. He always had these classic one-liners. This one was in regard to the game of Chess. He said, "The queen is the only piece that could move anywhere on the board, and it's your move." I filed that piece of information in the annals of my mind. Mickey called a few days later and said that he missed us, and wanted me to come back. Unfortunately Bobby didn't fare so well. He was 86ed from Max's for many months to come. Bobby is the only man to date that I ever asked to come live with me.

**Bobby Neuwirth, right, talking with Donald Lyons** (photo by Billy Name)

rebellion

**i**n June 1971, when failed ventures and Mickey's tax troubles threatened to close Max's down, all the artists who frequented Max's—de Kooning, Warhol, Rauschenberg, Lichtenstein, et al.—contributed artworks for an auction to save their favorite watering hole from going under. They became stockholders in what Mickey coined "the Chick Pea Conspiracy."

**JERRY ORDOVER, ART ATTORNEY:** I'd come down with my suits and ties and the bouncers didn't want to let me in, but I'd mention Mickey's name and they got to know me. I brought Frank Stella down one night, he had never been there even though he traded with Mickey. He gave his tab to his studio assistant named Robert Gordon. He wasn't going to bars. In the old days he went to the Cedar because his studio was cold. It had no heat. He was living on Jones Street. I think it was around the time of the Chick Pea Conspiracy, the auction to help Mickey pay back taxes. I think he contributed a piece and I convinced him; I said, "Lets go over there." I was one of the foreman

# steaklobsterchickpeas

## max's kansas city   max's terre haute

**213 Park Avenue South · New York, New York 10003 · (212) 777-7870**

October 8, 1971

Mr. Ronnie Landfield
31 Des Brosse
New York, N. Y.

Dear Ronnie:

As a Stockholder in Chick Pea Conspiracy, Inc., Jerry Ordover will be mailing you
your shares of stock very shortly. But I also want to take this opportunity to
thank you for everything you have done for Max's. The mere fact that we are still
open is proof of how much you did as there is little doubt that we could not have
survived the summer without the proceeds of the auction. This is not to say that
we still don't have substantial problems but hopefully, with the remaining money
and with the new spirit, we will be able to solve them and keep growing.

As to what your money did, first of all it has paid off some of the old debts that
had accumulated during the past two lean years. Secondly, we are redecorating the
old place a little to make it more comfortable. Incidentally, it's interesting
how many people have objected to each change no matter how small -- resistance to
change, etc. But after five years, I guess it was time to do something. So far
we've carpeted the floor and walls on the first floor and are about to repaint the
ceiling. Also we've recovered the bar and front of the store with aluminum. Next
on the agenda will be some new furniture on the first floor and a general refur-
bishment on the second floor. In addition, we have started a policy of live entertainment and extended our dancing to every night of the week. As an incentive to
Chick Pea Stockholders, you will be charged only half price for the live entertainment and of course all Stockholders will be allowed in for the dancing free of
charge.

I hope, now that you have a vested interest in the continued prosperity of Max's,
you will all make some suggestions that will help make it a more interesting,
and hence a better place. I am usually around during the afternoon as well as at
night, and would love to hear any ideas or suggestions you may have as I rely on
my creative friends for ideas.

Enclosed is a Max's T-shirt, a small token for all of you. I am also asking that
each of you come have dinner for two one evening as Max's guest. This is not only
intended as a small dividend and as a tangible way of saying thank you, but also
has a selfish motive. It will give each of you the opportunity to make what I hope
will be some constructive criticism of the menu and the food. I hope that you'll
take advantage of this as soon as possible.

Once again, thanks for the second chance and we'll see you soon.

Sincerely,

of the auction. Tanya Neufeld worked at *Artforum*. Ed Ruscha was the art director. She ended up going off with Tony Weinberger.

**JEFFREY LEW:** I had a piece in the auction. One day Mickey told me that the piece didn't sell but, he said, "a lot of pieces didn't sell, so don't feel too bad." I went to the auction then I didn't know what had happened to the piece, and then I got this call from Rauschenberg, and he asked me to come over. I had been a guard at the Jewish Museum when Sandra Hunt was doing the best curatorship that anybody had done. Mel Bochner was a guard there, and Brice Marden had been. They had introduced me to Robert Rauschenberg, who I literally fell in love with. Bob was my mentor, and as a person he was dynamic and funny. He had this sensitivity that nobody else in the art world had. I kissed his ass. I would kiss it to this day.

So I go over to his loft and he's sitting at the kitchen table and he says to me, "I'd like you to come upstairs, follow me." I said, "Where we going?" And I'm thinking, Here it comes, do I want to? Can I do this? Anything for Bob. And he brought me right into his bedroom and I'm thinking, This is it. He pulls open the shade and there was my sculpture out on the platform. He had installed it. I started laughing and he asked me what I was laughing about, and I told him. He thought it was very funny.

**LARRY BELL, ARTIST:** A lot of the artists sort of resented in a way giving a piece for the auction, because they didn't feel like supporting Neil and John.

**HELEN HARRINGTON, WAITRESS/ARTIST:** We got a bill from Mickey and it said, "Congratulations, you now owe $3,000." We just looked at it and laughed. He really kept Brice going in the early days when he didn't have any money, and he could eat there and charge. I think Brice was actually one of the people that actually paid it. With the auction he gave a painting. He actually gave back to Mickey.

**BRICE MARDEN:** When Mickey had the auction in 1971 the artists who donated work were given stock in the bar. I gave him the proceeds from a work sold in a group show, which kind of settled my tab.

# AUCTION

June 15th, 1971    59 Wooster St

**Max's Kansas City**

Carl Andre

Arman

Richard Artschwager

Edward Avedisian

Fred Brandes

David Budd

Rosemarie Castoro

Dan Christensen

E. Castro Cid

David Crum

Mark di Suvero

Peter Forakis

Clement Greenberg

Ken Greenleaf

Alex Hay

Danny Johnson

Jeffrey Lew

Roy Lichtenstein

Al Loving

Ken Noland

Sven Lukin

Tanya Neufeld

Bob Povlich

Brigid Polk

Larry Poons

Richard Serra

Ken Showell

Robert Smithson

Donald Judd

Joseph Kosuth

Ronny Landfield

Sam Leavitt

Marisol

Malcolm Morley

Forrest Myers

James Monte

Peter Reginato

Larry Rivers

bert Raushenberg

Bob Stanley

Michael Steiner

n Soffer

Marjorie Strider

Richard Van Buren

Andy Warhol

Jack Whitten

Don Wyman

Neil Williams

Chris Wilmarth

Larry Zox

Larry Bell
Mel Bochner
John Chamberlain
Billy Copley
David Diao
Peter Downsbrough
Jane Logemann
Sol Lewitt
David Prentice
Frank Roth
Alan Shields
John Tweddle

# Max's According

Red table-cloths in the Sunset,
Dan Flavin's pink-red Fluorescent
        Sculpture
 In Taylor Mead's Corner,
Warm elegant fireplace glow
for the Back Room.
Volatile crowd generally Subdued
On juicy well-cooked shrimp and
    big many dressed salads
        your Choice,
Suddenly Andrea "Whips"
    Feldman, future suicide, on
    table with bodice bared screaming "Show Time!"
Something going on Under a
    Table or two, God knows
            what!?
Jane Fonda and Roger Vadim
        Slumming with
Candy Darling and Andy
    Warhol Farthingale,
Hunched over the round table
    in the corner looking anonymous.
Taylor Mead shouting at Bill
    Graham "You owe me 30,000
            Dollars!"
    Mistaking Bill Graham
    for Ben Barenholtz who
probably does owe him 30,000 plus
    for unlimited showings of
famed badly edited film "Brand X"
conceived and mutilated
by Wynn Chamberlain,

hanger-on of the Art World,
    Hangers-on not allowed
in Back Room, or in
front door by suave
    magical Mickey Ruskin,
Some sneak by and float
    like seaweed around real
    denizens, choking off oxygen.
Nights of swimming upstream
    against seaweed.
Taylor tells David Bowie
    he doesn't like him, because
    he doesn't know how to smile.
Taylor orders famed Italian movie
    star to leave Back Room, because
Movie Star objects to Taylor's
    Fans sitting on floor around
    their table. Taylor also owes
Movie Star money: "Get
out of here you second-rate
Italian Movie Star!" he
shouts at fleeing figurine.
Back Room takes it in its
        Stride.
In long narrowish (because
of Bar) Front Room,
    famed artists John
    Chamberlain and Neil
    Williams are mixing it
up fisticuff-wise.
Finally reconcile and
Each grabs a bottle of

high on

## to Taylor Mead

Martel, or Grand Marinier,
And Splits (Put it on the
    Charge!)
Delicious hot snacks appear
  in afternoon for business
  and starving artist types who
  order only a glass of water.
Mickey would like Some
  Bills paid!   I come up
  with a thousand some
  years' ends; if the family
comes through.

"Mickey," I say "it's not all
of us who owe you money
that are ruining you—some
of your "help" is screwing
you out of thousands.
He calmly answers: "I know,
Taylor; the last four years
has just been a party for my
    friends."

Taylor Mead
163 Ludlow St.
NYC 10002

rebellion

Andy Warhol, *John Lennon*, 1985–86. © Copyright The Andy Warhol Foundation for the Visual Arts / ARS, NY. Courtesy The Andy Warhol Foundation, Inc. / Art Resource, NY.

I was once on a book tour and someone said to me, "Where did you grow up?" And I said, "The back room of Max's Kansas City."

—Steven Gaines

**sex, drugs, and superstars: the back room**

**n**ew York was reinventing itself and moving at hyperspeed in the days of the back room's Warhol era—from 1966 through 1972. It seemed as if everyone was on ups. And even those who weren't, were subject to the rabid new pulse and pace being set by the speed freaks. LSD deepened and enhanced the frenzy. A buck a hit for pure, potent, and plentiful acid. The crazies in the back room dropped it right on top of the speed. They also smoked pot, took downs, and drank. The energy, the rush, "the electricity of life" was at an all-time high. Not since Fitzgerald and Zelda had things been so gloriously out of control. Nightlife was "to die for." Unfortunately, many did.

Overall, the tendency in all the areas of Max's was toward cliques, and the competition for a pecking order and hierarchies was fierce in both the front and the back rooms. Several of the artists up front despised Warhol, his art, and the power he seemed to exude once he took over the back room. They accused him of exploitation

**Backroom characters**
(photo by Raeanne Rubenstein)

and blatant commercialism. They didn't feel he was an *artist* in the true sense of the word. "We used to call him Wendy Airhole," quips Rosemary Castora. When a new young artist attempted to emerge as a part of Max's inner circle, his work was challenged and scrutinized before he was accepted as part of the establishment.

• • •

**GLENN O'BRIEN, WRITER:** The back room of Max's Kansas City was the center of fashion fucking art, music fucking fashion, art fucking music, etc. The Superstar atmosphere where everybody was "there" or on the way, was the center of the sixties, the central happening of multimedia, the beginning of the happening. A painter throwing a punch at a guitar player is a multimedia event, but this was a multimedia world. Every art and every class and every trade and every state of mind was there drinking with each other, showing off with each other, and going home with each other.

**LOU REED:** It was a party every night. It was not the kind of place you could buy your way into, you either belonged or you didn't belong.

**DAVID SMITH, WRITER/PHOTO ARCHIVIST:** It was very intimidating at first. There was that amazing atmosphere that if you didn't somehow belong, you were an outcast, which was intoxicating. That's what you wanted to accomplish in New York.

**LARRY ZOX:** In the beginning, around the early part of '66, the back room was just the back

rebellion

room. People went there when it was really crowded up front and they wanted to have a conversation or a private place to eat dinner. The back room happened kind of slowly. It was like the degenerate room. Warhol started coming to the back room pretty early on. He was not aggressive, and neither was anybody else with him. The reason he could always take the round table is because back then nobody else wanted it.

**GLENN O'BRIEN:** The back room was thirty by thirty feet square. Everybody in it could see everybody else. All of the tables had red tablecloths and red napkins with wine lists and little bowls of chick peas meant to induce thirst in drinkers, but frequently used as projectiles for flirtation and aggravation. In one corner was a big Flavin fluorescent sculpture which bathed the room in a reddish light, earning it the nickname *Bucket of Blood*. In the opposite corner was the round table, a black vinyl banquette. Like the Round Table at Camelot and the Roundtable at the Algonquin, this table ruled the roost. This is where Andy sat.

Andy was there every night, to watch and listen and pick up a few tabs and meet a few new kids. It was an all-Superstar cast. It was the best show in town. The stars of the music scene came. They would watch the show or be in it. It was exciting but anonymous. Jim Morrison could gently nod into oblivion behind his shades, sitting with Nico without anybody asking for autographs. Even Janis Joplin was treated like a lady.

**IRA SCHNEIDER, FILMMAKER:** I met Janis Joplin there in 1967 before she really became famous. I said, "You're Janet, aren't you?" She

**Warhol at round table with Viva**
(photo by Billy Name)

112

high

said, "No, my name's Janis. Buzz off." I saw her a month before she died and she looked like hell. Whereas Jimi Hendrix, it was a mistake. He didn't intend to die; he wasn't depressed.

**STEVE GAINES, AUTHOR:** They called that table in the left-hand corner of the back room closest to the Flavin sculpture "Paranoia Booth" for a while because that room was permeated in red. The blood-redness of it. The atmosphere was thick in Max's. I always used to feel a little bit like I was swimming. It was almost like that sense of chlorine that you feel when you're in a swimming pool. It was a warm, thick feeling—the physical setting of the place, the gray carpeting up the walls, and that blood-redness. So we called that booth the Paranoia Booth. Then the round table on the right hand side was considered Andy's table.

**MICKEY RUSKIN:** Andy started coming to Max's in the spring of 1966, and that really shaped the character of the back room. The only people I can remember who started drifting back there before Andy was one time about twenty or thirty people started dancing around back there and I said, "Hey, you can't dance here." And that was Joan Baez and her crowd. Andy attracted the whole underground theater crowd, who in turn attracted a lot of film and media people, adding to the writers, poets, photographers, and models who'd begun going back there. Then when Danny Fields started bringing in musicians every night, that made the mix complete.

**LEEE BLACK CHILDERS, PHOTOGRAPHER/ROCK MANAGER:** At the very beginning of 1968, Andy Warhol moved the location of his notorious Factory from Forty-seventh Street to a more spacious and less dangerous (he thought) building just across Union Square from Max's. It was just two or three years after Andy had begun to expand his activities from paintings and lithographs to include very peculiar movies and an even stranger rock band, the Velvet Underground. Besides vocals by Lou Reed and Nico, the band featured a whip dance by Gerard Malanga and a fantastic light show. The actors in his films assumed names like Ultra Violet, Viva, and International Velvet. And all of these actors and musicians Andy dubbed Superstars.

And so it came to pass that besides the regular bunch of scruffy artists surreptitiously propping up a corner of the bar, Mickey found himself playing host to the likes of Edie Sedgwick in a silver tissue minidress and seven pairs of false eyelashes, Ultra Violet in a black patent-leather body suit with manacles and chains, Baby Jane Holzer dressed like a cheerleader on acid, and a bonanza of others. But instead of complaining, he loved it. If the regular customers couldn't eat their steaks with a vampire at the next table, that was their tough luck.

It didn't work the same way with the Superstars, however. They didn't come there for steak dinners. They came there to take pills washed down with wine, to gossip to flirt, to take off their clothes if they felt like it, to sleep or sing or dance. And they didn't much like doing whatever they were doing in the midst of a bunch of stockbrokers and their dates munching steak and salad and discussing the art on the wall.

rebellion

And thus the back room was born. Back past toilets and the pay phones and the kitchen and the galley and the pantry was a room, a gloriously empty room. And why not? Nearly every restaurant is cursed with such an unfortunately located room or alcove—the area known to the waiter or maître d' as Siberia, where no sane person could enjoy his meal. But these people were not sane and for them it was perfect. Not too large or too small. (In its heyday you could probably have squeezed a hundred people into it.) There were booths down both sides, tables in the middle, and in the front corner, a fabulously large round table. Clearly a focal point. Certainly destined to become a stage.

Mickey was kind enough to install red lighting in the room to match the laser which was already there. Red light is flattering to everyone, from teenagers whose red spots magically disappear, to aging beauties whose crow's-feet melt deliciously away. Many a romance blossomed in the warm glow of the back room only to die a startling death in the harsh glare of streetlights at the end of the night.

Soon the back room of Max's Kansas City became the most glamorous and talked-about haven in New York. Although, miraculously, tourists never seemed to invade, the crowd remained otherwise very diverse. They were actors, writers, artists, rich, poor, famous, unknown, men, women, drag queens. It could be argued that in that one room in New York, in the late sixties, the people who were to become the most innovative and influential in the future of the arts ate, drank, and made merry. But for most of these, the back room was just a part of their lives—a phase through which they passed on to other and greater accomplishments. For some, however, the back room became the highlight of their lives, where they blossomed as they could nowhere else—a hothouse for their own rare beauty. Some of these went on to fame and wealth. Others wandered off disillusioned. Some died. But for them all, Max's would remain a focus of their existence.

**TONY ZINETTA, DIRECTOR/ACTOR:** The thing about the back room, the whole thing about gender and sexuality...nobody thought anything of anything. It wasn't gay, straight, this, that, black, white. It was all mixed. There were all kinds of people back there. It was pretty much self-selecting. You basically decided whether you should go in or not. A lot of people were afraid to go in. You knew where you belonged in the place, and everyone sort of got off on everybody else.

**PAUL KILB, MODEL/CARPENTER:** There was the ordinary heterosexual crowd and then you had the Warhol crowd, which was kind of a pioneer, and later in the seventies became so prevalent. It became the rock style. Those were the first drag queens on that kind of level—a crossover drag queen, not a ghetto drag queen. Kind of a crossover Third Street-style Theater of the Ridiculous, which later produced Charles Ludlam and all those people.

**DONALD LYONS, ENGLISH PROFESSOR, RUTGERS UNIVERSITY:** There was an atmosphere of great tolerance and sexiness about it because it was very permissive. It was an atmosphere of bizarre self-display. All the people who went there, they were all there when they weren't doing their thing. And for many of them, their thing, their whole thing, was to go to Max's. Simply going to the back room and putting themselves on show, simply creating a kind of theatrical display of themselves was their career. This was their desire, was their fulfillment.

**HOLLY WOODLAWN:** The back room was a room to make the grand entrance into. First you'd walk down that long corridor and you'd hear all this whispering, "You know who that is? That's Holly Woodlawn." So you just carried on even more, blew kisses to everyone and stopped at this table and that table and talked about nothing. It took a good twenty minutes to make it into the back room. The front room was for impressing the peons who came to Max's to see, and the back room was our territory.

**STEVE GAINES:** When you first walked in that back room, no matter how hip you thought you were, or how far-out or avant-garde, you got shook to your bones. There was a real electricity about it.

**SUSAN BLOND, PUBLICIST:** When you'd walk in the back room, suddenly everybody looked pretty because of the Flavin light sculpture. There would be these different groups. In the first booth to the right as you walked in, that's where Eric Emerson, Andrea Whips, and that "Showtime" group would sit. Andrea was a real Showtime kind of person. She would get up on the table and yell, "Showtime!" then she would sing some song and dance and always be kind of out of it, but kind enough to actually finish it.

The drag queens were there too, and they were the most glamorous people. Candy Darling, Jackie Curtis, Holly Woodlawn, and the young Warhol stars. Jane Forth, Geraldine Smith, and Donna Jordan were the stars of my time. And Cyrinda Foxe was unbelievably glamorous then— blonde and Marilyn Monroe–ish. Then there were people like Steve Paul, who was already in business and doing quite well. He had The Scene, which was an unbelievable, legendary club too. And Shep Gordon was there just starting his Alice Cooper empire.

The *New Yorker* wrote about me at the time, and they said, "Susan Blond, famous at Max's Kansas City and elsewhere." In other words, I didn't have a job, I was really nothing. Yet, I was considered famous in the back room because I wanted to be famous. We all thought we were artists, everybody back there. Of course, Andy was an artist, so if you saw him do something with butter on a plate, you'd save it. And the fun was, you never knew who'd turn out to be a famous artist someday.

**STEVEN GAINES:** There was a girl who hung out in the back room who I am pretty sure sold belts on Eighth Street at one of those little peddler stands, and that was Fran Lebowitz. You could be there and know somebody who was selling belts on Eighth Street and they'd say they were one day going to become famous, and sure enough they did become famous.

**FRANCES GRILL, PRESIDENT OF CLICK MODELING AGENCY:** There was one night before Fran Lebowitz became a professional writer when we were sitting at a table with Toscani and

Donna Jordan. Fran was sitting there doodling—she was always doodling. I really didn't know who she was. I think it was the first time I had met her. A boy named Bill sat down at the table with us. Nobody knew who he was. Fran looked up from her doodling to say, "Bill just sat down at the table. Bill is gay. If Bill wasn't gay, there would be nothing to say about Bill." After she said that, I knew she was somebody I wanted to get to know better.

**HOLLY WOODLAWN:** There was definitely a hierarchy in that back room. There were the music people, which Danny Fields was the center of, the Playhouse of the Ridiculous people, and the Warhol people, who were at the top of the heap. Before we became Superstars, a lot of us were sort of envious of the Warhol table, because we wanted to be there. Most of the time we were like court jesters, hopping from table to table, whichever had a bottle of wine.

**TERRY NOEL, DANCER/DJ:** The right side of the back room was mine! I knew everybody. The first checking account I ever got in my life, I wrote my very first check in Max's, and it bounced. I came in and Mickey goes, "Terry!" I said, "I know, I know…." I wanted good credit—I felt so bad.

There was the whole anti-Warhol and -Terry Noel thing that went on. I always felt that Andy was doing everything wrong. I'd sit with Andy at the Factory and I'd say to him, "Andy, why are you doing what you're doing? You just sit there nodding your head saying, 'Oh, that would be nice' in that soft voice." Someone would say, "Oh, I'm going to shoot up with a needle now," and Andy would say, "Oh, that'll be nice." I felt it was wrong. He was someone that people looked up to, and he had all these people around him dying. I said, "This isn't right." His people consequently did not like me. They wouldn't even talk to me, his whole crowd, except for Pat Hartley and Karen Reeves.

**RICHARD BERNSTEIN, ARTIST/DID A LITHOGRAPH OF MAX'S BACK ROOM:** There was a pecking order of preferential seating and people would spend hours dressing for it and performing there on tabletops.

**RUBY LYNN REYNER, MODEL/ACTRESS, PLAYHOUSE OF THE RIDICULOUS:** One of the best moments of my life is when I had just finished a performance of *Heaven Grand and Amber Orbit*. When I walked into the back room, Danny Fields and everybody stood up and applauded because they had been to the show. To me it felt like I was a Superstar. I mean I wasn't really, but it felt like it.

As a waitress, I hated working that back room. We called it "the punishment room." Mickey would put a waitress there when she had broken one of the rules, like eating shrimp. The only waitresses I knew who didn't mind working the back room were Ellen Gofen (we called her "Mama Cita") and Debbie Harry.

**GEORGE ABAGNALO:** Ellen had the patience of a saint. We all loved her. She was like the Mama of the back room. I once asked her if she ever left because she was in the back room every night. I guess she was eternally punished.

**ALICE ZIMMERMAN, ONE OF MICKEY'S ORIGINAL WAITRESSES, WHO LATER MARRIED ARTIST LAWRENCE WEINER:** Mickey would never put you in the back room on your first night. That would be too cruel. The back room was for punishment or for Ellen. She could handle all that stuff. But every time I was put back there it was for punishment. If you found someone to replace you when you didn't want to work and Mickey didn't like the way it worked out, that was it—bam!—you got the back room. What was so bad about the back room? People pulling off their clothes, yelling and screaming, customers never having anything straight, their eyes were always dilated, and NO TIPS."

**DANNY FIELDS:** I remember lots of nights just taking my coffee cup and walking around from table to table. Sometimes it would be fun if you walked in and the round table was empty and you wanted to do something, you could sit down. I would not be nervous about being the only person sitting at the round table; some people would have been. They would have thought everybody was looking at them or it was presumptuous. Perhaps in the beginning I felt that way, but over a course of time we called it "starting a table." Or else you'd be sitting at another table and it would be vacated and you'd say, "Let's start the round table." You'd start it and then people would come in and join you.

But sometimes it wasn't so handy because if you were stuck in the middle of that table your mobility was cut down. People would be crawling on the floor to get out. It was more like a photo opportunity than a wonderful place to be. Sargent Shriver came in one night with Germaine Greer, who was a friend of Donald Lyon's and mine through Lillian Roxon, a fabulous rock-and-roll journalist from Australia. Germaine was a great friend of Lillian's and she had been on my radio show on WFNU. So she came in this one night with Sargent Shriver and we were sitting with Jackie Curtis and I said, "Oh, Jackie, that's one of the Kennedys." Jackie sat up and just turned on the charm and wouldn't let go of his hand and even pulled him down to sit. They had sort of a tête-à-tête conversation.

**MICHAEL GROSS, WRITER:** I was going to Vassar and I had a girlfriend whose whole orientation was NYC. She took me to Max's. Nineteen seventy-two. I was twenty. Before that I had been going to the Fillmore East and I had read about it. My girlfriend found a twenty on the street so we all had a lot to drink that night. That was my first night. I quickly realized she didn't kind of know what was going on there because she stood at the bar. I realized there was more to the place that met the eye. I started writing articles and going on tour with rock bands. I wrote for hippie magazines like *Crawdaddy*; then I started writing for *Circus* and there were all these flash people who liked young guys who were rock stars. Chris Makos was the photographer. Steven Gaines was the editor. I always thought that most of the people I met in the record business were into young boys, and the record business was a great place to find young boys. I was into it because I got free records and concert tickets, and a free social life.

I hung out with loose women and rock stars. Max's waitresses for me were absolutely untouchable. They had far too much attitude for a mere amateur like me. I fished in the pond of the booths.

**VICTOR BOCKRIS, WRITER/BIOGRAPHER OF WARHOL, LOU REED, AND OTHERS:** Andrew Wylie had moved to New York in 1971 and he had gotten himself a storefront on Jones Street. He came to do an anthropological investigation of New York nightlife with an emphasis on poetry and literature. We were running a small press called Telegraph Books based in Philadelphia. Aram Saroyan was the third person in the company. He lived in Cambridge. Andrew started going out every night with the idea of meeting hip people, and to pick up girls. He would get dressed up every night in a very particular way and he would go to Max's. I think he used to go at a certain time every night around midnight. He was only in the back room. He formed a good relationship with Mickey because Mickey was cashing checks for him.

I'd come up once a week for a day and a night. I'd stay at Andrew's and we'd spend the day working on this press. This was 1971 when Gerard was still associated with Warhol. He still had that great Gerard Malanga look. I remember being very scared to meet Gerard because he might beat me with some big black whip. I wasn't hip, I wasn't in that scene. I was very naive, and young. I really didn't know anything.

Then I moved to New York in 1973 and I got an apartment on Seventeenth Street, literally half a block from Max's. I inherited it from Jennifer Lee who was sometimes a girlfriend of Gerard's, and married Richard Pryor. She had been a model. Gerard got her apartment for me. I moved to New York specifically to work with Andrew as a writing team. We called ourselves Bockris Wylie like one name, and we wrote as if we were one person as if Bockris Wylie was a character. We were poets. We had a column in an underground newspaper called *The Drummer*, published in Philadelphia, sort of a gossip column with a humorous edge. I had published ten books with Telegraph Books. We published Gerard Malanga; and a collaboration by Ted Berrigan, Ron Patrick, Tom Clark; then Patti Smith's book; and then a book by Brigid called *Scars*—she would get famous people's imprint of scars. We were never really in it to make money. It was like a showcase. Nobody had heard of Patti Smith at that time.

Poetry was wobbling on its edge and Patti Smith was the perfect example of it, because she originally really wanted to be a poet. She really wanted to be taken seriously as a writer. Between 1970 and '73 that's what she did. She had a column in *Dream* magazine which was a very hip magazine, and had a lot of record reviews and articles, and then she published her poetry and she was making it as a rock writer. Many of the rock writers involved themselves in a new way, involving themselves as characters in the writing of the review. Lester Bangs and Richard Meltzer, for instance. Patti was one of them, *Cream* was the leading magazine for that. At a certain point Max's was the only place to go, at least for people who weren't in the high-society crowd.

**NORMAN HOLDEN, PAINTER:** Lillian Roxon brought me to Max's for the first time; it was around 1967. I'm a painter. I was known as Norman Billiard Balls back then. That's also when I met Ronny Vial. Ronny was the maître d' at Max's when it first opened. A friend of mine had said to me, "Do you want to meet the connoisseur of sleaze?" and he introduced me to Ronny Vial. Ronny used to hold court in that back room. He made necklaces all day and gave them away all night. John Vaccaro, the director of the Theater of the Ridiculous, said he was the only gentleman speed freak in New York. Then he got arrested for a shipment of hashish from Thailand that was sent to his uncle's house. His uncle opened the package and turned him in. He disappeared; no one knows where he is.

**BOB FEIDEN, RCA RECORD EXECUTIVE:** I'd go in at night and sit down, and it was like a show all around me. There was something very real about it, and earthy. It was almost like the eighth wonder of the world for someone like me who came from an upper-middle-class Jewish family, had gone to private schools, was an attorney, and had a nine-to-five job. I'd meet these people I had never met before, and just loved them. I had never seen a drag queen before. My idea of a drag queen was somebody that changed for fun, but it was not someone like a Candy Darling who seemed to be a woman and a lady.

There were all these characters. Eric Emerson in his filthy leather hot pants, with his cowboy boots, and his blond curly locks. He'd get up on the table and yodel. I was told he was hired to teach this group of kids to yodel for some movie.

**LYNN EDELSON:** I walked in one night just after going to the premiere of *HEAT*, and Eric was sitting at the window when you first walked in, and I walked over to him and I said, "Wow, you were really great in that film." He didn't say one word, he just grabbed me and shoved his tongue down my throat.

**STEVEN GAINES:** I became totally addicted to the back room. The thing is, everybody was entertaining. Everybody was very witty and had a lot of things to say, a lot of stories. Everybody was a struggling designer or artist or actor, and you knew that these people were going to be something or go somewhere. My girlfriend and I went to Florida for a week and when we came back I dropped her off at the apartment with the luggage and I was supposed to be finding a legal parking spot for the car, but I couldn't resist going straight to Max's back room. She really had put her foot down, too, about me going to Max's all the time. But when I dropped her off, she said that she was exhausted and was going to get right into bed, so I figured I could say that it took an extra twenty minutes to find a parking space. "Goddamn it, I drove around forty minutes looking for a space." And we lived on Eleventh Street, Max's was just at Seventeenth. So I go to Max's, parked the car, went to the back room, and someone immediately introduced me to this young guy Marjoe. He had all this curly blond hair and I sat down and started talking to him. He said that he was a former evangelist, that he was ordained when he was four years old, that he had married a couple when he was five years old and that he had met somebody who wrote for the *Village Voice* named Howard Smith, who was going to make a documentary about him. And I said, "Can I write your book?" I had never written a book before. It was just total bullshit. And he said, "Yes, you can!" And it happened. *Marjoe* won the Academy Award for Best Documentary of 1972 and my book, *Marjoe*, was an enormous success. When I got home, of course, my girlfriend was ready to give me hell and I said, "But you don't understand. I met this guy and I'm going to write a book about him." And of course she said, "Yeah, yeah, sure, sure, Steve." But it absolutely all came true and that was part of the magic of Max's.

**BOB BRADY, ACTOR:** The first time I met Ultra Violet somebody said, "See that girl there? she was Salvador Dali's lover." Then the next thing I knew, she was Chamberlain's lover, then Ed Ruscha's lover. She was actually gorgeous.

**ULTRA VIOLET:** Mostly when I went to Max's, it was with Andy, and we'd sit in the back room. Andy was always an observer, but he was also a taker. In other words, he seemed to be very detached, and not involved, yet if there was a pretty boy in the room he would spot him immediately. It was a fishing ground for Andy, for movies and for everything, because Andy was interested in everything, he capitalized on everyone. He had charisma. He had magic. He was like Hitler, in fact. People were drawn to him, they couldn't resist.

There was the regular Andy crowd, meaning Andrea Whips; sometimes the Velvet Underground; Ingrid Superstar; International Velvet; Susan Bottomly, who was from a very prominent family in Boston; her boyfriend David Croland; Edie, of course; Brigid; Paul Morrissey; Gerard Malanga; Chuck Wein; Ondine, on occasion when he didn't go to listen to opera; Billy Name, but not too much. And of course there was Candy Darling and Jackie Curtis and Viva, who first saw Andy there. She used to sit in the front room and see us go by and one day I think she got her courage together and came to Andy and said she wanted to be in his movie. A lot of people would do that.

I had come to New York from Paris, I was about eighteen, and the first person I met was John Graham. I was going to an exhibit at Leo Castelli when John Graham had a little room on the top floor of that building on East Seventy-seventh Street, in 1959, when Castelli wasn't yet known—just to tell you how far back I go into art—and I saw this very strange man coming out of the elevator that only two people could get into. He said, "Where are you going?" and I said, "I'm going to Castelli's show." "May I take you there?" he asked me. I said, "Sure!" He was an extraordinary man—he died in 1961. He was responsible for establishing the abstract expressionists in Europe. He took artists like de Kooning, Sam Francis, and Pollock to Paris, and he said, "Those people are painters." He was Russian-born, but he spent a lot of time in France, and knew very well the art scene of the twenties and thirties. He bridged the gap between European art and American art, which was essential. In Europe they didn't know they could have painters in America. And he was a painter in his own right. But he was very esoteric, therefore he wasn't really well known. Now he's been rediscovered. And he was my first big love affair.

rebellion

Anyway, I met Salvador Dali, and we had a very long friendship that lasted five years. One day Andy Warhol came for tea, with Dali, and that's when I met Andy. It was a lucky strike. He was one of the most *interesting*—famous is beside the point—artists in America. Andy said, "Let's do a movie." I said, "Fine, when?" And he said, "tomorrow." So I went to the Factory the next day—that's when it was on East Forty-seventh Street, and eventually we ended up in Max's Kansas City. I wasn't Ultra Violet when I met Andy. My real name is Isabelle Collin Dufresne. It was too hard to pronounce and remember. After I did my first movie, Andy said, "We have to find a name." "No thanks," I said, "I'll find my own." That night I was reading an article in *Time* magazine on light, which fascinated me, and they mentioned ultra violet. I thought that was a great name. It just popped out of the page, and I told Andy.

**PENNY ARCADE:** The same people went every night, and they were like layers. One layer was the brilliant people, who were not famous, who tuned in and dropped out, who refused to be fabulous. And they were the bottom line. They were the ones who got there at nine-thirty. Then there were the fabulous trendoids, many of them fashion people and male homosexuals—the pretty people who were just satisfied to be beautiful, who didn't have to be artists. And they would show up around eleven P.M. And somewhere between eleven and twelve the crazies like Rene Ricard would show up, and whoever was in town, like Vali, the girl with a tattooed mustache.

**VIVA:** I switched from the front room to the back room when I started making Warhol movies. For some reason I was in love with John Chamberlain—don't ask me why, there was no basis in it. All he did was complain....Andy would come into Max's and just sail through the front. He'd say, "Viva, what are you doing with all those heavies?" And Andy would just not deign to even nod in the direction of my old buddies. So I was kind of embarrassed and I'd sometimes sneak back up to the front to sit with Johanna and John and Neil, then I'd go back to the back room. I had to switch from being one of the guys in the front to this haughty character who swept in ignoring everyone and sat at Andy's right and did his talking for him, basically. That was a tough switch to make. I always thought I was being disloyal if I associated with the heavies.

Andy was always trying to promote dissension among everybody. When you sat at Andy's table there was really no conversational pleasure. It was really business. The other table I associated with a lot was the Danny Fields, Donald Lyons, Paul Morrissey table. I enjoyed talking to Donald Lyons. The conversations were intellectually stimulating. We conceived of what actually started my writing career at a table in the back room of Max's. It was a piece that I wrote in 1967 that was a satire on the Berrigan brothers pouring duck's blood on the draft files. It was finally published in *The Realist*. *Downtown* rejected it as being too dirty. I went home and wrote it after a conversation at that table:

```
Women of the world unite
Drop your Tampax strings
```

```
Type of thing
Organize for a massive
       Washington D & C
Bleed on the draft files
The hell with this imported
       duck's blood.
```

When the then president of Putnam read it, he asked me to write a book.

**DIANE QUINN, WAITRESS:** I was working the back room the night Joe Dallesandro came there to meet Andy. He was standing at the entrance to the back room and I walked up to him and said, "Can I help you?" He said, "I'm here to meet Mr. Warhol." I think I asked him if he had an appointment. You know, it was like an office. He said, "Yes, I do." I went over to the table and Andy said, "Yes, tell him to come over." He was so beautiful. I said to this guy Bruce who hung out there all the time, "Who is that?" He said, "Oh God, one of Andy's fags picked him up in New Jersey in a phone booth or something." That was Joe's entry into the back room scene.

**JOE DALLESANDRO, ACTOR:** I met some friends of mine in New York who were going to the apartment where Andy was going to be making this film and they said, "Come along and meet him." And I didn't know who he was. They said, "He's this famous artist who makes Campbell Soup." I was just a kid, I was seventeen at the time. I just went along for the ride. That's how I met Andy.

**BARBARA HODES, DESIGNER:** Don Johnson used to come into the back room. He was a boy toy at the time as well as Patti D'Arbanville's boyfriend. He sort of looked like Eric Emerson. Patti's mother let her bring him home. She was very, very young.

**Vali** (photo by Anton Perich)

Joe Dallesandro (photo by Anton Perich)

**BOB FEIDEN:** I actually got in there very early one night and I was sitting in the back room with Steve Gaines. Suddenly we hear this drunken southern whale saying, "Where are the Superstars? Where are the fucking Superstars? I came here for Superstars!" I'd heard this voice before and I go to look to see who it is, and it's Tennessee Williams, very drunk. He said, "I thought this is where the action was. Can you find me Superstars?" So I got on the phone and I called Paul Morrissey. Paul called Andy and between them, they got a group together and all these people showed up for Tennessee. He couldn't have been more thrilled.

**RUBY LYNN REYNER:** One time Warren Beatty was sitting in the back room with sunglasses on, just waiting for people to come over and flock around him and be sycophants to his stardom—and nobody did. People were more impressed with the freaks they loved who were hanging out there.

**LEEE BLACK CHILDERS:** Peter O'Toole came into the back room one time and was just sitting there drinking and the usual crowd was there. Ingrid Superstar was doing some number and there was a photographer in the room taking pictures and the flash would go off. Peter O'Toole was getting visibly crazier and crazier and started to appear very irritated. Mickey walked into the back room and Peter O'Toole called Mickey over to his table. "Excuse me, but could you tell those photographers enough is enough. I am here privately and do not wish to

high on

be harassed." Mickey said, "You're here privately, what does that mean?" He said, "Those photographers, they keep taking pictures of me." Mickey said, "They aren't taking pictures of you, they're taking pictures of Ingrid." He said, "But I'm Peter O'Toole." To which Mickey replied, "Oh, are you a painter?"

**KERRY RIORDAN, MODEL/MAX'S REGULAR:** I've only been a fan of somebody I didn't know once in my life, and that was Jimi Hendrix and I met him at Max's. We ended up going to Switzerland the next night with a friend of his named Ian St. James....We got stoned in Switzerland—literally, thrown rocks. When I met him, the guys that I was initially attracted to were usually heavily into heroin and very depressed. He wouldn't let me do any heroin. Jimi put wires in my hair before they had braiding and braided all my hair in right angles. So in Switzerland, I had hair down to my waist with these braided wires and that's when we got stoned by some Swiss drunks who thought we looked like interracial hippies. Here I am in my fantasy and I got stoned. I did not get to do anything else but get stoned. There I was with Jimi on the nod, crashed against some wall. After talking to him—he was an extremely intelligent, sensitive man—he became more real. It was like meetings of the skin. It was a very meaningful time, but it was also like a shedding of the dream.

**DENISE MOURGES, MAX'S REGULAR:** Rick Lloyd introduced me to this guy at Max's, this real funky-looking guy, very beautiful. He was living in Cambodia in this mountain village. He was like this king. When the Vietnam War was going on, they had a helicopter with a red cross on it and they would fly into battles in this fake-red-cross helicopter and pick up the weapons on the battlefield and resell them to the other side. These were the first gunrunners I ever met. He was American but he lived in Cambodia. You never knew who you were going to meet at Max's, from Janis to Emmett Grogin, to the gunrunners and people like Jimi Hendrix....It was such a magnet for an international cast of unusual suspects. There was this great individualism and pizzazz. It encouraged individuality and uniqueness. Your uniqueness was your calling card. You could really express it there.

**DAVID AMRAM, COMPOSER/CONDUCTOR:** Kris Kristofferson was back in town one time—we had played together in the past—so he gave me a call. He was kind of down, because he was being interviewed by all these different music magazines and his record company was send-

**Leee Black Childers and Ava Cherry**
(photo by Anton Perich)

rebellion

From left, Cherry Vanilla, Leee Black Childers, and Jackie Curtis (photo by Anton Perich)

Taylor Mead and Fred Hughes (photo by Anton Perich)

Maria Smith and Richard Bernstein (photo by Anton Perich)

Taylor Mead with a belly button
(photo by Anton Perich)

Mick Jagger (photo by Anton Perich)

Rene Ricard (photo by Anton Perich)

ing him out on a promotion tour, and Kris being a Rhodes scholar and a brilliant warm person, felt like he was being put through the grinder. He was going crazy because he didn't have one minute to relax. So I said, "Well, let's just go down to Max's." Ramblin' Jack Elliot was with us, and he being a walking encyclopedia oral historian of the world, he was giving one of his discourses, and we sat there for two hours and people would stop by the table just to say hello, and we were all just hanging out having a good time, and finally Kris said, "You know, this is the first time I've even felt like I was alive on this trip to New York, this is saving my mind." Just to get out and have that interchange was refreshing. And it was great to see how it cheered him up just by being there.

**IGGY POP:** For me there were two Max's. The first Max's was the back room, behavioral New York, gay intellectual performance-art Andy Warhol credit-card Max's. And then there was the other Max's which was the rock and roll venue. The old Max's was for me. I was a kid from the Midwest who had some exposure, mostly through books and records, to both the outrageous and the arts. Coming into that room was kind of like a University of Dementia. I'm sure I came in the first time with Danny Fields who was my mentor and my Addison DeWitt in showing me around town.

The people I gravitated to most of all were people like Donald Lyons. It was the first time I met older educated people who had some sort of straight positions who looked very straight, who I could talk to as if they were still kids. Some of them looked like my parents on the outside and yet it was like talking to kids but not the kids from the Midwest, interesting kids, and I felt a kinship with these people. And then there were these other people like Taylor Mead and I just liked to watch him act out, and I thought, What a witty, and strange kind of twisting, turning individual. He had a very serpentine quality to him. Then Jackie Curtis who was basically a Warhol actor. She was doing some of the plays and was in the Tony Ingrassia scene.

Jackie, Leee Black Childers, and Glenn O'Brien were three younger people that maybe in another era these people would have been young preppies perhaps working as interns at the White House or they would have been Senate pages. They would be doing their internships in this kind of twisted place and wearing dresses every other day. They had a certain Waspish good sense behind it all, and a very youthful sensibility. And then there were the rock people—Lou and Bowie and myself—that tended to come in less and be more musicianly. Probably in Lou and my case, a little more peaks and valleys.

**MICHAEL POLLARD:** Once I threw a drink in Lou Reed's lap. I was a little stewed. He was really mad. He said, "Let's go outside," and when we got there neither of us could remember what we went outside for, so we went back in and continued to drink.

**DENISE MOURGES:** I had the biggest crush on Lou. For years I had the biggest crush on him. One night at Max's, somehow Lou and I got thrown together and he was like, you know, "Do you want to come home with me?" And I was like, "Yeeeessss!!" I was so excited. So we went back to his place. He lived nearby. It was within walking distance of Max's. We got there and I'm like, Here I am with Lou. He had lots of comic books in the apartment. And he sat there and started reading comic books and kept on reading comic books. And kept on reading comic books. And I was getting so frustrated. Here I am, my big shot with Lou, and all he could do was read comic books. And I didn't realize that he was on speed. He was just speed reading. I soon after excused myself and left, because my idea of a fun time was not watching him read comic books.

**LYNN HARRITON, WAITRESS:** The first time I went to the back room of Max's, I came in with the Jefferson Airplane. My friend Nicole was friends with Jack Casady and I was paired off with Jorma Kaukonen. By the time we got there I had a lot more drugs than I could handle. There were more drugs than I had ever seen. I came into a scene where I did a lot of psychedelics, but not a lot of speed and no heroin. But when we were hanging out with the Airplane, there was just everything. So after a week of hanging out with them, I was pretty much a psychotic mess, and by the time we got to Max's, I deeply wanted to get out of there. I hadn't slept in five days, and I was no longer having fun. Everybody else was having a good time, they were throwing chick peas and laughing. We walked in, and we were given the best table. We were treated like stars, but I was feeling deeply self-conscious, like a little kid. Years later when I got over the intense feeling of psychotic hysteria, and had the opportunity to work there, I realized what a fun place it was.

**JOAN VOS, WAITRESS:** I was the unofficial script girl on *Ciao! Manhattan* and I had a small role in the film. I started going to Max's with the people from the Factory, and I became friends with Edie Sedgwick. I was helping Edie out. She required help even in those days. She was pretty neurotic. By the time she started filming *Ciao! Manhattan* she was doing a lot of drugs, mainly downers. When I was taking care of her I was supposed to be her social secretary. She needed someone to point her in the direction she was supposed to be going. Anybody who worked on that film did some taking care of Edie. She was with Neuwirth at that time. They were staying at the Chelsea.

**TAYLOR MEAD, ACTOR/POET/WRITER:** I met Andy in 1963, when he came to some of my poetry readings. I was reading all around town, at the Deux Megots, which is where I probably first met Mickey. Andy, Henry Geldzahler, and I drove to California, because Andy wouldn't fly. At the time, I was beginning to have problems with Andy and other people making promises and not keeping them, so rather than kill them, I got on a plane and went to Europe. I got on a Finlandia airplane, where you have to stop somewhere before you go on, and due to some bureaucratic nonsense, they had to change the number of the flight in Iceland, and I didn't realize it. So they announced this flight number, and there's only one big plane out on the runway. Then they closed these big shutters so you can't go out on it, and I'm wandering around the air terminal, and I see this plane starting to take off. I said, "Hey, that's my plane," and I jumped the fence and ran out in front of the plane, waving my hands like it was a taxi. The airport personnel came out frantic—a few more feet and I would

rebellion

**Nico, Taylor Mead, and Louie Walden**
(photo by Billy Name)

have been dragged into the propellers. So they stopped the plane, and I went to Europe.

I went to Paris and got into big trouble immediately. But then I ran into Mickey there in maybe 1967, '68, and he said, "Taylor, I have this great place in New York. You'll fit right in. You've got to come back." And then Andy came and showed *Chelsea Girls*, at the Cinéma in Paris, and half the audience walked out. That's when I said to myself, "What am I doing in *La Dolce Vita* land?" And I went back to New York to Max's Kansas City. Max's was all very normal to me, because I had spent all my time in Paris at La Flore and La Coupole. Although it was much more intense. La Flore and La Coupole were a lot more laid-back. I used to dance naked in Paris, so the back room at Max's was as normal as blueberry pie. And at the time, we were all on legal drugs, bipheta-mines and Tuinals. Of course, some people were shooting themselves up through their blue jeans. Every night somebody would come in on a different trip. I love when a restaurant has a good sound to it, it's music to my ears. The jukebox was one of the best around. It wasn't too loud. There was good food, nice people working there, nice lighting, and there was such a good cross-section of customers. Jack Nicholson used to come to the back room. One time he was dressed up in a suit; he didn't fit.

**MARY WORONOV:** Taylor was always fabulous. He was on this new drug that nobody had ever heard of before from France; it had this funny name: Quaaludes. It was the land of amphetamines. Everyone always looked very angst and wore dark glasses. Warhol was great, the Velvets were great, but when all those people got together, it was probably one of the most impolite, disastrous things that ever happened. But, it was very hot and very sexy. It was a great period in my life.

**DAVID JOHANSEN:** We were sitting at this table one night with National Velvet and there were all these people and she says as she points to each person, "You're on a trip, you're on a trip, you're on a trip, everybody's on a trip but me." And someone at the table says to her, "But National, you took six Tuinals." "Yeah, but I'm not on a trip!"

high on

**LOU REED:** I was sitting in the back room and Danny Fields comes in and walks over to me. "Lou," he says, "you have to come out and meet Brian Epstein, he's the Beatles' manager and he wants to meet you. He's thinking about managing the Velvet Underground." So we got outside in front of Max's where his limousine is parked. He sticks his head out the window, introduces himself, and says, "Get in," and offers me a joint. I looked down on people who smoked grass in those days. We spoke for a few minutes, and I went back into Max's.

**RITTY DODGE, NIGHT MANAGER:** One good thing about working the back room is when the lights came up, you could pick up enough pills to last you the week. At the end of the night when I told the back-room characters that it was closing time and to pay up, absolutely everything would come flying at me. You had to duck!

**DEREK CALLENDER:** There were enough drugs in that back room to cause genetic defects. That was pill city.

**From left, Jim Jacobs, Larissa, Danny Fields and Lou Reed**
(photo by Anton Perich)

rebellion

**LYNN MYERS:** We would have evenings in Max's where we would all sit in one of the booths and play "Guess the Drug." We would swallow a pill or two and try to figure out what it was we were on. Those drugs were mostly like mescaline. There were some we never did identify.

**RUBY LYNN REYNER:** Brigid would stand up on the round table in the back room, the Warhol table, and take out a syringe and plunge it through her clothes into her fat ass and announce, "I'm up!" Then Edie Sedgwick would be sitting there with her head down, nodding at the the table with Jim Morrison.

**HOLLY WOODLAWN:** In those days Brigid was evil. Her mouth, her look. I think it was that paranoia from that speed, and basically being unhappy. She always scared the hell out of me.

**TOM O'DONNELL:** Brigid was the best person I met at Max's. Of all the people I met there, she was the funniest, most intelligent. I never had a bad minute with Brigid. I used to hang on every word she said. She would play me these tapes of her mother and father eating dinner. She had all these incredible tapes. One of Viva's sisters was going out with Kissinger and she put a tape recorder in her bag, and had her tape their conversation.

**LAURA KRONENBERG:** Viva's sister Mary Beth was going out with Kissinger, and Brigid was there and egged her on to calling up Henry and putting the phone bug on and taping his phone conversation. She played that tape 'till there was nothing left of it. "Oh no, no, no, you mustn't tell anybody about it." But everybody heard it. "Oh darling, if they caught us behind the state curtain, if the Secret Service had caught us, it would have been such a scandal!"

I learned the hard way that you had to watch what you said around Brigid or on the phone with her. She would call and tape your conversation without your knowledge or consent. She could be vicious. She got me one time, and I wasn't aware until after the fact. She was asking me questions about Bobby Neuwirth like: "Was he a good lover?" "Did he have a big cock?" I don't remember what I said, but a few weeks later, there was a night we were all sitting at a table, I think both Neuwirth and Mickey were there, and she pulls out the tape recorder with this particular conversation and puts it on the table, turned it on, and let it run. I was flabbergasted, and Neuwirth was not happy. He said, "Yvonne, don't you know she records all her conversations? Never talk to Brigid about anything personal." It thought it was very cruel, and embarrassing to say the least. Sometimes she'd wait for you to leave the table then she'd play the tape.

**DAVID AMRAM:** Everything seemed to start to turn sour in the late sixties. It was a combination of history, of the assassinations of Martin Luther King and Kennedy, the Vietnam War, proliferation of LSD, the encouraging of people to use drugs, and that combined with drinking. And then the younger generation coming up being told by sort of major degenerates like Timothy Leary that getting stoned out of your head and not doing anything with your life was really a wonderful goal that you should pursue. He wasn't totally to blame, but the fact that he was on the cover of *Time* and *Life* magazines with the story that he had turned on the Loud family, who were then in their late middle age, to LSD and they thought he was a guru. This legitimalized the use of LSD in a way.

**TONY INGRASSIA, DIRECTOR:** The first time I took acid was at Max's. I was working this crazy office during the day to support myself and there were a lot of drug people working in the office. I was working on a play at night and I was exhausted. So one of them said, "Take this, it will perk you up." And unfortunately it was speed cut with acid. I had never taken an acid trip. I began to giggle a lot and they sent me home. I worked near Max's so I walked down there and went inside. I met Ondine there. I told him that they gave me this black pill and I walked outside and said, "Gee, Ondine, look at the trees." And he said, "That's not a Black Beauty! You don't look at trees on a Black Beauty."

**J. P. RADLEY, MAX'S ACCOUNTANT:** Tiger Morse, who I was seeing at the time, told me she learned how to shoot speed from Max Jacobson. Max was the original dealer of speed in this town. The original Dr. Feelgood. My mother, Pauline Trigere, went to him for a while. He was one of the big quacks. He put more people on speed. Tiger used to tell me that her family was somehow instrumental in saving Max from the Nazis. He was Jewish and being persecuted and they helped get him over to America in the 1930s. Tiger went to work for him as an assistant at a fairly young age.

I went to see him once on my mother's recommendation. There was this waiting room full of people and you wait and you wait. You go in and Max sees you and he gives you a cocktail in the behind. Tiger said she used to help mix the speed up. Prepare the injections. Many famous artists, actors, musicians, went through that place and got hooked on speed through Max.

**HOLLY WOODLAWN:** Once I was so high on speed I spent thirteen hours in front of the mirror putting on makeup. By the time we got to Max's it was closing time.

**RUBY LYNN REYNER:** Every week we would sit in the back room and say, "Whose birthday can we make it?" Because whoseever birthday it was, Mickey

From left, Jennifer Lee, Michael J. Pollard, Gregory Corso, and Taylor Mead (photo by Anton Perich)

*rebellion*

133

would buy us a bottle of champagne. Mickey came in the back room one time and said to me, "Ruby, how many birthdays have you had this year? This is enough already!"

**PAUL MORRISSEY:** Mickey allowed people to hang out in the back room and not pay if they were eccentric. It was odd that a guy would run a restaurant without making his customers pay their bills. It really made the place a magnet for a certain crowd. There was nothing else like it. Andy picked up the bills for the Velvet Underground because he was managing them and trying to make them famous, which he did. Andy also allowed other people to sign checks and then paid for the bills with artwork. A lot of people Mickey just let go—he would let them run up bills without collecting on them. The people who made it colorful were the people who had no money. Because of their peculiar status, they felt they had to put on a show—stand on tables and scream, or get especially drunk and fall down. People who have money tend to behave themselves, but people who don't, tend to compensate by acting wild. That's what gave the place its life, and Mickey knew that.

**TAYLOR MEAD:** I began running up bills but I always paid up. Around Christmas I got extra money from my family. Of course I could have signed Andy's name, he would give various people permission to sign, but I wouldn't. He wasn't paying the bill either, I'm sure. I had my own little table in the back room, next to the corner booth, on the back wall, under the Flavin sculpture. I loved the color, I loved the feeling in the room, and I loved the observation point. Also, I was paranoid. I like to keep my eye on the door wherever I am. One waitress told me that they voted on who was the best customer at Max's and I won. I thought I was the worst customer. Actually, Neil Williams and John Chamberlain were the worst customers. I thought I was doing a big number if I charged one or two grand a year. They were charging fifty.

**CHERRY VANILLA, ACTRESS/SINGER/PROMOTER FOR BOWIE:** Most of us in the back room just didn't eat, or at least we didn't order a meal. Because of the way they served the salad in that big bowl, family style, only one person at the table had to order it, and the rest of us could all have a little, and could keep asking the waitress for more bread. And most people got wine by the bottle or a carafe, and would offer you a glass, which you could nurse all night long if you had to. Then there were the coffee and the chick peas. Since the coffee machine was right at the entrance to the back room, it was sort of an unauthorized but well-established practice of the regulars to get up and get your own coffee. And it became a real status thing in a way. Like if nobody stopped you then you knew you'd arrived, you were in. Some nights I'd have money and I'd be the wine and the salad provider. But many a night I'd have none and I'd just live on the coffee and chick peas. The chick peas were the protein and the coffee was the speed.

**MIKE QUASHIE, THE LIMBO KING:** You could be sitting in that back room eating and someone would come and put their hand right in your salad and pick up a piece.

**GERARD MALANGA, POET/ACTOR/WRITER/FORMER WARHOL SUPERSTAR:** I hung out mostly in the back room with Rene Ricard, Richard Bernstein, and various girlfriends including Benedetta Barzini and International Velvet. We would have these chick-pea wars where people would throw the chick peas at someone if they wanted their attention. Occasionally the place would erupt with chick peas and bowls of chick peas flying everywhere.

**FROSTY MYERS:** Taylor Mead slipped on one of the chick peas that was used as a projectile in one of the chick-pea wars. As he was getting up from off the floor he said, "I'm going to sue Mickey for everything I owe him...."

A piece of cheesecake was a big thing in the back room, or a baked potato, or the salad bowl. Debbie Harry remembers the salad bowl: "Mickey actually created the salad bar. He had these big bowls of salad you would bring to the tables with lots of different dressings, except there was only one ladle." The snowballs were another big thing. The crazies back there would order five spoons with a snowball, which consisted of three scoops of ice cream covered with chocolate sauce, whipped cream, coconut, and a cherry on top. They'd order one thing at a time spread out over the entire night. You'd bring a baked potato to the table and someone else would say, "Oh, maybe I'll have one." They'd have you running back and forth to the kitchen and the bar all night. They'd let an hour or two go by in between each one, because they knew they were biding their time. They liked to sit there with dilated eyes, deep into their conversations, not stopping for a minute to think that they might be driving the waitress crazy. They'd act a little sheepish and guilty sometimes—there was that slight courtesy, but not much of a courtesy. They lacked a certain regard. And you would end up making ten dollars in tips for the whole night while the waitresses on the other stations were pulling in around a hundred.

Not everyone back there was like that, of course. People like Danny Fields and Donald Lyons and Taylor were always very sweet to the waitresses. Andy was pleasant, not much of a tipper, but there was usually an entourage of pretty people at his table, especially young boys, because Andy always picked up the tab. I'd say Danny Fields was definitely competition for Andy when it came to the pretty boys. We called them the "back room nymphets": Andy Paley, Rocco, Joe Dallessandro, Octavio, Tim Buckley, Don Johnson, Jackson Browne, Eric Emerson, and Jay and Jed Johnson were just a few that fit the bill.

**HOLLY WOODLAWN:** There were a lot of beauties back there, the new kids in town. And the next week they're big stars. If they were cute little boys in a band, Danny got them. And if they were cute little boys who belonged in movies, Andy got them, or Jackie Curtis. She was always asking

rebellion

the young boys, "Do you want to be in an Andy Warhol movie?" There were also plenty of female beauties: Viva, with her dark eye makeup and frizzy hair; Susan Bottomly, aka International Velvet (the girl who was on the cover of *Esquire* sitting in a garbage can naked, symbolizing the female fatalities from the new "Youthquake"), was more of an Elizabeth Taylor type; classical beauty Nico, who was a heavy woman; Candy Darling, before I got my foot in the door. Then when *Trash* came out I didn't bother looking at anybody else.

**DAVID SMITH:** It was sort of common knowledge that Jackson Browne couldn't stand the heat in the back room, and that was why he moved back to California. Danny Fields wanted to manage Jackson. He was totally focused on him. Jackson was determinedly straight in his way, and it was just too much pressure for him. And I think the girls who were after him there were too closely aligned with the gay guys. He was really not equipped to handle that scene. He had to go to California where it was easier to deal with life. I can remember romancing Jay Johnson, and Dorothy Dean coming right over to the table and screaming at me that she didn't approve of me for him. Dorothy Dean was the meanest bitch in show business. She was one of the door ladies at Max's, a black Harvard graduate who thought she was white, who was usually drunk and obnoxious. She was the only person who ever really came close to driving me out of there. I would say, "I'm not going to do this to myself. I'm not going to ever deal with that woman again," but I always went back.

**IGGY POP:** Gerard [Malanga] was…If you can have a crush on a guy without being gay, I had a crush on Gerard. I liked his…ah, I liked the way he looked and he had a certain balance. There was something about the guy that I admired very much and I always felt, Boy, I'd like to be…I thought he was a pretty cool guy and I had met him there, and about a year after I met him he took some pictures of me and one of them is probably the favorite picture of me that was ever taken. I was penniless and down and out and kicked off a label and dirty and very determined, and he took my picture in a bare bedroom of a deserted apartment that he managed to help me get into, he and Terry Ork.

I really didn't know any of these people…It was all superficiality in those days and everybody was hungry in their way to get somewhere and you didn't get to know each other so much as individuals—it was more you found out what you had to find out.

**LOUIE WALDEN, ACTOR:** Nico would bring her boyfriend, Jim Morrison, to the back room. He copied Gerard Malanga's look, wearing black leather pants. They'd sit there and I'd be sitting with Brigid and she'd be whispering to me, "Look at her. She has that awful Doors character with her who pulls his pee-pee out on stage."

**EVE BABBITZ, NOVELIST/JOURNALIST:** I knew Jim Morrison from Los Angeles. In fact, I met him just before his group decided to call themselves the Doors. In New York, I introduced Jim to Andy Warhol—it was love at first sight. Later on, of course, Jim became an insane Max's person.

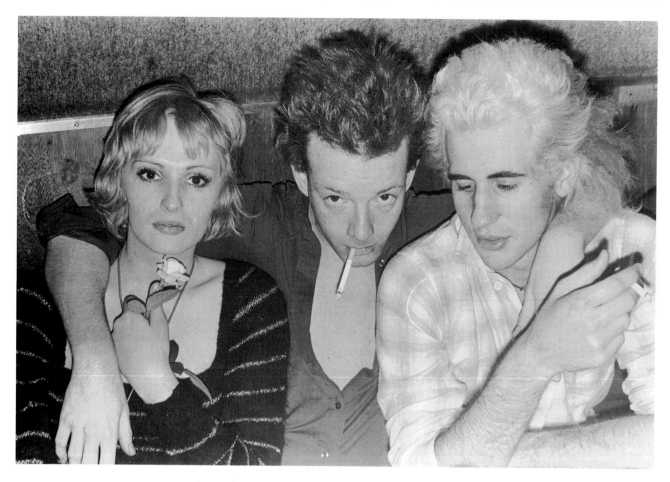

**DANNY FIELDS:** Jim Morrison and I were sitting at a table in the back room, and he pees into a bottle of wine that we had been drinking. He gives it to the waitress and says, "Oh, by the way, this is very good wine. I saved some for you." What a card!

**From left, Candy Darling, Jackie Curtis, and Rocco**
(photo by Anton Perich)

**JEFFREY NICKORA:** Before Jim was famous, he was hanging out at Max's and he would call two and three times a night to see what was going on and who was there. The phone was to the right of the cash register and there were four or five lines and people were always calling in. There was only one instrument, four lines, and a hold button. That phone was heavy-action duty. He didn't want to come out, didn't want to be out, but he wanted a life line.

**DAVID JOHANSEN:** Danny Fields would always try to talk me out of getting into the music business. He'd say, "You're such a nice boy. What do you want to get into this business for?" He would come in with Jim Morrison, and Jim would take acid and drink. He would go to the bar and get a glass of whiskey, this huge glass, and drink the whole thing down. I would look at him and he'd go, "Ah, takes the edge off!" I would sit at Danny's table and talk with Jim whenever I could. I thought he was just so great. But I never understood how he could drink like that.

**SUSAN BLOND:** The most humiliating moment of my life was when Mick Jagger was sitting in the back room with Fred Hughes from the Factory. I was working at the Factory at that point and Fred was one of the bosses. I was very bold in those days, and seeing that I did work with Fred, I didn't think it was being that bold to go over and for a second, be introduced to Mick. I walked over and Fred didn't say anything. I just stood there and he didn't say a thing. It made it even worse because all eyes in the back room were on that table.

**DEBBIE ROSS:** Yvonne called me the first night Mick Jagger came to Max's. She said, "Debbie, come over quick, Mick Jagger is sitting in the back room." I came over and we went back there and the room was packed with gawkers like ourselves. People who usually didn't go to the back room were there milling about and sitting on laps. Usually the Max's habitués didn't fuss over celebrities, but the Stones were a major sensation in the U.S. at the time. I think it was their first trip to New York City. Mickey was very angry with everyone, especially us, because he prided himself on the fact that celebrities were treated just like anybody else. He wanted their privacy respected, but we couldn't help ourselves—Jagger was a special attraction.

**JEREMIAH NEWTON:** Geraldine and Maria Smith are sisters that hailed from Driggs Avenue to the north of the Williamsburg Bridge. As children, they had dreams of becoming famous in the city across the river that they would look at through their window. Maria wanted to be an actress and Geraldine a model. When not engaged in warfare, they perfected their own individual style and learned how to dress chic, throwing together odd pieces of clothing. The challenge was on—making it in the big city. And they went out well prepared. Geraldine appeared many times in *Vogue* and traveled across the world and Maria got a lead part in the flick *Lords of Flatbush*, where she made use of her Brooklyn accent. Both sisters also appear together in Francesco Scavullo's *Book of Beauties*. Geraldine was a champion of the underdog and tried her best to protect people like Andrea Feldman, who was helpless, and faithfully protected Candy Darling through her final illness. Maria likes to spend her time in Ravello with the author Gore Vidal, where they discuss story lines.

**GERALDINE SMITH:** We never had any money. We never worked but we all wore the best clothes. We wore the most expensive Paraphernalia clothes. Plus, we would steal clothes. One time I stole a dress in Countdown, right off the dummy. Everything was a trip. We were on acid a lot. A friend of ours, Roberta, who had an apartment on Park Avenue and Thirtieth, took us under her wing. Her husband paid for it. He was very rich and she had divorced him, but he still paid for everything. So we started living there. Roberta introduced us to Tiger Morse, the hip fashion designer. She

designed clothes for the Kennedys. Roberta would take us into Tiger's store on Madison Avenue and Tiger would dress us and take us into Max's. Tiger was so ahead of her time. She made those silver short, tiny dresses. No one could touch her. She was always on speed. She and Brigid would get on the phone and they'd never stop talking. Brigid was always playing tricks on you. She would put the tape recorder on and talk about people and make you talk about them and you wouldn't know the tape recorder was on, then she would call them up and play it back. Mickey would 86 us regularly, usually because of Andrea—she would really get crazy—or we would start fights. Then Mickey would 86 us and two weeks later he would let us back in. It was like having a parent who just let you do everything. He wasn't strict. What other restaurant owner would let the kind of shit that we pulled go on?

In all the other parts of Max's, people came to eat. Even the artists ate. Ninety percent of the back-room people did not eat, they took drugs. And besides the drugs, nobody had any money. "None of us had any money," remembers Lou Reed, "so we were there every night eating and drinking on Andy's tab. The thing is Mickey would never confront you about your bill. Once in a great while he might make a remark when you were coming in the door." Danny, Andy, Donald Lyons, and a select few, were the only ones who seemed to have any money and a job. Just about everyone else back there was free-loading. Mickey loved them, though. Maybe it was because he knew they needed a home more than the others. Everyone knew that the artists were Mickey's first love, the ones who sat in the front room, the ones who made it worth his while to be there day to day and night after night. "By the time I opened Max's," Mickey once stated, "it was fixed in my mind that the smartest people in the world were artists."

But the backroom people fascinated Mickey, they were part of Mickey's family. Of course, he never knew how to deal with them, so he just kind of left them alone back there to do their thing. Every once in a while he'd pop his head in, just to let his presence be known.

## Excerpt from VITAMIN G
### by John Giorno
*Culture Hero*, #5, Summer 1970

Bridgit Polk is in love with German art dealer Heiner Friedrich and here's how it began in her own words. "I was sitting in Max's at the big long table at the entrance to the back room and this blonde boy with glasses was standing there staring at me. I became very bothered and could only look down as he wouldn't split and wouldn't take his eyes off me. He maneuvered his way to our table, and somehow got someone to insert a chair next to mine and there he was. He had a German accent, and he kept saying 'You're Bridgit, aren't you?' I didn't answer him and finally I got so mad I took my cigarette and put it out on the back of his hand." Heiner is giving Bridgit a show of her polaroids in Munich this September. Andy Warhol said "He probably liked it and wants you to do it to him again."

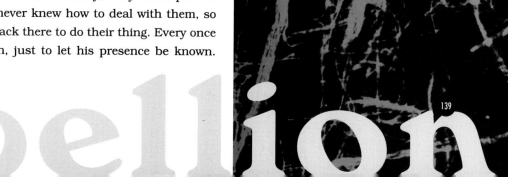

Then he'd kind of smile and shrug and go back up front and let them have their fun, whether they were spending any money or not.

**LEEE BLACK CHILDERS:** When I first arrived in New York in 1967, coming in from the airport I saw "FREE CRISIS" spray-painted on walls. And I thought, What's a "free crisis"? Later I found out it was a drag queen in Greenwich Village who had been locked up for being a drag queen because that's what they did to you then. When the police came, the drag queens would run. In 1969, they really cracked down around the time of the elections and that's when they had the Stonewall Riots....

Years before the Stonewall Rebellion, the attitude at Max's was permissive toward gender and sexual role experimentation. In the sixties, there weren't a lot of places that let drag queens in, but Max's did. You'd be in the ladies' room primping, and Jackie Curtis and Holly Woodlawn would be in there with you putting on their make-up, chatting and carrying on like women do about their menstrual cramps and what-not. You'd forget. It was just like talking to one of the girls. I'd walk out of there thinking, I'm very confused.

**TERRY SOUTHERN, WRITER:** Max's was like one of the lower circles of Dante's Inferno filled with Bosch and Breugel characters. I used to go there with Larry Rivers. We would pick up fantastically beautiful girls, wine and dine them, and then bring them back to Larry's studio on Fourteenth Street, only to find out that they were artful deceivers—drag queens. One night we tried to get Miles Davis to pick up one of these "girls," but when we got to his booth, he spotted her right off.

**DONALD LYONS:** When they talk of the revival of elegance of the seventies, I think it really began with people like Candy Darling, who, in the middle of a very mannerly decade, really stood in the certain sense for very high manners and for the high social comedy which could be associated with, say, Carole Lombard. She had a raucous sense of fun, if you look at Andy Warhol's film *Women in Revolt*. This was a film originally called *Pigs*. Candy's sense of life was that it should perpetually be beautiful and elegant, but it so often wasn't. It was because of this great tension with Candy that she carried it off with an almost religious conviction and really intense devotion to art.

**LOUIE WALDEN:** I was rehearsing for this play in this little bar on Seventh Street. Next to me was this very attractive blonde. She had on high heels, a satin dress, but when I looked at her and she smiled at me, she had these rotten teeth, but her role was a whore in this play so I figured that was part of the role. There was something about her, but I couldn't put my finger on it. She was really striking. Then while we were reading for the play, I noticed that she was a he. I'm thinking, My God, this is a man! So I said, "God, you have got to meet Andy." So I took her over to the Factory and he wasn't there. They had all gone to Max's. So we rushed across the street, over to Max's, and

**Drag queens**
(photo by Anton Perich)

when we get to the front, Candy grabs my arm real tight. "Louie, I—I—I—I can't go in there"—
Candy fumbled with her words. "What do you mean, you can't go in there?" I questioned indignantly. "You just walk in on my arm. Everybody will be there and I'll be there and I want you to meet Andy." "I—I—I can't," she stammered again. "It's against the law. If I go in there and a vice cop catches me, they will close the bar down." I convinced Candy to go in with me, just for a minute. So she was the first of the transvestites ever to walk into Max's. We walked into the back room but Andy wasn't there.

**ANDY WARHOL (FROM *POPISM*):** Candy was the most striking drag queen I'd ever seen. On a good day, you couldn't believe she was a man.

**ROBERT HEIDE:** I first met Candy Darling toward the end of the sixties through Ron Link. She had brown hair; not toothless, but not great. She looked great when she was in Tom Eyen's play, something about *Good-bye to Off Off Broadway*. Then I ran into her all the time at Max's later—she and Jackie Curtis. But they both started at Tony Bastiano's Cellar Studio. Jackie had written *Glamour, Glory and Gold*. Ron Link was the director and Robert De Niro played all the male parts.

I was there with John Gilman and we were sitting at a table with a kind of fat man in the back room. There's this man in the dark blue suit, dark glasses, fat—he looked like a gangster. We were

rebellion

**John Waters**
(photo by Anton Perich)

somehow sitting with him, Candy is sitting at another table, and this man turns out to be Burtowski, the great Polish director. I had heard about him. I had friends who were supposed to go study with him for seven years and develop this incredible sense of theater, but they would always come back. They couldn't stay the whole time. But he was as much of a kind of image as Tom O'Horgan, who directed *Hair*. Seeing him was just the opposite of what I would have imagined, but the one thing he was interested in was meeting Candy Darling. He was kind of drunk and was inviting her to join this Polish lab which is the farthest thing she was interested in. She was more interested in, "How am I going to get Andy to pay for my capped teeth?"

**JOHN WATERS, FILMMAKER:** Divine met Candy Darling at Max's—well, they first met at the Factory and then they had a little thing where the two of them got together at Max's. It was great, because I think they were both, at the beginning, wary of each other—you know, drag wars.

Then when *Pink Flamingos* opened, [Divine] came to Max's and was most definitely a star there, because he would show up looking like he did in the movie, so he wasn't exactly not noticed at the time.

**KERRY RIORDAN:** When Divine came to the back room he looked liked a lizard. Maybe I was tripping or something. He had on this dress that was red jersey and it had a cowl and so it was like the neck came all the way up and covered his bald head. The lipstick out to there and fingernails like Fu Manchu. I had not seen the movie yet; it was opening the next night or something. I didn't know who he was. All I knew was that the personage was sitting in my direct line of sight and food had just been delivered and I couldn't eat I was so grossed out by the look of him, but then when I got to know him I totally reversed my thinking. He was fabulous.

**GLENN O'BRIEN:** I lived across the street from Sam Green on West Sixty-eighth Street and Candy Darling was living with Sam at the time so she was often my date, because we would share a cab down to Max's. I was there one night with Candy when *Pink Flamingos* had just come out. Fran [Lebowitz] and I had become friendly with John Waters, so I had the pleasure of introducing Candy to Divine. It was like two great Hollywood movie stars meeting: "Oh, I am such a big fan of yours...." "Oh no! The pleasure is all mine. I'm *your* biggest fan..."

**SUSAN BLOND:** The drag queens, especially Candy Darling, worked harder than any girl to look good. Any money that came to her was put to get electrolysis or whatever she would do to get more and more beautiful. She really studied what it was to be a woman.

high on

## Candy Darling
### by Leee Black Childers

The most beautiful of the famous Warhol drag queens, Candy Darling, was born Richard Slattery on Ronkonkama, Long Island. Even as a young boy, Candy always looked like a girl, and loved the attention it brought her. In the early sixties, nice girls didn't "put out." But Candy soon learned what the horny young football players at high school liked, and was thrilled to be able to provide it. She was *very* popular—in her way. It did not take long for her to find her way to Greenwich Village where she soon fell in with the bizarre underground community that was then growing into a major artistic movement. She was fascinated by their talk of art and sex and drugs. They in turn were delighted with the emancipated girl/boy with the snow-white skin and red, red lips. She and Jackie used to panhan*dle* (accent on the last available syllable, please) until they had the money for the movies, and then they would sit in the darkened theaters for hours until they knew every line of dialogue, every move, every nuance of makeup or attitude of their favorites. Candy's were Kim Novak, and the cheaply styled movie star Beverly Michaels. Jackie went for Marlene Dietrich, even so far as to adopt her lisp. As Candy entered her late teens, she became a great beauty, envied and often insulted by the other Village queens. This bothered her not at all. "Why must they envy me? I can't help it if I was born beautiful…and they weren't." She became a favorite of Warhol and he gave her a role in *Flesh* and then in *Women in Revolt*. Jane Fonda loved her, often accompanying her on rounds of the Village that always ended in the back room of Max's. Candy had a walk-on role in *Klute*. Then, Tennessee Williams gave her the starring role on Broadway in *Small Craft Warnings*, a role she was particularly proud of because she was playing a woman, and no illusions were ever made to the truth…that she was still a man.

**Candy Darling** (photo by Anton Perich)

rebellion

143

**Holly Woodlawn, left,
and a Cockette**
(photo by Anton Perich)

**SIERRA PECHEUR, ACTRESS:** Dick Gregory's campaign manager had this show, *Strip for Peace* in 1968 when Dick was running for president, and we all worked on this show. I said, "You've got to do the Statue of Liberty strip, and we should get Candy Darling because she has the profile of the Statue of Liberty." Well, I managed to talk her into it. I got her twenty-five yards of silver lamé, and I dressed her up with the book, the sceptre, and the crown, and she had a blue sequined top and a red sequined bottom with a flashing red star, and balloons filled with red paint. She stood at the top of the dais and there were stairs. She walked down the stairs unwrapping this twenty-five yards of silver lamé, got down to the bottom...In the back was projected the American flag on a pure blue sky floating in the wind. This was in the Billy Rose Theater—you had the lunch crowd jerking off under their hats there—Candy was fabulous. She came down walking perfectly, got to the bottom, dropped the lamé, popped the two balloons with pins, and blood poured down her body. Flames leaped up around the flag, dollar bills flew out of the sky, and topless go-go dancers came out onstage. These guys were totally entranced. No one knew she was a man. She made it all the way to Broadway. I think she was the first transvestite ever to play a woman on Broadway.

**DANNY FIELDS:** I was the press agent for the Cockettes when they were here in 1971 to do their shows. It was full-blown. The first night I brought them to Max's, no one could believe it because they were all dressed up and one of them wore a toilet seat around her neck. This was their first night on the town in New York before the play opened. I think I saw them in San Francisco and then I became their press agent. Then they were all divided up and living with different people. I got Pristine Condition....

I met Fran Lebowitz because she wrote a bad review of the Cockettes and I was mad. I used to see her at Max's. She was writing for *Changes* at the time, She was walking past my table and I stopped her and I said, "Oh, come and sit down, I have to ask you about that mean review you wrote." And then she sat down and we became friends.

**MICHEL O'DARE, FILMMAKER:** The Cockettes were a group of twenty-five transvestites that came to New York to do some kind of operetta. It was a big bomb. Some producer had the idea that it was going to be really big in New York. They all came completely in drag and dressed up. It was quite a scene. They were in the bathroom—the men's bathroom, the women's bathroom—and everybody was probably having sex and stuff....It was like an incredible vision.

**BOB GRUEN, PHOTOGRAPHER:** I went to Max's because they served good food and I usually got the surf 'n' turf, which was an excellent meal, with the baked potato and the sour cream. Late at night, the kitchen was always open; you could eat well after working hard and going around drinking hard all night. It was the night the Cockettes were in town, a cross-dressing theatrical troupe from San Francisco, and they put on a big show on the Lower East Side. They were celebrating after the show in the back room. They were all carousing about, being loud and drunk, and they got up on the table and started doing a striptease. They were these very queenie guys, but with beards. They had glitter and lipstick in their beards and hair. They were dancing around with their slips and their panties and bras, and after they stopped, Eric got up on the table in his shorts and his T-shirt and he whipped off his T-shirt, then he whipped off his shorts. He was completely naked and he said, "If you want to strip, strip—don't just pretend," and his dick is like a two-foot-long schlong hanging right over my meal. He jumped up on my table. I lost my appetite. It's not my kind of meal. I think it was the last time I ate there. I stuck to the chick peas.

**LEEE BLACK CHILDERS:** Once Jackie was confronted at a party by one of those intense revolutionaries that were so numerous and vociferous in the late sixties. Wild-eyed, frizzy-haired, and with little droplets of California hearty burgundy spraying as she talked, he pulled at her dress, pointed at the glitter on her eyelids and lips, and shouted, "What do you think you're doing? Do you realize there's a revolution on?" Jackie looked at him and replied, "I do more for the revolution just walking down the street every day than you do with all your leaflets and pamphlets and crap."

Jackie Curtis was a man. Her grandmother, Slugger Ann, owned a bar on the Lower East Side, and her mother was a taxi driver during the war. Jackie became a celebrated playwright and actor, but one day he decided he liked the roles created for women, and adopted his controversial lifestyle:

rebellion

"To be a woman on the stage, you must be a woman on the street." But what a woman! Dresses made of ripped curtains and tablecloths held together with safety pins, old lady's orthopedic shoes spray-painted metallic silver, garish dyed red hair, and her signature—glitter makeup day and night. Once so attired, she turned to me and said, "One day everyone will look like me," and then doubled over with laughter. Of course, she has come close to being proved right.

Among the well-received plays Jackie wrote and starred in were *Femme Fatale*; *Glamour, Glory and Gold*; *Heaven Grand* in *Amber Orbit*; and *Vain Victory*. She starred in two Warhol films, *Flesh* and *Women in Revolt*. Robert DeNiro had his debut stage performance in *Glamour, Glory and Gold*, playing all ten male parts.

**JOHN HAYES, JOURNALIST:** Jackie and I were very close. She would always say, "Come on John, let's get high, and then let's go eat dinner. Mickey will treat us." And we'd get high and go off to Max's. Jackie would just sign Mickey's name like she was family.

**PHILIP LOCASCIO:** The only time Mickey almost fired me was when Jackie started this scam with me of signing Mickey's name to charges. For some reason they went unnoticed. Jackie somehow convinced me that Mickey said she had carte blanche and could sign his name. I did a lot of drugs in those days. So I okayed Jackie signing Mickey's name to about $1,000 worth of charges. Mickey came down from the office one afternoon and asked me, "What the hell is this?" So I ended up having to pay every single penny back. Here's Jackie wining and dining Rita Redd and Candy, and I'm okaying all these charges. I don't know why I never asked Mickey about it. He really tore into me, "Who told you to okay these? Are you crazy?"

**Jackie Curtis, left, and Divine**
(photo by Anton Perich)

# Decorative Veneer
## by Jeremiah Newton

I dressed for the occasion.

Max's Kansas City was a dark bar. Doubly so if you entered on a hot summer's day as I did one afternoon in 1968 wearing a loud Carnaby Street tie and limp Brooks Brothers seer-sucker suit I'd bought off the rack at one of those great thrift shops that once lined the east side of the 59th Street bridge. This lauded occasion would be my first time inside Max's.

I'd passed Max's many times, usually at night, and watched the comings and goings of its patrons but never dared to enter even though I knew plenty of people who had the credentials for entry and I could have gone right in with them. Psychologically I wasn't ready and made all sorts of excuses why not to go, sort of the same logic as the reasons of holding on to one's virginity. I heard stories told in MacDougal Street cafes—usually by old beatniks who sneered through their yellowed teeth at Max's and the whole Warhol scene—that there were some cool people who did not make the grade and were refused entry. These poor souls—judged by their peers to be instantly unhip, were left outside dick in hand, so to speak.

My fragile teenage ego did not want to risk death by rejection. And did I want to go inside? Would it be everything I imagined it to be; the cradle of chic, as *Vogue* called it? However, like a traveler to an out-of-limits foreign land, a land so exotic and appealing that I would become a lotus eater—an addict; I now possessed the right credentials to enter and would take that giant step forward.

The stars and planets were in the right conjunction. It was now or never. This was "the" time and as I stood wilting outside under a bright sun, I swallowed hard and stepped through the door. Momentarily blinded by the dark interior, I stood a minute rubbing my eyes and when I opened them, there he was, but I guess he was there all along: Mickey Ruskin, Max's owner—the wrong person to bump into when you were trying to act cool but were in reality an unknown teenager from Queens.

"Looking for somebody?" he said.

I was quick on the uptake.

"Umm. . .Candy Darling. Is she here?" (I had known Candy since 1966 and knew

rebellion

her star was on the upswing because of her small role in the Warhol/Morrissey film *Flesh*.) He smiled ever so slightly, stepping aside.

"She's in the back room. Know how to get there?"

The back room. I'd heard about the back room and the stories connected with it. It was "the" place to hang out—once you got into Max's itself, it did not guarantee you a seat in the back room. Mickey watched over the back room ver-r-r-y carefully making sure that the right mix of actors, models, filmmakers gathered there.

'Sure," I said bravely and followed the line of the bar and made sure I didn't bump into anyone else or end up in the kitchen. And I didn't.

Max's during the afternoon was empty with only the sounds of a muted juke box playing Hank Williams and the steady drone of voices coming from the back room.

"Does not."

"She does."

"Does not."

"She does."

In the back room booth under one flattering light sat Candy Darling carefully redoing her makeup and sitting across from her wearing a torn sweatshirt applied with sequins was Jackie Curtis. They were arguing the merits of Kim Novak's hand and foot size.

"I'm telling you Candy," Jackie said, "Kim's hands are never in a scene, neither are her feet. They're too big like yours."

Candy shut her compact with a thud.

"That's a vicious rumor started by demented woman haters like you. Kim has small hands and small feet."

"Does not."

"Does."

"Does not."

"Does."

Candy saw me.

"Jeremiah, come sit with us. Now Jackie, here's a young man with a totally fresh point of view." I sat uneasily next to Candy on the worn booth.

Jackie glared at me. I knew he was on speed. Anything could happen. I looked nervously at a heavy ceramic plate of chick-peas near his rough-looking hand accented with chipped red nail polish.

"Now Mr. Curtis over here (she put an emphasis on "Mr.") says that Kim Novak's hands and feet are so big that they never appear on screen. Isn't that the most totally ridiculous thing you've ever heard in your life?"

My life to date was 18 years old. I wasn't an expert on anything yet, let alone Kim

Novak's shoe or glove size. I didn't know what to answer. Whatever I said would sound dumb to two rabid Novak fans.

I closed my eyes to think. Minutes passed. The Ronettes were singing *Be My Baby.* "Wel-l-l," Jackie said looking at me. "What's your opinion?" He paused and said slowly, "Or don't you have one?"

Of course he has an opinion. He's been to college!" Candy said adjusting her lipstick while holding a small mirror. Jackie passed gas.

Candy made a face and whispered, "Do you think my beard's showing?"

I shook my head and spoke.

"The way Kim Novak is shot, it's difficult to see her hands, let alone her feet. But that doesn't mean she has abnormally large feet or hands."

Jackie snorted, his face as red as his hair, "Naturally a friend of yours would side with Miss Darling."

Jackie got up and walked away, heading towards the front. He must have collided with a waitress because I could hear the sounds of breaking dishes and curses.

"Tsk, tsk," Candy said shaking her blonde head. "Poor Jackie thinks he knows it all but he doesn't. None of us do. He's on his James Dean trip today. Do you think he looks like James Dean?"

The image of Dean's lean handsome face transposed on Jackie's red puffy one made me shudder.

"No way," I whispered, not wanting Jackie to hear me. I'd seen plenty of fights because of ill-timed words.

"C'mon, let's go to the Factory to see Andy."

**LEEE BLACK CHILDERS:** I was hanging out on Christopher Street on the stoop and Jamie Andrews, who has since passed away, sat down on the stoop next to me. "Leee, are you going to Jackie's wedding?" "What wedding?" I asked. He said Jackie was going to marry Eric Emerson on a rooftop the next day. "You should go," he said, "it's going to be great." So I went home and said to Wayne County, who I was living with at the time, "Jackie Curtis is getting married to Eric Emerson, I want to go. Let's go." "Leee," Wayne says, "Jackie and Eric can't get married, they're both men." "It doesn't matter," I said, "I'm going anyway."

Wayne wouldn't go, so I went on my own. I climbed the stairs to the roof, ran into Jackie wearing her wedding gown, which was some fabulous gown that someone happened to borrow from Bendel's. I went up to the rooftop. Now, I had read magazines, but I never knew people like this really existed. I looked around, it was incredible: drag queens; boys in makeup; Ricky Tappy Toes in his little white outfit with his tap shoes on and his Twiggy makeup; Holly Woodlawn, Jamie Andrews, Tony Ingrassia, Ruby Lynn Reyner...a tall, lean, luscious, redheaded model was maid of honor, David Peel was performing, and Elsbeth Leacock, daughter of filmmaker Robert Leacock, was filming the whole affair.

**TONY INGRASSIA:** Jackie is in this humongous white dress with three days of growth coming through, a big bouquet, streamers in her hair, and there's no Eric. That was the first theatrical event I had gone to, so I told Jackie, "You know what we'll do, we'll go get him." We ran down the stairs to look for a taxi, and a friend of mine's brother passes by in a car. I yelled, "Take us to Max's." We piled in the car, and he drove us to Max's. We ran through the door, it's the middle of the afternoon, and there was Eric standing at his post. I said, "Why aren't you marrying her?" It was so funny. And he says, "I can't, I'm working!" I said, "That's it, Jackie, we're finished with him." And we turned around and got into a taxi and went back. So Jackie married Stuart [Lichtenstein] instead.

**LEEE BLACK CHILDERS:** After the sun came down, Andrea Feldman walked in. I had never met her before. I looked at her and she was just so beautiful. All this hair, and she was wearing this lovely powder-blue dress, all different layers of chiffon. Somehow she decided to latch on to me. She walked over to me, "Oh, d-a-a-aling, you must come with me. Come with me to the reception at Max's." "Well, okay, I'll go, sure I'll go." That was the first time I ever stepped into the back room of Max's. I went in with Andrea.

You can imagine what it was like that night, Jackie's reception. Mickey did his usual of pretending to be aloof from it all. There was champagne, of course, and since I was with Andrea I was immediately right in there. Jackie asked me to go with her to get some of her things. She was living with Ruby Lynn Reyner and they had been arguing. The electricity had been turned off. It was pitch black. There I was in the pitch dark with this drag queen in her wedding gown. We were trying to find shoes and clothes and I'm thinking, What the fuck am I doing here? We did get her stuff and went back to Max's and hung out. I was totally entranced. I just couldn't believe it, and I was being

high on

accepted by these people. This was my total dream of the lifestyle I wanted to live.

I went home that night and told Wayne everything. So we went to Max's the very next night. Wayne was very nervous; he was a very shy southern boy. We sat in the very back corner booth. They used to call it the paranoid booth, because it was under the red neon Flavin light. Wayne had this little hanky and was constantly drying the moisture from his face, and Andrea and her friend Geraldine and Jackie were there, so Wayne got completely involved, so we started going there every night. Then a few days later Jackie moved in with us, and two weeks after that, Holly Woodlawn moved in, then Rita Redd moved in and then Rio Grande. So in a one-bedroom apartment on Thirteenth Street between First and Avenue A, there was me and five drag queens.

**STEVE GAINES:** It must have been only my second or third month as a regular going to Max's every night, when a girl named Rita Redd gave me a blow job under the round table. And I swear to God, I didn't know for a year that Rita was a guy.

**JOHN HAYES:** I remember Devon, Jimi Hendrix's girl-friend, coming in one night and Bianca Jagger was there, and there was absolute daggers, because Devon had a brief liaison with Mick. Supposedly, she had a dalliance with Bianca in London. Devon was bisexual. They had a big cat fight that night. Devon eventually O Ded in a bathtub at the Chelsea.

**PHILIP LOCASCIO:** We were sitting in the back room one night and Devon, Jimi Hendrix's girlfriend, invited us uptown to a party. We went with Devon to this girl's place named Shamalee. It was up near the United Nations. She was from India. Her father was the ambassador to the United States from India. There was Holly

**Jackie Curtis and Andrea Feldman outside Max's**
(photo by Anton Perich)

rebellion

and Larissa, Eric Emerson, myself, and a few others. We all got very high. Eric and Holly went into the wife's bedroom and started trying on all her clothes. About two hours later we all decided to go back downtown and here's Holly in this woman's clothes. I said, "Holly, what are you doing?" She says, "Trust me." We're all on speed; none of us had been to bed, and Holly decides to wear this sarong home to the Chelsea.

The next morning at around eight-thirty A.M., Holly puts this woman's sarong back on, and she's putting this makeup on. "Holly, where are you going in that thing?" I inquired. She says, "Don't worry, I'm going up to the United Nations, and we're all having dinner at Max's tonight on me." She pulls out this woman's checkbook, went out, got into a cab, and went directly to the United Nations bank and impersonated the ambassador to India's wife. She cashed a check for $300, came back downtown, and we all ate dinner at Max's that night. But that wasn't enough for Holly. The next day she did the same thing. I don't know how they found out, I think she used Max's as an address or something dumb like that. But we're all at Max's again the next night eating dinner, and who should come in but the United Nations police, the FBI. They handcuffed her. Meanwhile Holly is still in this woman's garb so they dragged her off to the women's house of detention on Greenwich Avenue, and told her to strip. These matrons are standing there and Holly strips. There she is with her big schlong hanging down. So they threw her in the truck and took her to the tombs.

**HOLLY WOODLAWN:** Candy and Jackie Curtis were into the Cafe Chino, which was Off Off Off Broadway. Candy was in one production, *Give My Regards to Broadway*, got a review, and got the bug. That's when I started hearing about Max's from her all the time. "That's where Andy goes. Andy thinks I'm wonderful." Andy this and Andy that. She thought Andy thought that she was going to be the next big Superstar. I went to Max's just once during that time. I went with Candy. It was one of the strangest places I had ever been to in my life. I wasn't ready. Everyone was so outrageous. All the models in every "vogue" magazine I ever had were there. All these people who were strange and wonderful. It was something I had to be a part of. I thought the people would be just sitting around drinking sort of informally, and being tasteful and very chic. I didn't think I'd fit at all, which I didn't. I was wearing something modish and feminine. You see, I always wanted to look like a model. That was my thing. Whereas, Jackie and Candy wanted to look like stars. They wanted to be Superstars. I just wanted to be Jean Shrimpton.

Every once in awhile I got a job. I worked in Saks Fifth Avenue as a model for a while, as a mannequin. This guy who hired me thought I was a girl. I was young, my hair was long, and I was on hormones. Then I met some speed freaks living in the East Village, and that's when I started taking speed and shooting up. They knew Andy, and they used to go to Max's a lot. So I went back with them about a year or two after I went the first time. By this time, Candy and Jackie had done *Flesh*, so now they were Superstars, and they were hanging out in the back room. Before that, I don't think they were eligible. I just went with my speed friends and we went upstairs to dance and shoot up in the bathrooms. All the bathrooms. We weren't picky.

**Holly Woodlawn**
(photo by Leee Black Childers)

When I finally met Andy it was at the factory. My friend George wanted Andy to meet me, because he thought Andy would be interested in me. *Flesh* had just come out, so he took me to the Factory. I was expecting MGM, not an empty loft with a couch and these dead people. Andy looked deader than all of them. All these people are making such a commotion over this? I asked myself. It doesn't even talk. I remember Morrissey, who was nonstop talk. The way *Trash* came about was that they were [making a] film about trashy people, and someone said, "Holly Woodlawn would be perfect for this," because they had a low opinion of me. And I went to Max's one night and Andy was there with Fred Hughes and Bob Colacello. I was sitting at another table, at the other end of the room, and Fred Hughes came over to me, like the true gentleman that he is, and asked me to join Andy at his table. And in total shock and horror, I joined them. They asked me if I would be in this movie, if I would do a scene that they were filming. I said, "Of course."

They instructed me to show up the following week to Paul Morrissey's basement, which turned out to be my apartment in the movie. I did the scene for them, and then they called me to do another scene, and then another. I did them at $25 a shot, which was a lot of money for me back then. That's when I started hanging out at the Factory, to see the rushes, and my name started getting around as being the star of *Trash*, even before the film came out. One day I walked into Max's and Sylvia Miles was sitting at the bar with these two young model-type boys. She had just come from

rebellion

**Sylvia Miles and Eric Emerson** (photo by Anton Perich)

seeing the rushes and she was going on and on about how wonderful I was in the film, and how I should be nominated for an Academy Award. And I was just playing myself. That's when I started becoming one of the stars of the back room. That was fun. Now I could sit with Candy Darling. Now she could sit with me. That's when the rivalry started, when *Trash* came out and it wasn't Candy Darling anymore. People were coming to the back room to look at me. Now I could sit at Andy's table whenever I wanted, and that's when Mickey started respecting me.

The back room was just one of the many scenes going on at Max's in the late sixties. The front room, including the alcove and the middle section, continued buzzing nightly with artists, photographers, filmmakers, writers, models, and others who had made Max's their home. And it wasn't uncommon to see some cross-pollination between the rooms, depending on who was in them at the time. Even some of the back-room crowd would, on occasion, take a table in the alcove (always my favorite station) for a quiet business dinner or romantic rendezvous, or sit in one of the banquettes in the middle section, to be seen in a different light or enjoy a different perspective.

The back-room crowd did not resent the front-room regulars. They enjoyed having their own territory. It was like a private club back there. The front room crowd, however, especially the homophobic artists, were clearly not enamored of the back room and rarely ventured back there except for perhaps Chamberlain, Rivers, and Rauschenberg (who was one of the princes of the back room). Once in a while one of the other artists or writers would stick his head in to check out the action.

Brigid Polk, who was definitely a Warhol person, migrated to the front room to familiarize herself with the art world. Apparently Andy made some comment at the round table one night about how uneducated she was about the art scene. Many of the artists up front refused to give credence to Andy as an artist, eventually acknowledging him only because of his commercial success, which in itself marked the beginning of a new "pop" attitude for these serious artists. "The back room was always

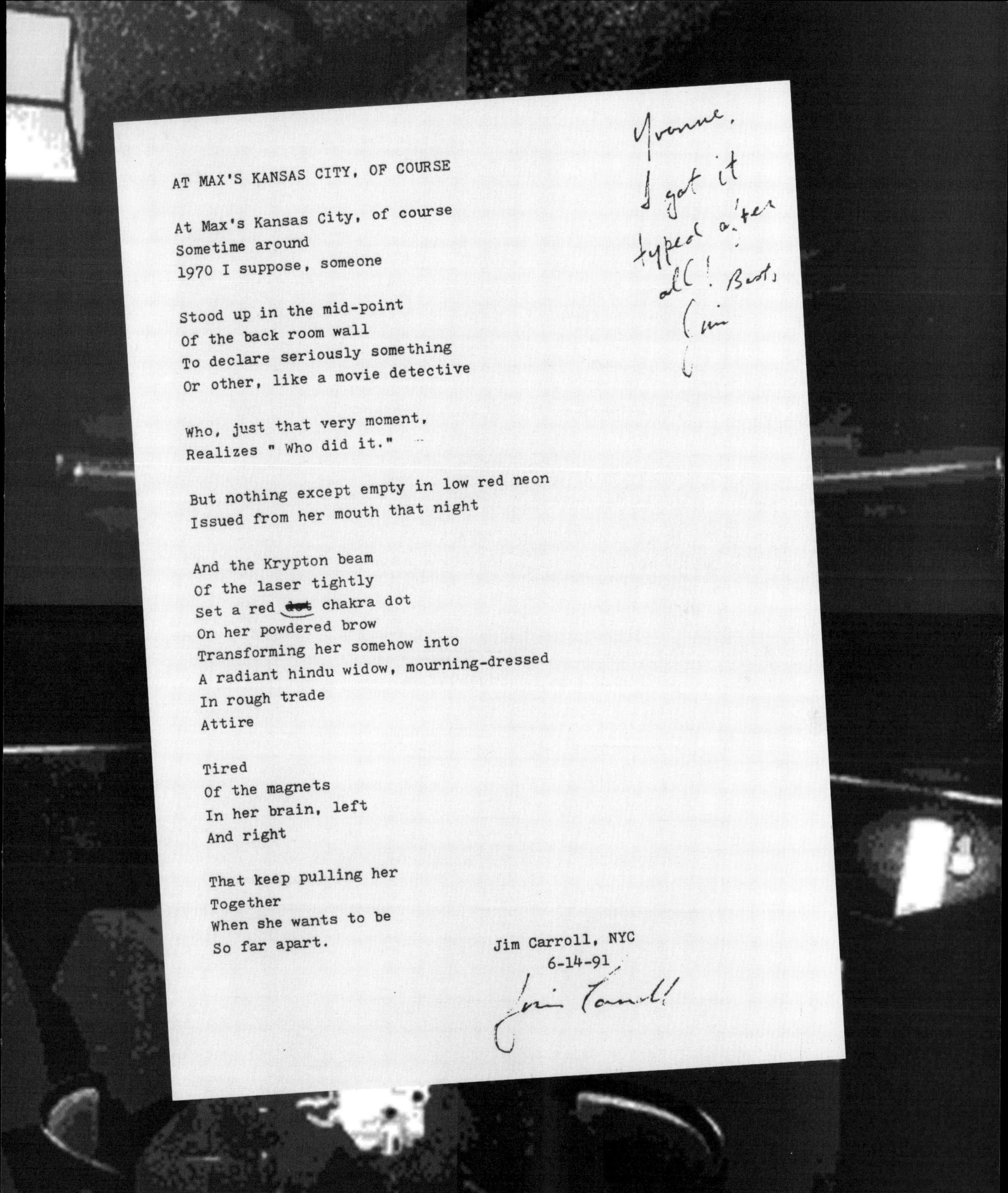

AT MAX'S KANSAS CITY, OF COURSE

At Max's Kansas City, of course
Sometime around
1970 I suppose, someone

Stood up in the mid-point
Of the back room wall
To declare seriously something
Or other, like a movie detective

Who, just that very moment,
Realizes " Who did it."

But nothing except empty in low red neon
Issued from her mouth that night

And the Krypton beam
Of the laser tightly
Set a red ~~dot~~ chakra dot
On her powdered brow
Transforming her somehow into
A radiant hindu widow, mourning-dressed
In rough trade
Attire

Tired
Of the magnets
In her brain, left
And right

That keep pulling her
Together
When she wants to be
So far apart.                    Jim Carroll, NYC
                                        6-14-91

Yvonne,
I got it
typed after
all! Best,
Jim

Warhol to me," artist Francine Tint remembers, "and I didn't consider him an artist. He told me he was never an artist himself. I worked with him on a fashion job when he was an illustrator. He was a great, marvelous businessman."

As the sixties began to dwindle and the seventies began to dawn, it was pleasure as usual in the back room. The beauties made entrances in new outfits from Abracadabra and Paraphernalia, while models like Twiggy and Veruschka flew in from Europe wearing the latest fashions from hip clothing stores abroad like Granny Takes A Trip. Tiger Morse, Annie Flanders, Betsey Johnson, Jackie Rogers, Michael Mott, and Steve Burroughs were the looks favored most by the back room's "fashionettes," although army surplus, thrift shop, originals, ethnic, and good old jeans looks were also quite in. Showtime was proving to be a super long-running hit and the sex and drugs and drag continued with unbridled bravura. But the balance of the back room was changing. It was, as the regulars would say, "getting too rock-and-roll." It might have been due to the music scene upstairs, which started in '69, or simply the fact that in both underground and high society, rock stars were replacing artists, writers, and actors as the gods of the time. The new young poets of the back room began to embrace rock as a vehicle for their words. Others were looking to the business side of it for a career. And still others were becoming "groupies," a scandalous new term of the time. But not all those who came to the back room came as patrons. There was, of course, Debbie Harry. The back room was Debbie's entree into that world. She wanted to be a part of that whole theater, rock-and-roll scene. I, on the other hand, was working at Max's not to be discovered, but because it was a great place to make money. If there was money floating around that back room the waitress never saw it. Eighty percent of the back room characters were on drugs and broke.

**JACKIE SHERMAN:** When I became senior waitress, they gave me this real young, plain girl from New Jersey named Debbie Harry to train. She was so sweet, this little face, brown hair, no makeup, really scrubbed face. She was into being a singer. She didn't seem to mind working the back room. Then she left and came back again to see us, after getting a job at the *Playboy* Club. She became a *Playboy* bunny and she had bleached blonde hair and makeup. Of course, in those days we were all against girls who wore so much makeup, because we were downtown girls. So she walked in with these eyelashes and rouge and bleached-blonde hair and we thought it was just so disgusting. But Debbie looked fabulous.

**DEBBIE HARRY, WAITRESS / ROCK MUSICIAN:** I worked at Max's for about seven or eight months as a waitress. I guess it was 1969. It was really just a fantastic place to be. Everyone went there. You were constantly meeting and seeing all these famous people every day. Andy and his entourage were there every night. As far as rock-and-roll performers go, there was Steve Winwood, Jimi Hendrix,

Lou Reed, Genya Ravan, and Michael Quashie (photo by Bob Gruen)

Janis Joplin—just everybody. And of course, Lou Reed was there all the time. I met Tony Ingrassia in the back room and started working with him. He helped me put my first group together—the Stilettoes.

**ELDA BRANCH, ROCK MUSICIAN:** I was sitting in the corner and all of a sudden I see Debbie Harry trotting up the stairs carrying a tray. I'm going, "Oh my God, oh my God, I want to see her get that to the table." I had known Debbie from the Dolls because she had a mad crush on David and she used to have this Chevy, this blue car, that she used to drive them around in all the time....I asked Debbie if she knew how to sing and she said she did. So I said to her, "Well, let's put a band together. She did have a band in the sixties for a year—Wind in the Willows—but I didn't know about that. I knew I could make her look good.

rebellion

**ELLEN GOFEN:** What was interesting was that there was a whole scene going on every night. Andy would show up and I used to like to watch how he operated. He was always very quiet and observing everything. There was a waitress who was a model, she was in *Ebony*. She was very pretty, very light skinned. When everybody had left and Andy was paying the bill she sat down next to him and she was talking about how she wanted to be in his movies. She said something to that effect. He said in that voice of his, "Oh, I wanted so much to talk to you to ask you the same thing but I was just too shy." It was interesting how he turned it around. Then that young girl came in all the time wearing Andy's jacket with the bullet holes in it from when Valerie Solanas shot him at the Factory. She had asked Andy for the jacket after he had gotten shot and he gave it to her. She was just a little girl.

**BARBARA HODES:** Lou Reed and his friend Roz, who he had gone to college with, were sitting in the back room one night when Valerie Solanas walked up and said, "I'm going to get all of you men." It was shortly before she shot Andy.

**PENNY ARCADE:** I went through this period when I got involved with Loudon Wainwright while I was still with Danny Goldberg and I didn't go to Max's for a week. I went with Loudon to his house in the country. When I got back, I was very excited. I walked in the back room and at the round table there's Danny Fields, Donald Lyons, Bobby Neuwirth, and some other people. It was me and all men. I was sitting next to Danny Fields and on my left was Bobby Neuwirth. All I knew about Bobby is that he was hanging out with Patti Smith. I'm sitting there and I had on this brown satin dress that kept sliding off the shoulder. They're all drinking tequila so I'm drinking tequila also. Neuwirth is expounding on something and the dress keeps sliding off my shoulder and I keep pulling it back up. Finally, Neuwirth reached over to me, took my dress, and rips it off me and says, "Why don't you pull it all the way down?" He accused me of trying to seduce him. Now, there were all these drinks on the table and I stood up, holding my dress up with one hand and said, "You bastard," and threw every drink in his face, one at a time.

Next to the round table were three short tables across the room and sitting at one of them was the Jefferson Airplane, and Papa John Creech is sitting back to back with Bobby, so while I'm throwing all these drinks at Bobby, Papa John Creech is getting drenched. Jack Casady and Jorma are hysterical. They don't like Bobby. The whole room is in an uproar. Neuwirth is beating me up, swinging with me on his arm. There's this huge commotion and Mickey comes running into the back room and turns on the lights—Mickey never turns on the lights in the back room until four A.M.—sees that it's me and Bobby Neuwirth, shuts the lights and leaves. Ritty comes and grabs me, throws me on a table on the opposite side of the room and pretends to be fucking me to get me unattached. Finally, I start laughing and go back to the round table. By now, Bobby is in the phone booth, calling Patti Smith, telling her he's been attacked by this crazy feminist. I turn to Donald Lyons and said, "Why didn't you help me?" And he says, "How can you do that to Bobby? He's such a sensitive guy."

high on

**Patti Smith, Jackie Curtis, and Penny Arcade rehearsing for Jackie Curtis' play, Femme Fatale (1969)**
(photo by Leee Black Childers)

## Profile of Patti Smith
### by Leee Black Childers

Patti Smith was probably the least glamorous looking of the back-room rock-and-rollers. But make no mistake, her "look" was just as carefully planned and executed as any of the others. When she initially started showing up with her friend, Robert Mapplethorpe, she wanted to be a beat poet, concentrating her considerable determination in the direction of Gerard Malanga, who had made quite a name for himself in this respect. Patti was very unsure of herself at first, but three things worked in her favor. First, her fierce ambition. Second, her innate New Jersey toughness. And third, she had rooms at the Chelsea Hotel. For the past hundred years the Chelsea had been the haven in New York for the weird, wonderful characters no respectable hotel would accept. Brendan Behan, Dylan Thomas, Janis Joplin, Thomas Wolfe, and Sid Vicious have all called the Chelsea

rebellion

159

**Robert Mapplethorpe**
(photo by Anton Perich)

home at one time or another. Patti was crazy over Keith Richards and Brian Jones. She wanted to be like them. Gerard encouraged her to do live poetry readings with him, and she always read with this wonderful cadence, this rhythm that always got the audience so involved. It was Lenny Kaye who encouraged Patti's rock-and-roll career. He began adding his rhythmic guitar counterpoint to her words, and one night convinced her to sing-not one of her own poems, but the old Kurt Weill classic "Speak Low." The audience loved it. Patti was on her way to becoming a rock star, just like her beloved Rolling Stones.

high on

**GEORGE ABAGNALO, WRITER/ACTOR:** Patti Smith and Robert Mapplethorpe started coming to the back room together. They were staying at the Chelsea. They would get dressed up in the kind of clothes that looked right for that time. They would come to the back room looking like they belonged there. They were very eager to become friends with Andrea. A number of people looked at them and said, "Who the hell do they think they are?"

**RITTY:** Patti Smith tried unsuccessfully to get into Max's several times. Mickey refused her at first, because she was so scruffy and dirty-looking. He'd say, "Tell her to go home and take a bath."

**GERALDINE SMITH:** I used to hang out in the Village with Andrea Feldman. We all met each other in Washington Square Park. Me, Andrea, and Patti D'Arbanville. We would all take LSD, hang out in the park, and run around the streets in the Village, up and down MacDougal and Bleecker. I lived with Patti at her father's house. I lived in Brooklyn till I was twelve and I'd go into the Village by myself....

**Patti D'Arbanville and Celia** (photo by Anton Perich)

We started to hear about this place, Max's Kansas City. It was 1967 or '68 and we decided we had to check it out. We walked in, me and Andrea. We looked very sophisticated, very hip, so we got in. We went in the back room and saw Andy and Paul and all these people and we just loved it. We said, "We've got to get in with these people. God, this is great!" So we decided to go there every night. We'd get all dressed up and Andrea—she was so eccentric—one night she wore a pink bath towel wrapped around her head and she had black eye makeup on and this white stone and she started to talk to Andy and tell him that she would get money from her mother for a limousine, that she was this rich girl from Park Avenue and she would take him in her limousine.

**GLENN O'BRIEN:** The main event in the back room for several years was *Showtime*. *Showtime* could be anytime. Everyone would be sitting there pretty calmly, although "really up there" as Andy would say, to describe a common condition of mind in those days, talking and sipping drinks, when suddenly someone at another table in the back room, or maybe even your table, or maybe even you, would get up and yell, *"Showtime!"*

The term itself is generally ascribed to Andrea Feldman, aka Andrea Whips Warhol, who was the undisputed inventor of *Showtime*, as well as the most persistently spectacular *Showtime* performer.

rebellion

Andrea Feldman doing *Showtime* on the table; foreground includes Jane Fonda and Roger Vadim

(photo by Archie Strips, courtesy of George Abagnalo)

# Showtime by Cherry Vanilla

Andrea growled in her deep demonic rasp, her beautiful wobbly legs straddling the huge bowl of salad in the middle of the table. "It's *Showtime!*" and she began to strip. This was New York in the sixties. This was "the back-room" at Max's Kansas City, the melting pot of New York's pop and avant-garde elite. This was Andy Warhol's neighborhood bar.

"A-a-a-acid," Andrea bellowed in a voice that seemed to come from one possessed. "Has anybody got any a-a-a-acid?" The forty or fifty people in the room sat transfixed. She was in some ways so tragic, this rich girl who'd run away from home and fucked up her chromosomes so badly. But she was also so electric, so immediate, so confronting...just like the era itself.

"It's *Showtime*," Andrea cooed, wrenching her young pastel body in a spastically sensual self-caress. Light from red fluorescent tubes fell on her shoulders. Chick peas rolled around her black stiletto heels. Some were broken and smashed into the red tablecloth.

"The Be-e-e-e-e-eatles," she wailed, plié-ing precariously over the romaine. "I want the Be-e-eatles!" Then suddenly she jolted up with outstretched arms, smiled a child's smile, and took a bow. The room broke into cat calls and worshipful applause. This was Andrea Whips, a SUPERSTAR!

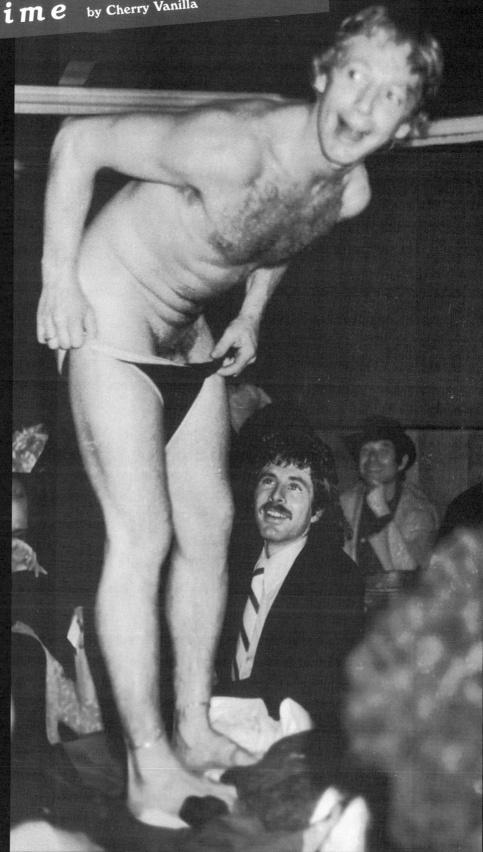

**Eric Emerson doing *Showtime*, with Steven Gaines in audience**
(photo by Anton Perich)

Jason Holiday, foreground, and Taylor Mead, background
doing *Showtime* (photo by Anton Perich)

**GLENN O'BRIEN:** Andrea would sing and dance on the tables, tell jokes and play love scenes with partners as diverse as Taylor Mead and a champagne bottle. Andrea, best known to the public as "the LSD Girl" in Paul Morrissey's Trash, was an exhibitionist to the end.

**CORY TIPPIN, STYLIST FOR WARHOL:** Something about Andrea's timing was perfect, because you felt that it was *Showtime* and Andrea wouldn't do it. She'd just prolong and procrastinate for another few minutes and not do *Showtime*...and suddenly, just when you thought that she wasn't going to do it, Andrea would jump up on the table, rip open her blouse and say, "Oooooo-kay folks, it's *Showtime!*"

**JACKIE SHERMAN:** Andrea had this Kotex that she took off and put around her head. Robin, the night manager, had to carry her out in a fireman's hold over his shoulder, and all the while Andrea's screaming, "Robin, I love you." She was on a weekend pass from St. Vincent's or Bellevue. She was in an institution. I don't think she was much more than sixteen years old. She had her Sweet 16 party there in the back room with her family.

**JEFFREY NICKORA:** Jim Morrison was a phone freak, and so was Andrea Whips. With Andrea if you couldn't talk to her because you were busy, she'd hang up the phone and call back. There was no way of getting rid of her, because if she had been 86ed for a week or three days, she wanted to be there anyway. And sometimes the people in the back room would have her call on the pay phone, and they would just leave it off the hook so she could hear. And Tiger, forget it.

**BOB FEIDEN:** I used to love the idea that people could be banished from the back room. Mickey would suspend people like in school. Many times Andrea would be suspended for *Showtime*. Sometimes she would urge people to keep it down instead of bellowing out *"Showtime!"* so loudly, so that Mickey wouldn't hear up front. She'd get this irresistible impulse.

## Andrea Whips by Leee Black Childers

Andrea was rich already–born rich. Unfortunately, she was also born crazy. Her real name was Andrea Feldman, and she lived alone in a huge, luxurious penthouse on upper Park Avenue, complete with terraces, statuary, and even a waterfall. Her parents set Andrea up in the penthouse, provided her bank account with a gigantic monthly deposit, and sent a doctor around every few months to see if Andrea was any crazier. If the doctor decided she was, they would put her away in a "rest home" for a while, after which she would return to Park Avenue. She was a striking-looking girl with long, thick blonde hair and a pixielike face. She wore lots of makeup, often inexpertly or even incompletely applied. She entertained often, and Wayne County and I became frequent guests. Once, when we arrived she had completely taken apart the air-conditioning system and had the parts scattered all over her living-room floor. She explained that she was looking for microphones planted there by the nuns from the Catholic school across the street, who she believed were watching her. She went to Max's back room nearly every night with Geraldine Smith, her best friend and star of Flesh. Frequently, at Geraldine's instigation, Andrea would suddenly shout, "Showtime!" and jump up on a table and take off all her clothes. One year she had her birthday party at Max's and arrived wearing the stunning black-and-white dress Cecil Beaton had designed for Julie Andrews for My Fair Lady. In no time at all, she had taken it and everything else off and was standing on a table shoving the necks of champagne bottles up her vagina and then serving giggling guests from them. She worshiped Andy Warhol and even changed her name to Andrea Warhola (Andy's real last name) for a time. But for her two screen appearances in Warhol's Trash and Heat she retained her real name, possibly at Andy's suggestion. Her performance in Heat was very well received. So much so that some very powerful producers asked to meet her. She invited them to her penthouse for dinner, which she said she would cook herself. Dinner was champagne and Hershey's chocolate bars. The producers stayed less than half an hour before making their excuses and fleeing.

**From left, Geraldine Smith, Tony Ingrassia, Candy Darling, and Wayne County** (photo by Anton Perich)

**LOUIE WALDEN:** Not everyone was used to all those speed freaks—Eric coming up to you and French-kissing you, Brigid getting up on a table and shooting up through her jeans, and all those crazy kids on acid.

**TAYLOR MEAD:** You'd always know who the most current celebrity was because Brigid would have them nailed down in the most intense conversation. Even if you were her best friend, you couldn't talk to her.

**ELLEN GOFEN:** It was very frantic and very sad in a lot of ways back there. There was a lot of frenzy, a lot of people who needed attention. Everybody was so into being a celebrity. Everybody was either performing or into voyeurism. It drove these people to perform. That was the whole idea with *Showtime*. Andrea was always pulling up her skirt, exposing her breasts, and Eric was always pulling out his dick. My husband, Jerry Gofen, was making underground films at the time. Ondine and Taylor Mead were in his films. So to me, it wasn't so alien.

**CHERRY VANILLA:** Somewhere around 1969, I started working with the New York Theater Ensemble, which was Wayne County, Leee Black Childers, Tony Zinetta, Patti Smith, Debbie Harry, Jamie Andrews—they were all part of this theater. Tony Ingrassia was the director, and it was a spin-off of the Playhouse of the Ridiculous, so Andy was involved. Whenever there was a play he would show up and bring a lot of friends. By virtue of my now being part of that world, I had won the right to sit in the back room, which in those days was really a thrill. Because when you walked back there you just didn't go sit down unless you felt you had the right. It was like a private club. They had a way of staring at people who came there and didn't belong. Debbie Harry was naturally the rock crowd's favorite waitress. Like a lot of us back there, she had a crossover love for both music and experimental theater. She was great to work with, very giving as an actress and very easy to get along with offstage.

# Cherry Vanilla by Leee Black Childers

CHERRY VANILLA was originally a nice Irish Catholic girl from Queens called Kathy Dorritie. She came to Manhattan to be a television commercial producer, at which she was very successful. On the weekends she was the DJ at an uptown club called Aux Puces. Her friends could mostly be found in expensively furnished Upper East Side condos complete with doormen and screening committees. And when she first started going to Max's, it was to the front room to entertain clients or be wooed by some director, or announcer wanting to work on a TV commercial. She began attending underground theater performances because their irreverence and bawdiness gave her a vicarious thrill. One day she learned Anthony J. Ingrassia was casting for a production of Wayne County's World, The Birth of a Nation, and she went for an audition. I was stage manager on this production and it was my job to interview her. I could hardly believe this obviously cultured, expensively attired lady was seeking a role in an underground play. I very tactfully explained that this play would very likely require her to indulge in profanity and humiliating simulated sex acts, plus there was no pay involved. She said, "Fine." She was thinking of changing her name to Party Favor. What did I think? So Party Favor got a role where, among other things, she simulated sex with a dead puppy and pretended to drink piss. She loved it. So did her rich friends who began to invite us all to uptown lavish dinner parties, where we soon learned that bizarre sex acts were not always simulated. (Holly Woodlawn loved these parties. The first thing she would do was excuse herself, go to the bathroom, and steal all the ups, downs, and in-betweens in the medicine cabinet.) Party Favor changed her name to Princess Charlotte Russe, became a back-room regular and a notorious groupie. I think it was while on tour with Leon Russell that she cooked up the name Cherry Vanilla, which she finally stuck with.

**CHERRY VANILLA:** I had taken a lot of psychedelics, but I was more sophisticated than kids like Andrea because from the time I was seventeen I had been working on Madison Avenue in ad agencies. I was pretty much already over speed and psychedelics by the time I was twenty-six and I wasn't into the white powders or all the three-letter shit, only pot. I wasn't as naive as the rest of them. I was a little bit more careful, which is why I'm still alive. Nevertheless, I was going through the sexual revolution and wanting to be in the forefront of it—just letting it all go, not only sexually, but artistically, emotionally, intellectually—getting up and performing a song, a poem, a dance, or anything at the drop of a hat, being an exhibitionist, as it were. I was very shy—a little Irish Catholic strict thing—and this was my letting-go period. It all happened at Max's. It happened for a lot of people there—Taylor Mead, Jackie Curtis, Eric Emerson, Patti Smith—they all did *Showtime.*

Meanwhile, the back-room people, via their own notoriety, were spreading the Max's mystique far beyond the confines of its art-adorned walls and out to the Pop-hungry public—thus increasing its legend and insuring its popularity for at least a few years to come. Even during the months that I worked there, the back-room people—be they Superstars, regulars, or celebrities who occasionally dropped in—were out there "doing their thing" on TV, movie screens, and stages, from New York to San Francisco to Paris. The Warhol Superstars could be seen in *I, A Man, Bike Boy, Nude Restaurant, Chelsea Girls, and ****, the 25-hour movie*—all of which debuted during those last few months of 1967, as did Jimmy Rado and Jerry Ragni's musical, *Hair.*

"Janis Joplin saw me in *Hair,* which was the hippest show in New York," remembers Paul Jabarra, "and she became infatuated with me. And I, of course, was infatuated with her, so we decided to go out on the town together. So we went to Max's, which was the hippest place in New York to go at the time. Walking in with her—it was kind of equivalent to being with Madonna twenty years later—we caused a minor sensation." Ultra Violet, Viva, Nico, and Brigid all made appearances on the *Merv Griffin Show,* and the Velvet Underground recorded their second album, *White Light/White Heat* for Verve. Jane Fonda and Roger Vadim's new movie, *Barbarella,* was causing a huge sensation in the press, while Jane and Roger came to sample the counterculture in Max's back room, causing a bit of sensation of their own.

**RUBY LYNN REYNER:** I remember when Jane and Vadim were hanging out in the back room—it must've been around 1968—and she and Roger liked Eric Emerson. One night Eric came prancing into the back room, stood at the doorway and yelled, "I just fucked Jane Fonda," and everybody applauded. He would talk about how Vadim had this long, skinny dick, it was hard to use or something like that, so they would invite select people over from the back-room crowd and Vadim would watch Jane fuck them from the balcony. It became a trend there for a while. Everyone had their tall tales and skinny-dick stories.

**FIELDING DAWSON:** Eric told me that he was with Jane and Roger, and he saw Roger ball Jane, and that Roger had a cock that was really something.

**HOLLY WOODLAWN:** A lot of stuff went on in the bathrooms, a lot of fucking, heterosexual fucking, too. Once I walked in on Jane Fonda, Roger Vadim, and Eric Emerson doing a lot of heavy petting in there.

**PENNY ARCADE:** Jane and Roger were in the back room sitting at a table with Jackie Curtis. I was with Jackie and she had been spending a lot of time with them. We were all on acid and demented. Everybody was buzzing that Jane and Roger were there. I was table-hopping and when I got to Jane's table, she turned to me and said, "I just love being in the back room because of the buzz of excitement here." And the buzz of excitement was about them. It was like that all the time, whether it was the Jefferson Airplane or Janis Joplin. There was always a constant state of foreplay in the back room.

One night me, Jackie Curtis, Rita Redd, Jane Fonda, Roger Vadim, whoever the blonde waitress in the back room was, and Eric Emerson went over to this town house in the West Village, and through music and lighting the room started to change imperceptibly, and Jane came to me and said, "Come on, let's dance." There were these cubes around the room and Jane was on one and I was on another, and we were dancing away and all of a sudden I started thinking, Something very weird is going on. Then I looked up and there was this little balcony, and there's Roger Vadim smoking a cigarette, watching this whole thing. I jumped off the cube and went over to Jackie and said, "This is a sick scene, and I'm getting out of here." What they had been doing was taking people out two by two, and getting them coked up, and they hadn't reached me yet. And Jackie said, "But Penny, it's so glamorous." Jane came over and said, "What's going on? Get back and dance." And looking up at Vadim she said, "You know, Penny, you're the kind of person who picks up on too much for your own good. You're going to get yourself in a lotta trouble." This was shortly after the Tate murders, around 1968. Jackie and I ended up running out of the place and going to the Pink Teacup.

**JOE LOGIUDICE, ART DEALER:** This chick walked in the bar one night, went into the back room and her man is back there under the table giving head to somebody. She marched out of the back room and I'm sitting up front on the rail with Mickey. This chick walked up to the bar and proceeds to give blow jobs right down the line to every guy at the bar. Mickey is just sitting there watching this whole thing. So I said to Mickey, "What do you think of that, what's going on?" He says, "Yeah, her boyfriend, that son of a bitch, still owes me a lot of money."

**CHRISTINE LOMBARD, WAITRESS:** I was working the back room and René Ricard ordered some food. I came with the plate and he was under the table giving somebody a blow job.

rebellion

**EVE BABBITZ:** I introduced Eric to Andy. Eric was gorgeous—he had this cherubic blonde hair—and everyone would fall in love with him. He opened a shop on Ninth Street that had an aquarium in the window where he put an iguana. Once he went away for two weeks and the iguana died in plain sight of everyone. It was horrible, but that's what that whole group was like, they were crazy. They would just forget cats and dogs and animals and wives and husbands and clothes and jewelry.

**BOB FEIDEN:** When Eric started living with Jane Forth, Andy was very against it. He thought that Eric was drug trash and he was very against it. So Andy would call Jane at home and he would pretend that it was Eric and start saying all these filthy, rude things to her on the phone and she would say, "Andy, I know it's you, Eric is right here sitting in bed. Andy, hang up, I know it's you."

**CHERRY VANILLA:** Eric Emerson was the embodiment of the child-man—a little curly-haired blonde whose features hadn't yet taken on any of life's hurts or cruelties. He looked at you full-on, fully open—with the trust, curiosity, and wonder of a five-year-old boy. He approached sex in a way that was so light and refreshing, so playful and adventurous. Much like the way the Tom Hanks character approaches it in the movie *Big.*

Eric and I never had any kind of a boyfriend-girlfriend relationship. We never slept together. We never even fucked in a bed—or even on a floor for that matter. We only fucked a few times—always standing up, and always in the upstairs phone booth at Max's. When we fucked, it was fast. It had to be. But it was always fun. Eric and I were not into spending any time alone together, other than our time in the phone booth.

"C'mere," he'd tempt, grabbing my hand as I'd reach the top of the front staircase at Max's. He always seemed to appear somehow out of nowhere, usually dressed in as little a pair of shorts as one could possibly get away with in public, and sporting a sad-puppy glance as if to say, "If you don't come with me instantly, my heart will be forever broken." It was all a little game in a way. But in those days, our whole aim seemed to be to blur the lines between what had formerly been split into two separate worlds—fantasy and reality.

Disease? Who cared. The kinds of diseases that were around then could most often be cured by a needle in the ass. And we all loved needles in the ass anyway. We took 'em to get high. So what was one more needle filled with antibiotics? This was a great golden age. We could fuck our brains out without condoms or fear. We didn't even have to seduce or plot and plan. We could find instant love almost everywhere. And we weren't ashamed or afraid to call it simply SEX!

God, he was good at maneuvering in that phone booth. Little as he was, Eric was built like a rock—all muscle and cat and ballet. People would pass by, peer in—often seeing a bare ass smashed tightly up against the glass. Some would knock in fury, wanting to make a call. Some would walk away in desperation, saying, "Oh forget it, that phone's gonna be tied up for a while." Eric would always say something stupid like, "Just give us a minute, we're making a call," but would never lose the "Fuck you, I'm in ecstasy" smile from his face.

It would have been easy to fall in love with Eric. But I didn't. I loved him, but I didn't fall. As I said, though, I was very, very young. And so I did get all puffed up with pride that this Warhol star (I had not yet joined the ranks, via *Pork*) had reserved this "secret" special place for fucking me. My bubble was soon broken, however, when I told Leee about it in the back room one night. "Don't you know, Cherry, Eric fucks all the girls in that phone booth, every night!" My tender heart sank, but even I was soon laughing at my own naiveté. If someone could wave a magic wand and offer me the gift of youth right now, I don't think I would take it. Because I know in my heart that I could never really be as young again as all of us were in our hearts and minds back then. And Eric Emerson personified that youth. So much so, that he never even got the chance to—like the rest of us—grow old. It's only now that I truly know how golden my youth was. And in my treasure trove of memories—phone-booth infidelities and all—Eric will always stand out as the most shiny, sparkly, impish, ageless, beautiful, golden boy there ever was.

**Eric Emerson in a French kiss**
(photo by Anton Perich)

**LEEE BLACK CHILDERS:** As the years passed, I became a good and close friend to Eric, but I never understood him. He was, of course, one of the very first Warhol Superstars, but he never talked about it. I had to learn about it from books and articles. He was a successful model, a talented musician, but he never spoke of that; you had to find out from other people. He was a whore—which he talked about all the time. He loved sex like he loved life, passionately and constantly. He was bisexual long before it was universally accepted as cool, and open and exhibitionistic about his sexploits to a point that would make Tallulah Bankhead blush. He knew he was beautiful and he knew everyone wanted to fuck him—and his reaction was, "Okay, I'll fuck everybody." And he did.

This does not mean he was insincere, quite the opposite—he was very sincere, very loving, very naive—it was the other people who were insincere. He had some luck—Elda Gentile, Jane Forth,

*rebellion*

and even Jackie Curtis truly loved and cared for him. But he was too driven by his appetites to allow too real a love to come too close—to him a blow job in a telephone booth was love. He died, like Jackie and Andrea and so many others, far too soon. Before we got the chance to truly appreciate his beauty, which was his simplicity. No, he was not a bus boy. He was the sultry-sweet madness that was the back room—he was the surprised wide-eyed youth when he sees his first cunt or hard cock and reaches out to touch it.

**EMMARETA MARKS, PERFORMER/WAITRESS:** Eric was so cute but he was always Kentucky Fried on the brain side. I used to call him Eric Love.

**GERARD MALANGA:** Eric Emerson and I were very close. I was probably in for a close second with the most sexual encounters at Max's. We obviously did share a few....We were both involved with Elda Branch. Elda and I were in love with each other before she got involved with Eric.

Eric Emerson came over to see me at my sublet one night shortly after I moved out on Mickey. He came with that big dog of his and he had on those lederhosen shorts that he always wore, the ones he would yodel in. He told me he always had this fantasy about fucking Mickey's wife and that he had never fucked a pregnant woman before and thought it would be a great experience. Likely story. But I ate it. I figured, What the hell, I had nothing to lose. I mean here I was with a baby in my stomach, Jessica, Mickey's and my two-year-old, sleeping next to me in her crib in this one-bedroom sublet, while Mickey was shacked up with some chick in our four-bedroom duplex. And Eric was the only one crazy enough to want to fuck a "very" pregnant woman. So we tried our best to get it on. It was a little awkward. We weren't too successful. He was very high on speed or some other sordid drug and I don't think he could get it up, so we finally gave up trying and he left.

**PAUL EDEN:** Andy came in one evening handcuffed to his boyfriend of the moment. He was this terribly thin sissy little boy. Andy was doing it just for the shock value. The boy was leading Andy but he was the complete opposite type that you would expect.

**CORY TIPPIN:** I stayed with Jay and Jed [Johnson] in their apartment on Seventeenth Street before I took the one downstairs. We would go to Max's and Andy would sit with Jay on one side of him and Jed on the other. He'd be squeezing their legs under the table. There was always something going on under those back-room tables.

**EMMARETA MARKS:** A lot of us during the sexual revolution had the attitude, "just don't bring any diseases home and don't let her sleep in my bed. As long as I don't see it, I don't give a shit."

**MICHAEL FINDLAY, SENIOR VICE PRESIDENT AT CHRISTIE'S:** Jane Fonda and Roger Vadim made a movie in the back room. They were seeking the flavor of the New York underground in a highly fashionable way. The whole thing was just phony and everyone knew it. Andrea Whips Feldman jumped on a table and announced very loudly, "Jane, you may be a great actress, but I am a star."

**GEORGE ABAGNALO:** Andrea invited Roger and Jane to her penthouse apartment on Park Avenue. She had a penthouse with two terraces, 1199 Park Avenue. She invited them for tea. She said to her doorman, "Jane Fonda and Roger Vadim are coming up for tea so let them right up." Of course, the doorman thought, Oh, it's just that crazy girl in the penthouse, forget it. When they did walk in, I heard that the doorman's mouth dropped.

**LEEE BLACK CHILDERS:** Andrea and I were engaged at the time and we were going to get married. It was sort of a ploy at first but it started to get serious. Her parents would commit her to Bellevue now and then to keep her under their thumb. Things seemed a little strange between us when I got back from doing *Pork*, a play we were performing in England. It was real wild for a while there, and Andrea was acting very strange toward me, like she didn't trust me. All of a sudden in the middle of all the mayhem, Andrea stood up on a chair and held a picture of Marilyn Monroe over her head, and she just stood there. And a couple of people at other tables said, "Oh, it's *Showtime!*" After a long time of just standing there, she said, "Marilyn died; love me while you can!" The next day, she jumped from the fourteenth-floor window of her uncle's Fifth Avenue apartment. That was her farewell to the back room.

**OLIVER RISH, REGULAR, COLLEGE STUDENT:** I was at Andrew Wylie's apartment the night Andrea Feldman called him and said she was going to kill herself, and he said, "Oh, Andrea, go back to sleep." Apparently she did that all the time, but this time she really did it.

**JACKIE SHERMAN:** She jumped out the window with her rosary and a Bible. And she was Jewish.

Of course, not everyone was thrilled with the way the back room was evolving. And by 1970 a few of the early back-room regulars had moved on—most taking up residence at Mickey's competition, St. Adrian's Company, or just making way for the new regime. Still, for many in the back room, the "second-wave stars" especially, the changing of the decade was absolute "prime time." Derek Callender recalls, "When the place got halfway punky, I found I was too old for the people, and I wasn't going to dye my hair green to fit in. Plus, it got down to a different language. I think what happened between the painters, photographers, and musicians was that the painters and photographers disrespected the craft of the musicians. When you paint a paint-

rebellion

ing it's there. You can't doctor the sound. We felt as though we were being run off by the punks." The front-room continued being very male-oriented as always, with all that hard-drinking macho camaraderie, the artists wallowed in up there, but the back room had always glorified its females. The female Superstars (drag queens included) always got much more attention than the males, and the female celebrities always seemed to create the biggest buzz. So, at the start of the 1970s, a dominant force in the back room was the rock-and-roll women, including Cyrinda Foxe, Gloria Stavers, Lisa Robinson, Alice Cooper's girlfriend Cindy Laing, Liz Derringer, Bebe Buell, and Tinkerbell.

MDA, PCP, THC, poppers, and angel dust were the hot new drugs—with cocaine just beginning to show up, but still with great scarcity and secrecy. Pot, pills, and acid were like everyday stuff, and heroin, though around, was still the ultimate taboo. In 1970, when both Janis Joplin and Jimi Hendrix died drug-related deaths, and Edie Sedgwick slipped into her alcohol-and-barbiturate decline, the impact of the consequences of our "turn on and trip out" attitudes, put a touch of tarnish on the back room's tinfoil twinkle. But no one really cut back on their intake of intoxicants. The danger, after all, was part of the thrill. Everyone in the back room was still having much too good a time to observe the subtle signs, but the Warhol era's peak was passing; a certain innocence was about to be gone. Only looking back can one clearly see how the glitter that had once looked so blithe and beguiling on Jackie Curtis, the Angels of Light, and the actors of the Playhouse of the Ridiculous, was beginning to look rather common and cliché on the new "glitter rockers." A lot of it had to do with the drugs. Glitter looks so rich and magical when seen through psychedelic eyes, but becomes so gritty and garish when one is high on opiates or cocaine.

Then in 1971, Andy gave the back room one more shot of the Warhol Pop it was originally about. *Pork*, the only play he ever wrote, opened at Cafe LaMama, with Tony Ingrassia directing Tony Zinetta, Wayne County, Cyrinda Foxe, Jamie Andrews, Suzanne Smith, and Harvey Fierstein in leading roles. Once again the back room was abuzz with theater talk as much as it was with rock. A producer from London was negotiating with Andy and Tony to take the play over there. Suddenly it was Andy and the actors' room again, and for a moment the old balance was back. Andy wasn't happy with the actress who played Pork (based on Brigid Polk, aka Brigid Berlin). He thought she was too much of a legitimate Broadway/TV type. So, in the summer of '71 when the play went to the Roundhouse Theater in London, he replaced her with Cherry Vanilla. Andy had apparently admired Cherry's humping of dead dogs and castrating of raw-hot-dog cocks when he saw her in *World*. Then, when she sang "Dear Lady of Fatima" for him at her audition and told him everything he wanted to

Joan Baez (photo by Anton Perich)

Liz Derringer and Geraldine Smith
(photo by Leee Black Childers)

Tony Pinck and Danny Fields
(photo by Anton Perich)

Larissa and Cindy Laing
(photo by Anton Perich)

know about TV commercials, he immediately decided she should be a Superstar. Leee Black Childers was *Pork*'s production manager, and besides working on the play together, Cherry and he became a really notorious team on the London music scene, interviewing and photographing the city's new young musicians for American rock-and-roll magazines—some real and some fictitious! Cherry invented a column called "Cherry Vanilla with Scoops for You" and created a scandal when she did some "blow-ing" of her own with the horn section on a B.B. King recording session. At one point she had a whole young band called Bronco living in her bedroom.

But in the fall of 1971 when Leee and Cherry returned to New York and the back room of Max's with the rest of *Pork*'s cast, there was one young English musician in particular who they talked about more than any of the others—David Bowie. Lisa Robinson, Lillian Roxon, Gloria Stavers, Danny Fields, and Danny Goldberg were all quite captivated by the pair's enthusiastic descriptions of Bowie's style, sexuality, wife (Angie), and guitarist (Mick Ronson). And since these young movers and shak-ers were all sponges for new talent, and in the business of telling the world about it, they began touting Bowie as the Next Big Thing in rock. Hints of his bisexuality, mime ability, and drag queen/spaceman stage persona added to the intrigue. So the buzz in the back room once again shifted to rock. Andy was as curious about this "outrageous new rocker" as everyone else, but Andy was no longer hanging out at Max's. When Valerie Solanas shot him at the Factory in 1968, he'd stopped coming for a while, but eventually returned to take up his "knightly" position at the round table. By the end of 1971, though, when the *Pork* cast had turned into flacks for Bowie, Candy Darling had become a legitimate Broadway actress in Tennessee Williams' *Small Craft Warnings*, and Edie Sedgwick had died in California of "acute barbitual intoxication." Andy and his closest cronies pretty much stopped coming to Max's. With Andy gone, the round table was taken over by whichever regulars got there first, usually a combination of the music women, the Ingrassia group, Donald Lyons, and Danny Fields.

Cherry, Leee, and Zee (Tony Zinetta) were meeting regularly with Bowie's manag-er, Tony Defries, who was coming to town more and more to scope out the possibili-ties for his "product" in America. They were also working on Ingrassia's new play, *Island*, which starred Patti Smith as a speed freak and Cherry as a nude groupie. Joy Martin was the back room's favorite new waitress, Andy Paley was the pretty-boy musician of the moment, and *Showtime* was still going strong. At the beginning of 1972, Ingrassia directed a one-act version of Jackie Curtis's play, *Vain Victory*. Debbie Harry had a role in the play, and her brand-new band, Blondie, provided the musical score. Cherry, Leee, and Zee were once again working with Ingrassia on the play, but they were also becoming more and more official in their production and PR roles for Bowie. By summer, they had set up MainMan, a management office for him, on East Fifty-eighth Street, and were working full-time at securing U.S. concert dates, hiring tour personnel, and creating a media blitz. Though he paid them peanuts, Defries provided them with little luxuries like limousines and expense accounts. Defries encouraged everyone to spend recklessly, to create the illusion that MainMan was a company of great wealth. His chief executives had American Express cards, Bloomingdale's and Harrod's of London charge plates, and expense accounts at the Four Seasons and Max's Kansas City. Suddenly these formerly penniless Off Off Broadway theater kids who had lived on chick peas and coffee, were buying champagne and dinner for themselves and everyone they thought would spread the word of Bowie. They also took everyone for champagne-and-marijuana rides in their limos, and promised tickets, backstage passes, and Bowie himself in the back room come September. Everyone was geared up for Bowie's arrival in the States. He seemed to be the commercially viable embodiment of all that the back room was about. Perhaps one fabulous era had just passed, but for those who were there in the summer of '72, the electricity in the air made it obvious that another was about to begin. Then, as if on cue, as if a marker had been profoundly placed at that exact moment in time, Andrea Whips jumped out a window to her death. Three thousand miles away in Santa Barbara, California, Edie Sedgwick, another glamorous Warhol Superstar, died of a barbiturate-and-alcohol overdose. Andrea died just a few blocks away from Max's. It really hit home. It was the end of an era. The queen of *Showtime* was dead.

**STEVEN TYLER, ROCK MUSICIAN:** For some reason, when the shit started flying, you knew even the assholes were going to be famous someday. It was that kind of place. Everyone was fucked to the gills. We were like bubbling over with anxieties, nuances, and coolness, and hot and cold moments. It was like lighting a whole pack of Black Cat firecrackers all at once and throwing it in the room.

*the village* VOICE, *August 17, 1972*

# Andy Feldman, 1948-72

by Geraldine Smith

Andrea Feldman, one of Andy Warhol's superstars, jumped to her death on August 8 at 4.30 p.m. from a 14th floor window at 51 Fifth Ave, taking with her a crucifix and Bible she found in a church a few days before.

I met Andrea nine years ago in

—David Hoff

ANDREA ''WHIPPS'' FELDMAN

Washington Square Park and we were friends ever since. We frequently visited Max's Kansas City, where she performed for recognition, which she immediately received, by singing "Everything's Coming Up Roses" in her unique style. Eventually this led to her role in the movie "Imitation of Christ," after which she made "Groupie" and after this "Trash." By the time she did "Trash" she was a recognized superstar, an established personality. In the yet unreleased "Cleopatra," which brought out her comic talent, she was brilliant as co-foil to Viva's campy Cleopatra. Her last performance, in Andy Warhol's "Heat," is already movie history to the few who have seen its previews.

Andy identified with Marilyn

Monroe. She had many friends and yet never believed anyone really loved her. She gave of herself so much and she will never know how much we all will miss her. She said of herself, "This time I'm going to the top, to explode like dynamite." She said of herself, "I'm as unique as an antique," which she was. She also said, "No one takes me seriously because they think of me as a joke." Andrea was tormented constantly by her fear of not being loved, of unrecognition, of ridicule and not being understood. But Andrea was loved, and you can see this by the shocked expression on the faces of her friends who cannot believe she came to this.

Andrea had just returned from Europe where she was wined and dined, making a whole world of new friends which was her dream come true. This is why it is all the more tragic that her previous fears returned to torment her in her last days with us. We all stood by helpless watching her as her self-inflicted sufferings became reality and we were not able to do anything about it.

Andrea left a note addressed to everyone she knew, saying she loved us all, but "I'm going for the bigtime, I hit the jackpot!"

Just last week she toasted Marilyn's 10th anniversary with champagne, saying "Marilyn's gone 10 years, so love me while you can." It is ironic her own life ended so shortly after.

## Etching Class

Elaine Brieger will conduct a class in the techniques of etching and intaglio printing at the YM-YWHA this fall. For further information write to the Educational Department of the 92nd Street YM-YWHA, 1395 Lexington Avenue.

rebellion

**CYRINDA FOXE:** Living in the Midwest, I already had frosted hair and I knew I'd look good with blonde hair. I spent two days right behind the women's house of detention—there was a hair parlor—and for two days they stripped and worked my hair until I came into Max's with platinum-blonde hair. Of course, Candy Darling had a temper tantrum. Then Dana started to make me some of these clothes, and I'm telling you, in five minutes I was getting attention and I was now enlisted in this play, *Pork*. I'm at the rehearsals. I have no idea who this old guy is. He's cute. "Who's that cute old guy?" "Oh, my dear, that's your boss, that's Andy Warhol." It just started everything and Max's was every night.

I was hooked immediately. This is what I wanted. They were fun. I wanted a bunch of wild kids. It was like everyone back there had run away from home. We could dress like we wanted, do whatever we wanted. The first person I noticed in the back room was Candy Darling. She had on a spaghetti-strap dress…black satin…tall…"Woof," I said. "Gosh, she's gorgeous." I had no idea she was a he.

**David Johansen, left, and Cyrinda Foxe**
(photo by Anton Perich)

# Cyrinda Foxe
## by Leee Black Childers

CYRINDA FOXE was an army brat, one of thousands just like her. Her stepfather, a career soldier, was very strict. Her mother was loving and motherly. She was an only child. But for some reason, Cyrinda felt different from other kids. Of course, there was no Cyrinda at the time. Cyrinda was a dream. Her name then was Kathleen Hotzikian. And while the other kids living on the army base in the Philippines went to dances, Kathleen sneaked off-base to Manila where she found Filipino musicians who tried to sound like the Rolling Stones and look like Marlon Brando. Kathleen caked on the makeup and tried to look older. When her family moved to Oklahoma, Kathleen found little improvement. She fell in with a group of bikers who took a lot of acid and played very rough. She was beaten up so regularly that she grew to accept it and even expect it as part of lovemaking. She ran away with them to Texas where she was involved in a gunfight which left her badly wounded. After recovering back in Oklahoma, she asked her mother if she could move to New York. Imagining things couldn't possibly get worse, her mother handed her the bus fare. She went straight to the back room of Max's and was an immediate success. Within her first month in New York, she had begun working for Sam Green, a wealthy art dealer; she had gone platinum-blonde and gotten a boyfriend who designed fabulous fifties-style dresses for her, and she had been given a role in Andy Warhol's Pork at the Cafe LaMama. A few months later she was featured full-page in Life magazine as a symbol of the youth of the day. She became the darling of the Warhol set, who were becoming more and more socially upwardly-mobile and were in need of a glamorous real woman who wouldn't plunder their hosts' medicine cabinets. When David Bowie came to New York to begin his first American tour, he and his wife Angela both fell madly in love with Cyrinda. She joined the tour company and traveled across the country with them. David wrote "Jean Genie" for her, and wore her clothes and jewelry onstage and off. Angela no longer found Cyrinda so irresistible. Then Cyrinda grew tired of people thinking she got her fashion ideas from David when she considered it quite the reverse. They parted company. Cyrinda then met and married David Johansen, of the New York Dolls. They lived happily around the corner from Max's. The problem was that they had to live rather frugally. Between Warhol and Bowie, Cyrinda had become used to finer things. One day she met Steven Tyler, lead singer for Aerosmith. Steven was already many times a millionaire, with a mansion in New Hampshire where the entire roof slid away when the weather was sunny. Cyrinda divorced David and married Steven.

**CYRINDA FOXE:** We saw the Dolls and they were electrifying in a real funky way. They were extremely colorful. That's when New York City people wore color. It wasn't just black and gray and paste. We were all so good-looking back then. They became the New York "It" band. It wasn't Gary Glitter. It wasn't the English bands. I'd seen Johnny Thunders at Max's. That was David's entry into the back room of Max's. He had been hanging out on the Lower East Side with Charles Ludlam and that theater crowd. He took me to my first plays and that was really fun. I'm sitting in one of the booths talking to Leee and Eric, and David came in and sat down. Leee had him sit down with us. We were all excited. I guess they were getting some attention. Coming to Max's was very important for them because…all the press that hung out there—Danny Fields, Lillian Roxon, Lisa Robinson. And David—how we got together is he just kept knocking on my door. Oh hey, he was heterosexual—sort of, I guess. Geraldine Smith and I sat at this table one night and she told a table full of people that we had more sex with gay men than we'd had with anyone else.

**DAVID JOHANSEN:** I met Cyrinda Foxe in the back room of Max's. Shortly thereafter, we were married. Sometimes you have to get married to break up! Max's was so decadent. You didn't have to learn to do it, because you had already been doing it in high school for years at the soda-pop shop. It was the people who wanted to continue that sort of cafe society, except that we had real booze instead of egg creams. And it was habitual, because it was like you had to be with like-minded people, and you could find them there. Being an artist is very childlike, so it was part of the growing process.

**CYRINDA FOXE:** Leee introduced me to everybody. He also walked me down the aisle at one of my weddings. He said, "You know, we can leave, we can leave right now."

**LEEE BLACK CHILDERS:** I don't know what made me say that. That was at David's. It was about David when I said it, it was about life itself.

**LARISSA JARZAMBECK:** I didn't have money in those days but I wasn't really eating. A baked potato with sour cream. There was this piece in *Vanity Fair* on the different clubs—the Stone Age, the Gold—I was in the Oscars of the Platinum Age of clubs. I came over from Belgium. I always made my own clothes as I was trying to decide what to do, and someone said, "Well, you make your own clothes." So that's what I decided to do.

**BEBE BUELL:** I remember someone who has gone on to be very successful was giving her boyfriend a blow job in the phone booth. But the whole phone booth–bathroom scene at Max's was a riot. People would pee in cups in the phone booth because they couldn't get into the bathroom. It could get a little wet in there sometimes. It was so nice and dark….

I was seventeen when I came to New York in 1972. The way I went to Max's the first time was with Todd Rundgren. We went in the front room and everybody got very drunk and I took a trip to the bathroom and I thought, Hmm, this red room looks a lot better than this other room up here. I knew that Mickey liked me right away because somebody whispered in my ear, "He must really like you because he told you not to eat the chick peas." He leaned over to me and said, "Don't eat one of those, you'll have no career." So the very first time I went, I really didn't understand the whole social structure of Max's. I just went in there with Paul Fishkin who was the president of Todd's label, Bearsville. I remember going back to the table and saying to Todd, "I think we're in the wrong room. I think we're suppose to be back there." And he said, "Well, that's if you want to hang out. We're eating."

I remember thinking, I've got to come back and go in the back room, because it was extremely glamorous and different in comparison to where everyone was eating surf'n'turf. I did that. I got on the Second Avenue bus and came downtown and got off on Seventeenth and walked over and just walked in the back room. I had been in New York maybe five months. I was eager to be where I thought I belonged. I was completely alone. I could not get anybody from St. Mary's Women's Residence to go with me. All my roommates were soap-opera stars and they had to be up in the morning. They warned me I'd ruin my career if I went down there.

The first time I walked into the back room I met Andy Warhol immediately. He came up to me and asked me if I wanted to sit down at the table. I think Bob Colacello was

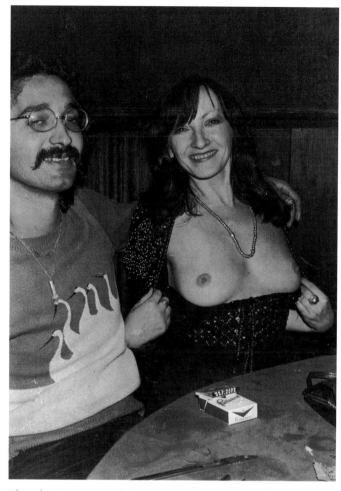

**Claude Pervis and Larissa** (photo by Anton Perich)

there and Patti D'Arbanville, maybe John Cale. Andy said, "You look rich. You look like you come from a really nice family. Where are you from?" I guess I looked a little groomed because I was from Virginia. I was wholesome and athletic-looking. I kind of felt like a princess because everybody wanted to meet me. I didn't have to lift a finger walking into that room. It was like a magic fairyland to me. I immediately made friends. People were giving me their phone numbers, then I realized I didn't get out of there until four in the morning. So of course everyone's warning about Max's having an effect on my career were correct.

**LEEE BLACK CHILDERS:** David Bowie was very entranced and intrigued with the idea of Max's and the back-room scene. He never felt that he fit into it. A lot of times he'd get completely out of his

People used to say, "Once upon a time there was a vacant lot on Park Avenue South, and there was a little lady sitting there on a chair, and they built Max's around her." And that was Larissa.
—Leee Black Childers

rebellion

**From left, Syl Sylvain, Wayne County, and friend**
(photo by Anton Perich)

mind, either drunk or stoned on something, because he couldn't understand the way the back-room scene was.

**LARISSA:** David Bowie was always saying, "Larissa, Larissa, where is Andy, where is Andy?" He always wanted to know where Andy was, and this was before anybody knew who he was. And then the weirdest thing is, here he was totally fascinated with Andy and then he ends up playing Andy Warhol in the Basquiat movie. It's such an incredible circle.

**BEBE BUELL:** I met Bowie in the back room of Max's. He actually came in with his wife Angela and they were very, very, very glam, dressed to the nines, very decadent. He came over and introduced himself to me. I think basically he and his wife were trying to pick me up. But I was sort of naive. Cyrinda hung out with Angela and David together. I hung out with David alone. By the time David called me and asked me to go shopping with him and to Radio City Music Hall and to do all these New York kind of things with him, Angela had already left. And he explained their relationship to me, which was a little puzzling. I hadn't been exposed to open marriagesand bisexuality. I certainly learned about them very quickly living with Todd. He was far from monogamous-minded. He wasn't the loving, faithful boyfriend, and I had to maintain my sense of independence.

At the time there was a glitter rivalry. I think Todd was very inspired by David's look. The most we'd ever seen of that was Alice Cooper and Marc Bolan. David had a different way of delivering the whole package. It was more reminiscent of our drag queens and our lovely Candy Darling. I think Jayne County—at the time she was Wayne County—had a lot to do with David cultivating his look. I think Angela, at the time, was the driving force behind him making these challenging statements. When David came walking in the back room in that beautiful blue suit with that spiked red-orange hair and a tie and everybody else was so scruffy, Angela had an incredible look with no eyebrows, the white hair, and the big, giant, feathered jacket. She took everything to the extreme. She was very tall and androgynous. For the whole

Bebe Buell and Todd Rundgren
(photo by Anton Perich)

week after he picked me out of the crowd to come over and say hello to, everyone was talking all week about it. Andy would come over to me and say, "What was he like? Was he fabulous?" Everybody was curious. I felt like Grace Kelly for a week. I hung out with him for about four days. We did all the New York kind of things. He was like a little kid. He burst into tears when he saw the Rockettes. I took him to see the New York Dolls at some place like Kenny's Castaways, and we kissed all through that show. That caused a big scandal. I was still with Todd, but that kind of nonsense went on all the time with us. There was a lot of temptation.

David and I were sort of buddies and our couple of feeble attempts at sex ended up in hysterical laughter. I don't think I was really his cup of tea in that way—I wasn't black and I wasn't weird. He would call me at all hours of the night to come over and rescue him from some emotional trauma. He was at the Gramercy Park Hotel and I would go rushing over there at four or five in the morning sometimes. Every time I got there, there would be someone leaving and someone coming. He just had a trail of women coming in and out all the time....

Todd had never really glammed out before. He had multicolored hair and he dressed in English fashions, tight velvet suits and stuff. It was very English, like Pete Townshend. He never wore makeup or glitter. One night I was at Max's with David and I was sitting with David and Alice Cooper, and I think Todd was starting to get a little jealous. He showed up, he walked into the back room so glammed out, he had feathers on his eyes and glitter, and he put this stuff in his hair and it was

rebellion

all shiny. He had on this silver jacket and skintight blue pants and he just came walking in and over to the table and said, "Hi," and sat down next to me. So here I am in the middle of Todd and David, and David burst into tears. And Todd said, "David, it's okay, I'm leaving to go on the road tomorrow, she's all yours." And then I went, "What do you mean, I'm all his? You're my boyfriend, he's my friend." Todd said, "You mean you're not having sex with him?" I said, "David, would you please tell him we're not having sex?" And David just sat there crying. And Alice was sitting there—he was very macho for a guy who carried a woman's name—and said, "What the hell's going on here with you guys? Smarten up!" Todd just turned around and walked out. So I chased him, of course. And the feathers were falling off of him as he was walking and I was picking the feathers up behind him going, "Todd, Todd." Todd and I finally managed to patch things up, and get over this hump and I'm lying in bed with him at four-thirty in the morning, and David calls, weeping. I don't think he was crying over me. I think he was crying because he just did. He was like a drama queen. Now that I look back on it I think it was the alcohol and the drugs. Plus he was extremely underweight. He only weighed 122 pounds. We're talking really skinny. He wanted me to come over and read to him. He in turn taught me a lot about makeup and fashion....

**BEBE BUELL:** The big thing was to get your picture above the cash register for that week. I remember Todd had gone on the road and I had a fling with Iggy Pop and I thought I would get away with it, and Todd would come home and everything would be normal. Todd and I come walking into Max's and above the cash register, I finally got my wish; it was a photo of me and Iggy Pop blown up the size of a house. And Iggy had Todd's jean cap on.

**MICHAEL GOLDSTEIN, PUBLICIST:** I never scored at Max's. The door became very complicated and who sat where became very complicated. I was more into naive young things and they could never get into the back room. I'm talking about nice young girls. Those like Donna Jordan and Patti D'Arbanville were using the place like their mothers used the Stork Club. They were all presenting very complicated lives to anybody who was willing to get involved with them. Even at eighteen, they were bringing an awful lot of baggage and complications to your life.

**CHERRY VANILLA:** There's a play called *Niteclub* by Ken Bernard in which a bunch of people dying in an air-raid shelter perform for each other until the last drop of oxygen is gone. It was like that in the back room in this era. Everyone knew a certain age of innocence was dying, and everyone was out to give it its last hurrah. It was a divine improvisation which could not go on forever, for soon the very air of it would be gone.

# The Age of Beauty
### for Mickey Ruskin
### by Gerard Malanga

```
        lobster
Steak       chick peas
Park Avenue South
Max's Kansas City
```

•

```
Dolores Valerie
Danny Fields
Viva, a/k/a/ Susan Hoffman

Jack Daniels
John Chamberlain, Signorelli

Dolores Valerie

Judy Bunce- "addressee unknown"
```

•

```
Geraldine, Andrea-
"the Back Room at Max's"
            like they say
'the chick pea wars'
```

•

```
Anna Karina,

fragrant,
full-bodied breasts
came thru

once
only
```

•

```
"Did you see it,
Did you see it!?

Max's burnt down!

That was incredible!"
```

```
                    -Benedetta Barzini,
            the immortal words
            New Year's eve, 1966
```

```
The night
Joy Bang
took me back to
her flat

Madison Avenue bus

East 74th street-

can't remember now, except

soft, moist
skin, tight
ass

take off clothes

moonlight-windowlight

shirt on chair

Christine Biddle

the floor below,
```

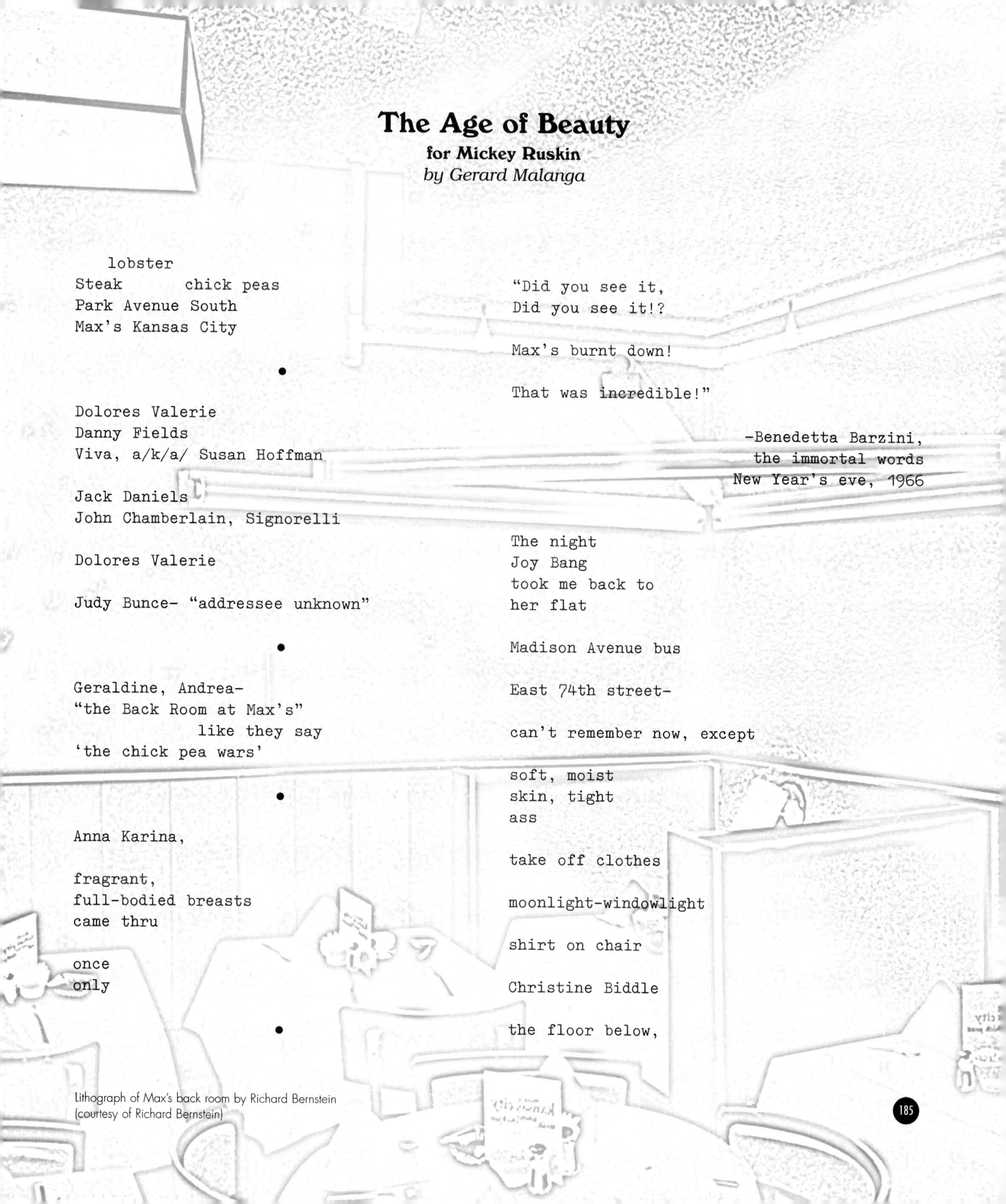

Lithograph of Max's back room by Richard Bernstein
(courtesy of Richard Bernstein)

downstairs,

presumably
asleep

next morning, breakfast-
Joy's treat

the night Peter Ardery
and I cinched the deal:

Charles Olson interview:
the Paris Review

the night
Dorothy Dean
slapped Bob Creeley's face
for no apparent reason

the night Taylor Mead attacked
Denis Deegan
for attacking
Andrea Whipps
in back room

•

Christina Miller,
encounter in snow-

Currier & Ives in New York City

reminiscent: the movie "Portrait of Jennie":
my Intro

to the Berkshires 1970

Lake Buel Rd

the Green River.

•

back in New York,
Tom Collins, tequila sunrise, Courvoisier.

Who is Max ?

-not Peter Max,

but last name Feinstein,
commune-living pioneer,

poet, New Mexico.
Years past,

•

now, not too late--

it's getting late

"Please
come

home
with me."

3:viii:80   East Hampton

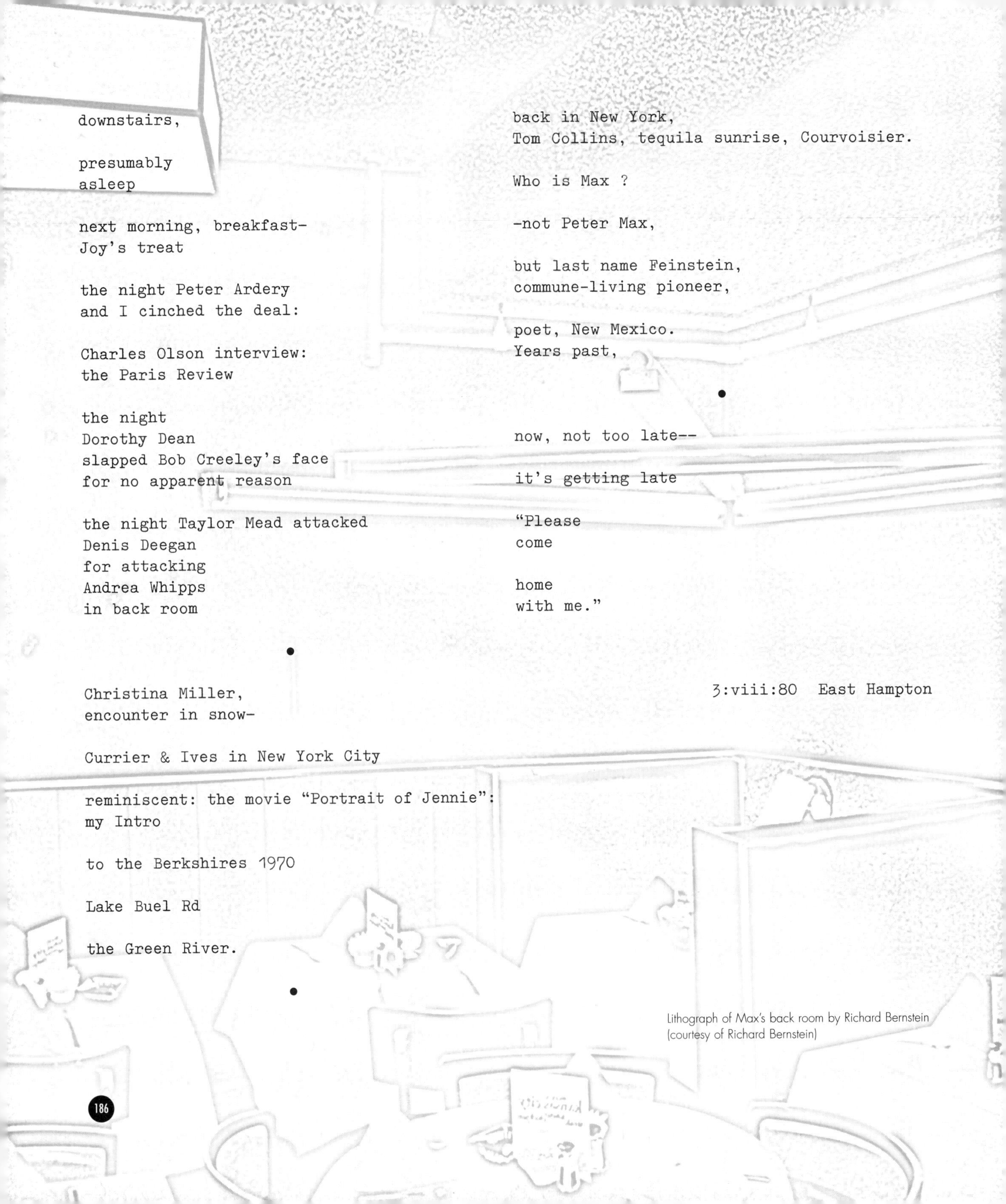

Lithograph of Max's back room by Richard Bernstein
(courtesy of Richard Bernstein)

186

ANDY WARHOL IN THE FACTORY
JANE FONDA IN THE MAX'S EPISODE
ROLLING STONES IN THE METROPOLIS

ARTCHIE STRIP

# THE MAX'S EPISODE

STARING

JANE FONDA   ROGER VADIM
CANDY DARLING   ERIC EMERSON   ; SUPRISE GUEST ANDRA
FROM THE OUTSIDE OF MAX'S KANASA CITY IT LOOKS LIKE
ANY OTHER RESTAURANT. BUT I WOULDN'T SAY THAT
ABOUT THE INSIDE- MIDNIGHT SETS THE MOOD IN THE
BACKROOM. FOR A BLEND OF ACTIVE PEOPLE-

CANDY DARLING - GLAMOROUS, GORGEOUS BLONDE IS A STAR BEYOND BELIEF. AUDIENCE ARE CAPTIVATED BY HER SEX BOMSHELL QUALITY IN FILM SUCH AS BRAND X AND FLESH WATCH FOR HER IN THE BAR.

SURPRISE GUEST ANDREA FEIDMAN, ALSO KNOWN AS **ANDREA WHIPS** - SUPERSTAR OF IMITATION OF CHRIST AND TRASH LIVES IN A PENTHOUSE ON PARK AVE.

**ERIC EMERSON** ACTOR AND SINGER, HAS BEEN FEATURED IN CHEALSEA GIRLS, LONESOME COWBOYS - CURRENTLY HE'S WORKING ON A NEW DISC -

(photo by Elliot Landy)

Max's became the showcase for all the fashion changes that had been taking place at the art openings and shows: now people weren't going to the art openings to show off their new looks— they just skipped the preliminaries and went straight to Max's. Fashion wasn't what you wore someplace anymore; it was the whole reason for going. The event itself was optional—the way Max's functioned as a fashion gallery proved that.

—Andy Warhol

**FERNANDO SANCHEZ, FASHION DESIGNER:** I worked for Revillon, the fur company, so I spent six months in Paris and six months in New York each year. There was nothing like Max's in Paris. It was much more provincial and old-fashioned than New York in those days. At Max's people would have on bell-bottom pants, big shirts with billowy sleeves, waistcoats, Afro haircuts, feathers, earrings, bracelets, necklaces, high-heeled boots, sunglasses, and there was a lot of grass.

**PIA KAZAN, PARIS EDITOR OF *HARPER'S BAZAAR*:** I was a model at the time…God, I guess I was about twenty and Max's was the place to go. It was a hangout for models, photographers, couturiers—all of the people in the magazine world. I would go with Chris von Wagenheim— he was a great photographer for Italian *Vogue* and *Harper's Bazaar*, dead now, sadly enough. We would have dinner with Pilar Crespi, Elsa Peretti, Giorgio di Sant Angelo, Halston…I think Jim Hotton, Daria Sacriman. A lot of the top models would go there: Marina Schiano, Veruschka. There were some heavy numbers at Max's: Giorgio and Halston, although neither was the *monstre sacre* that

**Francesco Scavullo
and Bianca Jagger**
(photo by Anton Perich)

they are today. We'd work with Giorgio and then go to Max's with him afterwards. I felt like I knew everyone there; also, when you were a successful model, people just opened up to you. It was like home—it was great!

**GIORGIO ST. ANGELO, DESIGNER:** I had just arrived in New York, and I wasn't into fashion yet. I was a cartoonist for Walt Disney, also working with sculptures and plastic. I was one of the first hippies to arrive in town. I had very long hair, a turquoise earring, and velvet pants. Max's was always a costume for me; every night was different. It was a very compact group. I met Andy through Diana Vreeland. The fashion I did at the time had lots of colors: one leg would be purple, the other yellow, and the top green—not really so peasanty as later hippie looks. I did an aluminum dress and a mini aluminum dress. Arto Gallanti did the frizzy hair on Penelope Tree, and I went around the world painting Veruschka's body. Lou Lou de la Falaise was my model for a time.

**ANDREA PORTAGO, MODEL:** When I came to New York from England, I wanted to be an actress. I started going to Max's because that was the place to go in New York. I met Bobby Neuwirth there, who became an important part of my life, as he was in so many others'—he helped the careers of Janis Joplin, Bob Dylan. I would see him at Max's and Kinky Friedman, who started a band, Kinky Friedman and the Texas Jewboys—they would play frequently at Max's. Bobby would have me do my audition pieces on the Max's stage after the bands had played and it was emptier. I became a model eventually. Nina Ricci had a perfume—Farouche—and I became the Farouche girl. At the time models and actresses would have their own perfume—Candace Bergen had "See." I met a lot of the artists at Max's: Brice Marden, Larry Poons, Dan Christensen, and the rock-and-roll world.

high on

**Egon von Furstenberg and Larissa**
(photo by Anton Perich)

**AGNES BENJAMIN, FASHION EDITOR, *HARPER'S BAZAAR*:** I was sitting at a table with Nina Simone, Melba Moore, and a photographer named Ira Mazer who was one of the top commercial photographers, whom I had worked for in the past as a stylist. And he was always on the lookout for new and interesting people and he said, "Who's that guy?" And it was Marjoe with his blond curls and all his American Indian jewelry. And I said, "Oh, that's nobody." So I went over and I asked him who he was and he said, "Nobody." But I got together with him and I ended up working with him on the documentary that was made about him by Howard Smith, the writer for the *Village Voice*. Then Marjoe and I had this mock wedding.

**ANNIE FLANDERS, DESIGNER/EDITOR:** In 1967 I opened my store. It was one of the first hip clothing boutiques, Abracadabra, at 243 East Sixtieth Street. I had been buying and merchandising in department stores and what was happening around 1965, '66, was that there were all these extraordinary people walking around in these extraordinary clothes which I quickly came to realize that they or their friends were making. And at the same time, I was buying for a boutique and

rebellion

a department store and there was nothing to buy from established Seventh Avenue manufacturers, so I realized that all of these clothes that I saw in the East Village and at Max's, were the clothes that the public was looking for and could not find. So every time I saw someone in one of those unique outfits, no matter where I was, I would stop them and ask them who made their clothes. Up until the mid-sixties, fashion was the same for all ages except maybe little children. There was no real differential in fashion.

All of a sudden, a lot of it started in England. Many of us thought it was Mary Quant. There was a slew of people and there was this energy and it was called the Youth Quake, and it truly was about young clothes for young people and they had the energy and excitement, and they were completely different-looking than anything there was before. In America we were still somewhat behind. Boutiques were opening and they were called young and individual, but there was nobody to buy from except Rudi Gernreich. There was really no one else in America in the mainstream who was making anything that represented youth. So I started collecting names and a few of these people had boutiques, all on East Ninth Street. East Ninth Street happened because the very first head shop in the U.S. happened on East Ninth Street. It was opened by a guy named Jeffrey Glick. The *New York Times* once wrote him up as the King of Psychedelia. That head shop spawned a whole lot of happening things on that block, Ninth Street between First and Second Avenues. That is where it was happening.

**JOHN HAYES:** Two young ladies named Stella and Colette had this marvelous store at 321 East Ninth Street with the fringe and leathers. They were designers for Hendrix, the Allman Brothers, and Miles Davis.

**ANNIE FLANDERS:** People were doing incredible things in their lofts or in their apartments in the East Village. Plus there were masses of people in the country working with leather and beads, and expressing themselves through clothes rather than mass-marketing clothes. Tiger Morse was the most incredible of all the designers and one of the first major influences on fashion in America. She did the first American flag shirts. She had her store up on Madison Avenue covered in tinfoil. She had a painting of a farm that was covered in plastic and in the back when you sat down there was one of those cow toys; when you sat on it, it made the sound like in a barnyard. She had trucks of antique clothes that she collected. She was originally one of the high-fashion ladies of America. Tiger would travel all around the world and buy all of these unique pieces, tapestries, jewels, and unique articles from strange countries, and incorporate them into the most elegant clothes. She designed clothes for Jackie Kennedy and all the leading society women in New York. And then she just completely went berserk. She left all her alligator handbags and fantastic thousand-dollar gowns when she got into speed and pills.

**CATHY DREW:** Tiger would come into Max's on her roller skates and designer sunglasses, with her lunchbox filled with drugs. She would wear all these different outfits.

**J. P. RADLEY, MAX'S ACCOUNTANT:** The peak of Tiger's fame was fourteen pages in *Life* magazine. Sally Kirkland, who was the fashion editor for *Life*, did the story. Tiger was definitely the fashion original. She was a visionary. She was trying to do with tinfoil what was done with Mylar. Mylar hadn't come out yet. She was educated, had read all the basic classics in American literature, spoke a decent amount of French, and had a feeling for politics. She was living in her loft on West Sixteenth Street where she was trying to do her light shows and slides. The slides she was working on, it was 1969, '70, she had in her head, a vision of what you see today and the kind of electronics that you see at the disco now. The kind of stuff with light and things floating and going on and off with the music, and doing things to people. She imagined and wanted to produce it with little slides when the technology wasn't there yet. She really saw that far ahead. A few years before that she had her ex-husband wire her in a dress with little lightbulbs all over it and some battery packs under her waist. We went to this function and all these lights were flashing all over her. She was wearing twenty-two pounds of batteries somewhere hidden on her body that her ex-husband was smart enough to figure out how to wire.

**DAVID JOHANSEN:** Tiger had those fur coats that she dyed Day-Glo colors.

**JOHN VACCARO:** Tiger had this fire and energy. She was one of the greats. She had those go-go dancers in the front window of her boutique. It was like tripping to go in there.

**DEREK CALLENDER:** Tiger was beyond description. According to Tiger she was the high priestess of fashion. As a matter of fact, according to Tiger Morse, she was the high priestess of everything. I was talking to her one afternoon at Max's, and she was carrying on about some sort of women's-lib thing. Well, I have no argument against it and didn't have any argument against it then, so I couldn't figure out what she was going on about but she was making a statement. The next thing I know, she reaches down and grabs my dick. Well, fine! It looked as though for a minute I was going to have to hit her, because I have this hostile woman grabbing my dick, and we're standing in front of this crowd by the hors d'oeuvres; it's early in the evening and I've got this appendage, a full-grown woman has attached herself to my dick, and it's Tiger Morse of all people. What finally happened is that I looked at her and it was just so goddamned weird that my face must have shown the shock.

**DANNY FIELDS:** Tiger was a brilliant invention that appeared every night. She would stand there with her costumes and sunglasses, yapping away. She was totally self-centered. She never talked about anything else but herself, but it was always okay. It was like the village Yenta comes in and she has to kvetch about something. She talked like it was a broadcast. *My Day* by Tiger Morse, and then she's gone.

**VIVA:** I couldn't stand it. Tiger came in all the time high on amphetamines, yapping away. It gave me a backache.

rebellion

**MICHAEL GOLDSTEIN:** I did get involved with one woman on speed—Tiger Morse. I was her boyfriend. I went out to Chicago with her once. I cut it out because she began to taste of the stuff. It was worse than cigarettes. It was literally coming through her pores.

**JASON CROY:** I used to go to Tiger's sales at her loft. She'd sit up on her throne, and she had all that stuff in shoeboxes. And you'd just be looking through stuff and Tiger would holler across the room, "Don't steal that." And I'd be looking at these plastic earrings and she'd be yelling, "Don't steal that."

**RONNIE LANDFIELD:** Tiger showed up at the Pace Gallery on Fifty-seventh Street when I was working there part-time, helping out with installations. She was wearing this short white fur coat and electric miniclothes made out of what looked like colored cellophane. She talked a mile a minute, and she was very loud. She was always moving around and taking everything in. I thought she was totally incredible.

I ran into her again at a Psychedelic Conference in Toronto. It was instant attraction, powerful and immediate, but not sexual, and we hung out for three days. We shared pizza with Allen Ginsberg, talked to Richard Alpert, hung out with the Fugs, and by the time we got back to New York we were pretty good friends.

Then in the seventies I had this disturbing dream that the phone rang and it was Tiger. She told me to come see her right away—she insisted. I told her no, and then she said, "Good, you stay home." We found out later that day that Tiger had died that night.

**BETSEY JOHNSON:** I had been working for a fashion magazine, *Mademoiselle*, for about eight months as a gal Friday, and this fashion boutique, Paraphernalia, was on the verge of opening. My fashion editor got me an interview with the guy who was hiring the young, pure, raw talent. I mean, you had to know how to make your patterns, your samples, your duplicates, there was no way that you could teach someone to do chrome this and that, and neon—that sixties formula now. You either knew what it was about or you didn't. Right off the bat it was my pure work, with my name on the label, but I had to pay my dues by designing a viable, saleable, junior "Youthquake" collection for Puritan. Max's was a test where I could see how people reacted to what I made earlier that day. I was working at this boutique called Paraphernalia that opened in 1965. It was a phenomenal, once-in-a-lifetime thing, like Max's. It was a designer boutique operation of the best imports like Mary Quant and Emmanuel Kahn. This crazy guy, Paul Young, got this big company, Puritan Fashions, now with Calvin Klein, to give us a division of this retail-franchise situation that any kid, tall, short, fat, skinny, black, or white could walk into, with no training in design. I was an art major. I met Edie, Andy's new Superstar, when Andy and the bunch were doing a shooting and needed silver clothes. They knew about me from Paraphernalia. I was always working when I met the Velvet Underground or Edie. I was able to make these kind of work connections because I was designing the kind of clothing that these people connected to; that wasn't going on anywhere else. The shop itself was chrome and glass, blasting rock-and-roll music with go-go dancers in the window. It was thickly layered with the Kennedys, Carter Burdens, Pam Sachowitz, and baronesses. Veruschka was always in the store.

It was at Madison and Sixty-seventh Street and Sassoon's was a block away. We were appealing to a young, wealthy, socialite lady, a woman who was very hip and aware of the new art, the new music, the new clothing. I was the street kid at Paraphernalia, I liked making affordable clothes. Patti Smith wore my clothes; Julie Christie was wearing my clothes when she was written up in *Women's Wear Daily*. I dressed Penelope Tree for Truman Capote's Grand Ball. It was run very nine-to-five and Max's was like an extension. I designed the clothes for the Velvet Underground. Lou thought I could cut a good pair of pants, but he was threatened by me, because John Cale, who I was seeing, was giving his attention to someone else. I was so excited about doing their clothes. I thought, "Boy, they are going to want to rock out," and Lou wanted gray suede, and a Levi's jacket and jeans.

My friends Diane and Pinky had the store 52 Bond at the time, and the only guy on the scene creating original designs, that I recall, was Michael Mott. Bunky and Nini were at Paraphernalia. We scraped our money together, and opened our own shop, "Betsey, Bunky and Nini." The sixties was like the back phase and then the seventies was the whole flower phase. For me the sixties formula was very wonderfully synthetic and unisex, rock and roll, hard-edged, completely opposite of the camouflage-and-jean stuff marching in the park. I had no idea that so many people wore T-shirts and jeans. I was so depressed. The only designer that was my God, was Rudi Gernreich. I used to see him at Max's. He kind of proved to me that it didn't matter who you were, or where you lived, or where you went if you hung out, everything was based on your work. He gave me the security to hang in there and stay in the fashion business.

**DICK NUSSER:** Barbara Hodes, Lou Reed's girlfriend, was crocheting these see-through dresses. I happened to be going out with her girlfriend at the time. and I would end up shepherding the two of them around in their latest frock. We'd go out and have cocktails and dinner or whatever, and then we'd show up at Max's about the time Lou was getting up, ten or eleven P.M. Here I was walking these two in their see-through dresses through the streets of the Village. I had to dress like a bodyguard. This was before the see-through clothing started to mushroom. Barbara would come into Max's with her new design and there would be a lot of people in there from Seventh Avenue picking up ideas. He designs started regularly turning up two weeks later in the "Scenes" section of *Women's Wear Daily*. Barbara would say, "Hey, that's my design." That happened all the time at Max's. Charles James, the designer, would come in there—he was the Erte of couturier—and he would let Barbara wear his museum pieces. She would sit there with this original creation which is now, I'm sure, on display in the Met. I didn't know Charles James from Adam but he'd be sitting with Barbara and I'd go over. He looked a little bit like Quentin Crisp. You'd talk to the guy and you'd find out marvelous things about how life was twenty years ago or about the Duchess of Windsor. That was what made Max's so absolutely special.

**BUNNY ROSE HARTMAN, WRITER FOR THE *SOHO NEWS*:** I met John Drane at Max's, this English guy. He was wearing a huge long coat and he looked exactly like Mick Jagger, and he had just come to New York. In fact, *Women's Wear Daily* was doing a story on the fashions and photographed him. I don't think he even knew what *Women's Wear Daily* was, but he knew to get himself to Max's, and landed on the pages of *Women's Wear Daily*.

**BILL SOLANO, PHOTOGRAPHER FOR *HARPER'S BAZAAR*:** Around the time of the man on the moon I did a lot of things with the girls sort of leaving the ground, and plastic-colored bathing suits, and I was very interested in space. I tried to get the girls to be very self-contained in mannerism and I surrounded them with ambience clouds—as if they were understanding something from another place. They were there, they were beautiful, but also somewhere else. I shot outside a lot.

**TONY ZINETTA:** Larissa was making those long sheepskin coats with beads and bones and skins hanging. Then there was the topless phase. Cherry Vanilla did it with *Pork* when she played Brigid. Then the unisexual look came in.

**WAYNE COUNTY, ACTOR/ROCK MUSICIAN:** Jackie Curtis was the first person I ever saw who shaved her eyebrows and wore glitter on her eyes. She wore ripped stockings, dyed red hair parted in the middle, and high heels. A lot of trends started right in Max's.

**VALERIE PORR:** Each individual's clothing was very free and expressionistic. People would wear pieces that they made or that a friend had made that were intrinsically wonderful. Everything was very individually creative so that no one got the effect of a uniform. There were some showstoppers like Jackie Curtis. Some night she would come in with her hair in rollers and a scarf on her head with slacks just like the neighborhood girls would wear in the Bronx. She would wear it like a costume. Eric Emerson was another one. He always wore those amazing outfits. Then, of course, there was Holly and Candy. I was teaching and painting. That was too much, so I started making things so that I wouldn't have to teach. I would make hats, things with feathers, flowers. I once went into a shop and someone asked me to make a feathered vest for Jimi Hendrix, which I did, and three days later there was an article on me in the *Village Voice*. It was like my passport at Max's. I was famous for fifteen minutes. I don't know if people in the real world understood that concept like you understood it at Max's, because whoever you met at Max's, sooner or later, you'd find their name in the paper. After that I started making clothes and sold them to Abracadabra. People continually compared me to Tiger Morse, but I never met her.

**MAXIME DE LA FALAISE, DESIGNER FOR YVES ST. LAURENT:** Before I started working for Yves St. Laurent I had my own label and made horizontal sportswear—silk T-shirts and jeans. They were innovative for the time. The thing I noticed about America was that you had to

rebellion

NELSON LYONS · BUDDY MEER · LIZ · WILHEMINA ROSS · GINGER WALLACER · CAROL ROSS · TONY MONTE · TIM SEGMORE

DONALD DREAMS · MICKEY + AMICI · YORK · EMERSON · JIM VISCONTI

PETE D'AGOSTINO · ROBERT OZAROW · SUZY RASHKIS · RUTH · JILL HAM... · CHRISS ANDREA · JOHN K... · MICHAEL MINICH

BARBARA MANN · ERIC CONNIGER · BOB PATTON · FRANK RIZZO · PATRICIA MARIE · MARJOE

(photos by Oliviero Toscani)

MISS BONNIE

ANDREW WYLEY

JOHN FORD

JACKIE CURTIS: A.W. SUPERSTARS

Warhol, re della pop-art, con tutta la sua cerchia di personaggi famosi, René Ricard, Jane Fonda, e centinaia di colorati personaggi dell'underground newyorchese. Dal 1965 ad oggi la scenografia del Max's Kansas City è via via mutata, come del resto (cambiano rapidamente le culture e le loro avanguardie) è cambiata anche la gente, ma due cose sono rimaste sempre tali e quali: il menù, a base di steaks e pochi semplici piatti, e la fama del Max's che sempre, con la sua atmosfera e la sua fantastica popolazione, rimane il numero uno.

JIM VISCONTI

DALE SEXTAN

ROBERT OZAROW

ELVIN MORGAN E MARY LAMBCHOP

ro Toscani con la collaborazione di Donna Jordan, ha piazzato il suo obiettivo, realizzando in due serate l'identi-kit di una pazza e divertente parte d'umanità. E il magico mondo del Max's Kansas City di New York, il ristorante aperto nel 1965 da Mickey Ruskin nella Park Avenue Sud, dove da anni si raccolgono le avanguardie più colorate del costume e della cultura americani. E si sono incontrati qui a mangiare e a sognare gli hippies delle albe di Kerouac, i Ginsberg della beat-generation e ancora ogni notte fino alle quattro Andy

VESUVIO E GEROME

WARREN FINNERS

JERRY SOBEL

RUTH E ROCCO

È una storia di sempre. Sedersi da qualche parte e guardar la gente che ti passa sotto il naso, e sempre con stupore accorgersi che è il più grande spettacolo del mondo. Andy Warhol (e prima di lui molti altri) ha ben raccolto questo messaggio, e non a caso da alcuni anni lo si vede girare con una Polaroid a fuoco fisso, che fotografa proprio tutti quelli che incontra sulla sua strada, mettendo insieme collages e caleidoscopi di tutti i colori dell'umanità. Così, dove il fantastico, il pop, l'incredibile fanno tutti parte di una stessa realtà, Olivie-

# IL MONDO DI MAX'S KANSAS CITY

DAVID GRANITE

GINGER L WALKER

DONNA JORDAN

GIALYA E GEORGE KIBLER

OLIVIERO TOSCANI

**Jackie Curtis
and Rocco**
(photo by Anton Perich)

fit in, and at Max's, if you were too neat or too clean, people would've noticed. Just like at Mortimer's today, people would raise their eyebrows if you are too sloppy. At Max's the dressing code was inventive/sloppy. There was a lot of high-spirited inventiveness in clothes: tying things into your clothes was the big style: people would tie scarves around their pants and boots. It reminded me of a Mad Hatter's tea party—with no grown-ups to say you have to go to bed.

**BERRY BERENSON, MODEL:** I started going to Max's when I first came to New York in 1968. My sister Marisa had already lived in New York a year and a half, and she was already having

high on

some success as a model, so it was possible that I was introduced to Max's through her. I was working for the back pages of *Vogue*, and every issue had four or five pages in the back devoted to new restaurants and new boutiques. I was introduced to Steve Barrow's Au Boutique. They made everything out of leather. It was very hip, chic. Everyone used to go there and then go to Max's because it was across the street. Then I met Richard Bernstein. He was my boyfriend for a while and we were doing all the covers for *Interview*, which used to be a little tiny magazine that folded up. I clearly remember the big painting that Richard did of Max's back room. I think he did it from a photograph. Everything was very red—from the red neon light. It was very beautiful.

**HOWARD SMITH:** Everyone noticed girls weren't wearing bras anymore in the mid- sixties. Girls were carrying attaché cases, but you could see their nipples. So, I thought it would be interesting to see how people, in a relatively straight situation, would react to extreme see-through. I lined up a whole series of girls to do this—they did it because they thought it would be fun to be in "Scenes," in a big photograph, and tell their story about what happened. So I did this series of places, and I decided midway that for the last one I should turn it around, and instead of seeing how straight places reacted to this, I should see how a hip place would react. How would Max's react? I couldn't just have a girl with *some* see-through, because that was a fairly common occurrence almost any night during that period. So it had to be very see-through all over. I had this outfit made up, a little Grecian-type mini-nothing, with no underwear top or bottom. I had a feeling that the reaction wouldn't be as cool as the outside world would assume it to be. I had to have somebody who wasn't known. She had to look like she belonged, but who they didn't know. We had to have a way to get her there, so we had a car and we stuck her between two people in the car. We also had to have a booth all ready without Mickey or anybody knowing it was a setup. Plus, it had to be the right time of night. I went in with a bunch of friends. We sat at one of the booths right opposite the bar, and we timed it so ten minutes later, she came in.

The bar was pretty crowded, but not mobbed. It was the usual hip crowd. At the bar, it's mainly the painters, who of course are the hippest of the hip, the ones who saw everything—Dan Christensen, Larry Zox, John Chamberlain—and in she walks. We instructed her to walk to the bar, opposite our booth. As she walked past the first group of people, we could see these guys literally double-take, but nobody's doing it where she can see it. Now remember, we are talking see-through all over. She was skinny, tall, blond, very fashion-model looking. She steps to the bar and when she does, several guys literally come in right behind her, looking up and down her body, but the second she gets the drink and turns around, as she pivots, they turn away, as if they haven't noticed her. She walked up and down the bar and wherever she walked, the men all reacted the same.

**ANNIE FLANDERS:** I made the blouse for Sarah, the girl who wore the see-through dress to Max's. We knew that when Sarah wore the dress uptown there would be all kinds of stares and remarks, but we expected at Max's it would be a cool situation, that she could just walk in there and everyone

rebellion

HENRY MAJOR

RICH WALTON

GARY SAYLOR

FARREL

FRED HUGHES

LARRY HAPPY

JUTTA E JOHN CLARK

ROBERT FLYNN

PATRICK

TOM PONZIO

CHEKE GRESWOLD TIN ZARYSKI

JAMES GILLRONS DOMINIQUE

RENÉ RICARD

MARCO ED EVA

RAY COLES

DONALD LYONS

STEPHEN ISRAEL

JANE FORCH E EMERSON

RUTH E GINGER WALKER

(photos by Oliviero Toscani)

SILVER DOLLAR

RITTI DODGE

ROCCO

TAYLOR MEAD

DENNIS KEELEY

BOBBY DUKES

BENTON QUINN

**Eric Emerson and Jane Forth**
(photo by Anton Perich)

would be really cool, but that was not the case at all. The guys were going nuts. Everyone was looking out the sides of their eyes and smirking and giggling and poking each other, but no one talked to her that I recall.

**JOHN FORD:** Weird stuff happened in Max's regularly. Like the elephants standing around. So this girl comes in, in this total see-through outfit, standing at the bar. You could see completely through this thing and all these heavy hitters are sitting around and they don't know what to do. One of my wolfhounds liked her; he wanted to smell, so he went over to give her a sniff and I decided to go talk to her. Shit! If no one else was going to, I was.

**CATHY DREW:** Tiger Morse was the first older person I ever saw wearing a see-through dress, and she was on roller skates.

**DONNA JORDAN, MODEL:** It was 1967. First it was Cory Tippin and the Warhol crowd for me at Max's, then it became more fashion. I was working at Paraphernalia at the time. I'd stay out all night and get up at seven in the morning. I met photographer Antonio Lopez in Central Park. Antonio got me into modeling. Of course, he picked up Jane Forth first because she was the beauty, and he started drawing her, then she got me into it. Every session after he drew us, it would be eleven or twelve at night, and we would say, "Come on, come on, hurry up. Let's go to Max's. Come on we've got to go to Max's." So Juan Ramos—Antonio's partner— Antonio, Jan, and I would walk in around midnight. Then I split and went to Europe and that started my Toscani phase. I hooked up with Toscani when I went to live in Paris. I stayed there for a year and modeled, and did this film, *L'Amour.* After that I went to Italy and did a show in Venice and that's when Toscani got wind of me. I was doing quite well at that time. My whole career culminated at the same time. I came back to the U.S. for a year and a half and Andy got us a house on Nineteenth and Third. It was Pat Hackett's old apartment. Toscani documented Max's. He was totally fascinated with it. He sold the idea to Italian *Vogue.*

high on

**CORY TIPPIN:** Donna and Jane were so easy together because Donna was the exact opposite of Jane. The first issue of *Interview* magazine was Donna and Jane. I was doing their makeup and dying their hair.

**DONNA JORDAN:** Cory made Jane Forth's look when she shaved her eyebrows and slicked back her hair. It was totally his creation.

**CORY TIPPIN:** There was a party upstairs at Max's when Cris Cross was the DJ at the disco. It was the first time I met Elsa Peretti. Elsa, who was a famous jewelry designer, in those days, was a model coming from a very wealthy Italian family, and she and Raina Schiano and Naomi Simms shared an apartment. They were the three top models of the late sixties. She came there with Jane Holzer. Jane, at that point, was totally out of the underground scene. She was married to Leonard Holzer, and became more of a mainstream society type.

(photo by Fred Lombardi)

rebellion

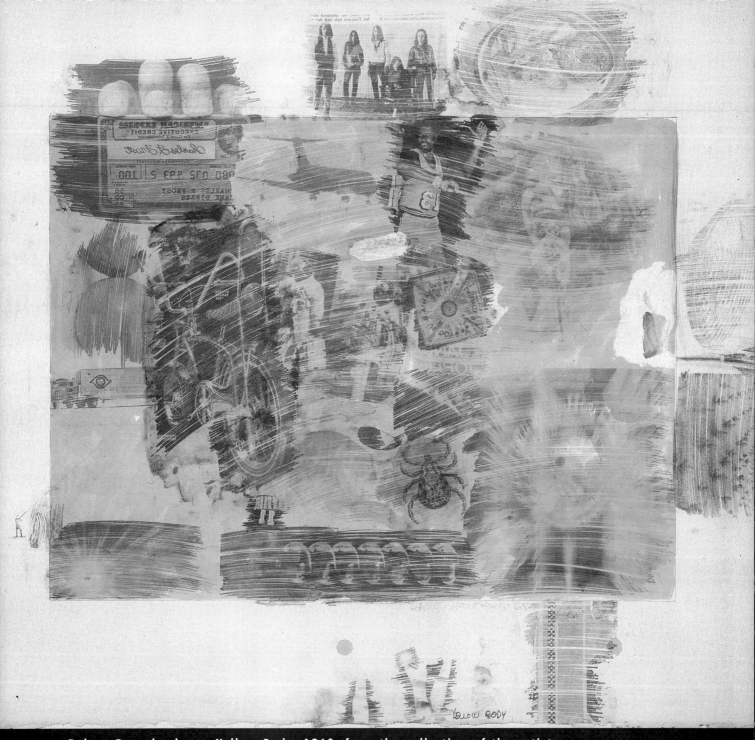

**t**he upstairs at Max's was first used as the locker room for all the Max's waitresses until Mickey opened it for the business from the bridge-and-tunnel spillover dinner crowd. There were times when there were lines around the block. Mickey said, "When that happened, I realized for the first time that I had a monster on my hands." And in the early days there was no kitchen upstairs. So we had to travel down the back stairs to pick up our order, then walk back up with plates piled sometimes five at a time up our arms—not an easy task when the place was packed and the stairs were many. We had to deal with not only impatient customers, but Izzy, Max's insane cook, who was constantly grabbing at your boobs and freely swinging the butcher knife. He was actually hired by Mickey out of jail on a murder rap. But, as Mickey always reminded us, "good cooks were hard to come by and waitresses were not."

By 1969, late at night after the dinner crowd had filtered out, the upstairs was transformed into New York's first rock disco. Unlike Arthur's—an uptown disco that you dressed up to get into—like everything else in Mickey's topsy-turvy, upside-down world, at Max's disco you dressed down to get in. And often one of Max's patrons would strip down to the bare essentials to the music chosen by Cris Cross, Max's first DJ. Artists like Robert Rauschenberg and European filmmakers like Toscani, danced next to six-foot bikers, hippies, and rockers. Just as Max's was a microcosm of New York City in the sixties, the dance floor upstairs was a microcosm of Max's. But like most of Mickey's innovations, the disco evolved somewhat by chance. Tiger Morse was having a rough time financially and she kept bugging Mickey to let her do a slide show to music. She also nagged him continually for a waitressing job, but he refused. Tiger was a speed freak and out of control at this point. But she and Mickey were close friends and he respected her talent so he told her she could do something upstairs with her slide show a few nights a week. She started a kind of media show up there with her slides and records, and people would come up from downstairs to dance like they were in a disco.

The music performances that Sam Hood organized for the upstairs room at Max's beginning in 1969 drew even more of the rock-and-roll crowd than was already hanging out there. The invasion of music caused quite a stir among the regulars at Max's, especially the artists. They felt that their territory was being invaded, and that Max's was starting to go downhill, a classic case of sibling rivalry. But, in spite of their criticisms, and feelings of being invaded, Max's became the hottest room in town for folk, country, and rock. To keep their public abreast of budding stars on the horizon, Sam and Mickey initiated talent-scout night to showcase new artists. Acts like Springsteen, Billy Joel, Alice Cooper, Aerosmith, and Bob Marley and the Wailers launched their careers upstairs at Max's. Very few people in New York had experienced reggae music until Bob Marley introduced it, when he debuted in the little room upstairs, with Springsteen as the opening act. Charlie Rich and Waylon Jennings all performed on that same stage.

Over time the styles and trends in music changed. Rock, folk, and country paved the way for pop, glitter rock and pre-punk. Punk began to surface with the emergence of groups like the Velvet Underground, the MC5, the New York Dolls, and the Patti Smith Group. Songs by the Stones, the Beatles, Dylan, Aretha Franklin, the Doors, Janis Joplin, the Jefferson Airplane, and country music, Mickey's great love, dominated the jukebox, which was the best in all of New York. "The Letter" by the Boxtops, played continually throughout the night. My favorite selection was "Love Me Two

Times" by the Doors. Up-and-coming acts like Alice Cooper and Iggy Pop were beginning to gain some popularity in New York, while in England it was Led Zeppelin and the Who. Like everything else at Max's, the mix of music was more than democratic.

Not just a disco and nightclub, the upstairs stage also showcased everything from Off Off Broadway plays to poetry readings and performance art, including Theater of the Ridiculous founder John Vaccaro's legendary play *The Mokeeater*. The upstairs also hosted the Who's New York debut party, a cast party for Zeffirelli's film version of *Romeo and Juliet*, the first New York press meeting for the rock group Cream, and Lillian Roxon's party for her book *The Encyclopedia of Rock*. Another book party—for composer David Amram—was attended by all the great musicians of the era, including Miles Davis and Bob Dylan.

**DICK NUSSER, JOURNALIST:** Eric and some of the Superstars started cavorting in the back room and Mickey would come through periodically and police the joint, with his sleeves rolled up and his hands on his hips. He came in the back and Eric was giving one of his little performances. He said, "Eric, if you want to do that, go upstairs. There is nobody upstairs, bring your friends and perform there." So we got to talking about encouraging people to do what they wanted to do. People would say, "I've got an idea for this," and next thing you knew, Eric organized these characters into some kind of loose cabaret. Then Howard Smith from the *Village Voice* said to me, "Dick, how long has this been going on?" He had just come down from the upstairs at Max's. I said, "Oh you mean Eric and the Troubadours." He said, "You ought to write about it in your 'Riffs' column." I was writing a column for the *Voice* at the time. I went back and wrote about it, that there was this burgeoning cabaret scene happening upstairs at Max's. The next thing you know, the crowd started coming out, and shortly after that it turned into a disco.

**BOB RUSSELL:** There was this bus boy named Cris Cross who

**Geri Miller** (photo by Anton Perich)

rebellion

**Charlie Rich** (photo by Lilly Hou)

was about to be fired. He was this real pretty boy and I didn't want him fired so I suggested to Mickey that he try Chris out as a DJ upstairs. He did and it turned out the position was well suited for him. He was Max's first authentic DJ....

Rauschenberg started going upstairs to disco every night as a regular. One of the things I learned from him was that you could make as big a fool of yourself as you wanted as long as you didn't hurt anybody. He never did anything at anybody else's expense. Sometimes he'd take his pants down by his ankles and chase people around and fall down in the aisle. People would help him back up again and pull his pants up for him. He'd be laughing and having a merry time just being a drunken fool.

**TISH, OPENED FIRST PUNK BOUTIQUE:** I remember seeing Patti Smith upstairs. I guess with it was sort of like a disco up there and she was by herself dancing. There was almost no one else in the room and she was just dancing by herself. I thought that was the coolest thing. I was thinking, she's so brave. She had this big raincoat thing on.

**BOB BRADY:** I would go upstairs to disco and there was this girl named A. She had the record for seducing the most men. She was wealthy, but she was not good-looking. She was daring in that she would like to have sex with an element of danger to it, while driving fast on the L.I.E.

**ELAINE GROVE:** The first time I went upstairs to disco it was such a different place than downstairs. The most striking sight was Eric Emerson wearing—it seems it was in the wintertime—his famous chaps with just his jockstrap on. So from the back it was like these bare buttocks, feather boa, and cowboy chaps.

**JOHN PUMA, AGENT:** We'd go up to dance and the crowd would always be very eclectic; you had Walt Frazier from the Knicks to Hud, the bizarre busboy. My wife and I were always compared to Sonny and Cher, people always thought we were them.

high on

**RON CUTRONE:** Eric and I were always dancing. We'd shoot LSD. We'd do a primer of methadrine. I'd go up there to disco, pull a girl off the dance floor, dance with her until she was too…to say no, and take her home.

**JOHN HAYES:** When Paul Eden was playing music upstairs at the disco, I don't know how we could hear it but we'd be downstairs in the back room, and there were those that wouldn't deign to go upstairs and dance, but when Paul put on "*Monkey Man*" by the Stones we would rush upstairs to dance, even Larissa and Rocco, who would never go up there, then we'd all come back down and assume our positions.

**DORY WEINER:** One time Andy brought Mick and Bianca, and I remember them coming up the stairs and Andy had this look on his face like, "Is she going to let us in?" Then I went into the ladies' room and Bianca was there and she looked so like, lost, and asked her, "Would you like a cup of tea?" And she said, "Oh, I would love one," and she gave me this beautiful smile.

**LOUIE WALDEN:** At one time some mafia guys came into Max's and I think they wanted to take over the door upstairs when Mickey was charging to get in and there were lines around the block. They wanted to put one of their men at the door. They were doing this all over Manhattan. Dominic, who worked for Mickey and looked like one of the mob and had connections, ran down and got this guy who runs Bleecker Street. He told these guys to stay away, to leave Max's alone. I think that's why he got the job as the doorman for the upstairs.

**CAROL WILBOURN, MICKEY'S FRIEND / *PLAYBOY* BUNNY:** Mickey came to me and said that he had to 86 Jagger, he said that maybe he could go and live with one of the *Playboy* bunnies. I was a bunny at the time. I said, "Well, what happened?" And he told me that Jagger had caught a mouse and brought the mouse in his mouth to Dory and she screamed. I said, "Yes, but he's only doing what a cat's supposed to do." Dory was not happy about the cat and the mouse, and Mickey said he needed Dory more than the housecat.

**MARJORIE STRIDER:** Hannah Weiner began organizing the "little bitty" events on Saturday afternoons upstairs at Max's. Artist Vito Acconci did one of his first pieces there. He sat at booths with his arm on the table. That was the event.

**Johnny Winter** (photo by Anton Perich)

rebellion

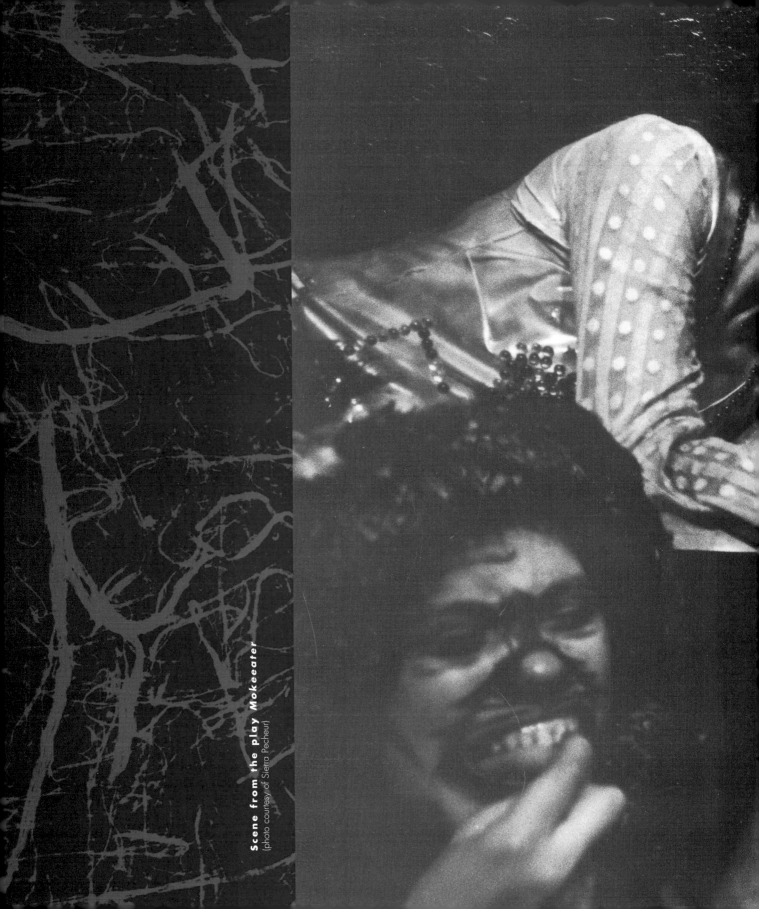

**Scene from the play** *Mokeeater*
(photo courtesy of Sierra Pecheur)

**Tom Waits** (photo by Lilly Hou)

**JOHN VACCARO:** We did this show at Max's [1968], *The Mokeeater*. It was August and it was so hot, we were rehearsing, and I had to give everyone salt pills. Bruce Pecheur was terrified of Sierra, who was playing the lead in the play. I introduced them on acid. Of course later they started living together. After they met they really fell in love. We all took acid together—René, Patsy, Bruce, and Sierra. I would stand there and say, "Kill him, kill him." And Sierra would say in the play, "The last person that came here, we took out his liver." Bruce was mutilated in the play and, ironically, he was killed by a junkie who broke into their apartment.

**MICKEY RUSKIN:** The upstairs was used primarily for the over-crowding we had on weekends. It was where I put the tourists, so that the downstairs would remain relatively pure. Then I had a major fire and I moved everything to my restaurant across the street for a week or two while we reconstructed the upstairs. But when we moved back in, my gross dropped in half and it never went up to what it had been. So Dave McShehee who worked at Dr. Generosity's, brought around Sam Hood, who owned the Gaslight. I had no idea at the time that Sam had been on a serious alcoholic binge, and was essentially sleeping in the street. David suggested to me that with Sam I could probably do something musically, utilizing the upstairs. So I showed Sam how small the room was, but he was still interested, so we started. I think we opened with a local group, Jake and the Family Jewels. Sam gave up drinking, went straight, got his head together, and we wound up being the major room for music in New York City.

**SAM HOOD, BOOKER MUSIC AT MAX'S:** The attention to the music scene really started with Elephant's Memory playing there and they were a terrible band. They got us the kind of action that we needed. What we needed was not just people coming in to pay their six dollars. That was important, but we needed industry attention so that we could start the kind of profitable relationship with the record companies that was really going to sustain us and allow us to do interesting things. In order to do what we needed the credibility. Also, the credibility came from the fact that John and Yoko were involved with Elephant's Memory. John Lennon actually called us and said, "Can you do us this favor? We need this place to work out of."

**CLAUDE HAYNE, ROAD MANAGER AND MEMBER OF ELEPHANT'S MEMORY:** We were introduced by a friend of ours, Jerry Rubin. He was using the facilities at John and Yoko's

high on

apartment, in the front half of their loft. John had explained to Jerry, because he was right there, that he was looking for a band to support him when he wanted to play out—a new Plastic Ono Band—and Jerry introduced us and John showed up to interview us, and to rehearse with us at Magna Graphics with Phil Spector. So the two of them showed up, and they liked the way the band played and that started the next act. We probably brought John and Yoko down to Max's and they liked the place and got a good feel for it, and wanted to rehearse upstairs. We were becoming the Plastic Ono Band. I guess that was the introduction. We started to do some rehearsal, and Mickey decided to open the room up and they put in a sound system and made a stage....We were the first people using the room upstairs.

It was just at that time we were receiving Lennon's equipment from England, and at one point I had thirty-five of his guitars brought into Max's. We turned around and the next thing we know there was a guy climbing out the window. He was leaving with one of John's guitars. One of our security guys grabbed the guitar, then grabbed the guy and dropped him down the back window from the top floor.

**JEFFREY BRENNAN:** I started out as a busboy at Max's, and worked for about a year, then suddenly I was made the upstairs doorman. Dominic Izzo, who looked like one of the mob, was running the door upstairs. My guess is, due to the fact of how much extra money Dominic was taking off the top as doorman, I got the job. Graham Parsons, Bonnie Raitt, Little Feat, Alice Cooper, Martin Mull, Andy Kaufman, Hall and Oates—most of them were unknown, and really working very hard. There was great comedy, great jazz like Charles Mingus. Billy Joel played there to a very mediocre crowd. I remember saying, "This guy will never make it." Tim Buckley played. David Allen Coe was a country singer who was in jail three times for murder. He murdered somebody in jail. This was his first time in New York and we were really nervous, because we had a murderer on our hands. The first night he was in a bad mood and said, "Fuck you all" to everybody, and walked off the stage.

**CARL GLIKO, ARTIST:** I remember when Mickey was putting on the music upstairs and he had booked Waylon Jennings and Billy Joel on the same bill. Everybody wanted to hear Waylon, particularly Poons. The sets finished and we went back downstairs to have some drinks and Billy Joel walked through the bar and we all booed him.

**TOM PUNZIO:** I came to work one Sunday and there had been a fire the night before. The restaurant had trailed off somewhat after that fire. Mickey looked spent. Meat prices had gone up. It needed something different. Then Sam Hood got involved and the music thing happened upstairs which brought a whole different element. Then the place really started having some interesting people come through the doors. Springsteen started playing there, the Doobie Brothers, Little Feat, and a lot of entertainers who are world-famous now. It had a second life as a club as opposed to a restaurant.

rebellion

**JOHN CLEM CLARKE, ARTIST:** Over time the place got to be really glamour, drugs, and glitz. It was great for artists for a long time because it was understated. The artists had been top dogs, and all of a sudden we're feeling second-rate, and they started moving to other places. Mickey was very loyal to the artists. He was always a little suspicious of the music people.

Max's had some great acts. I remember telling everyone to come see the Beans. They were great. The Beans became the Tubes. The first time I saw Tim Hardin perform upstairs, I was embarrassed for him. Here was a talent on a giant scale, with an obvious addiction that was dumping his career right into the toilet. The place was packed, and the crowd had tremendous enthusiasm, but Tim kept fucking up the verses. He couldn't remember the words to some of his songs. He could barely stand! He was a mess. What a waste. Drugs were definitely taking their toll and Max's seemed to be a breeding ground for them.

Tim returned to play Max's about ten months later. He gave one of the best shows I'd seen to date, but nobody showed. The room was practically empty. He had cleaned up—sadly, nobody knew it. His fans had given up on him.

**SAM HOOD:** They got the baby elephant upstairs. Tim Hardin was performing that night. The baby elephant waddled down the aisle to the stage while Tim was playing, and pissed on the stage while Tim is in the middle of a song. The elephant just pisses all over the front of the stage. Tim finishes the song, looks at the audience and looks at the elephant and says, "Everybody's a critic!"

**DANNY FIELDS:** In the spring of 1967, I had a quick freelance job doing publicity for Cream. The group consisted of Eric Clapton, Jack Bruce, and Ginger Baker. It was their first trip to New York and they were managed jointly by Brian Epstein and Robert Stigwood. My idea was to have a breakfast press conference at Max's so that the press could meet Brian Epstein because I knew he would be the draw and then everyone could talk about Cream, who at the time were not of interest to anybody in America, and so everybody came to see Brian. Mickey said it was the first music-business event to be held at Max's, and it was just a press conference. They were playing at Rko 58th Street with Simon and Garfunkel, Wilson Pickett, and the Who —all of them on one ticket. It was an amazing show. Then later, I brought Tim Buckley and the Doors to Max's.

**MICKEY RUSKIN:** When Danny Fields brought the Doors in Max's for the first time, I didn't know who the hell they were. He hands me a record one night and says, "Put this on the box," and it was something called *Break On Through*, and two weeks later he hands me another record and says, "Put this one on," and that was *Light My Fire*. Apparently he had been bringing them in regularly.

**ANDY PALEY, LEAD SINGER FOR THE SIDEWINDERS:** We were the house band at

220

Max's for a while. And we never made any hit records but we had this amazing core of people really rooting for us—Lillian Roxon, Danny Fields, Mick Jagger, Bowie, Neuwirth, Lou Reed. I was so impressed that all these guys were coming to see our band.

**JOE BIRD, BARTENDER:** We had a seat for Mayor Lindsey upstairs. He was still the mayor at the time and Koch was a representative. Lindsey would come up to watch the music. There was a sign on the second floor that said so much for admission, and so much for state tax, and so much for city tax, and of course the entire thing was off the books. There was the mayor coming to his own private table and the entire second floor didn't exist for city tax. Everbody who worked the upstairs was paid cash.

**RICHARD GOLUB:** Bob Marley and the Wailers played their first concert in America at Max's. I was outside with them before they went on and I remember how scared they were. Bob Marley was very scared and humble. They didn't know if they would be a success in New York. "Family Man" Henderson, one of the Wailers, was smoking a cigarette and shaking Marley, they were so nervous. The crowd liked them, but didn't go nuts over them.

**GLENN O'BRIEN:** Ronnie Cutrone and I were the only two people in the world who knew who the Wailers were. We had their first album, *Catch a Fire.* It had just come out and it was in the shape of a cigarette lighter and the top opened up and the record was inside. Ronnie and I were the music freaks. The Wailers show was pretty well attended. We had never seen anything like it. We were both standing there with our jaws dropped. Ronnie just kept saying, "They are so noble." It was the original band with Peter Tosh and Bunny Wailer and Bob.

**RONNIE CUTRONE:** I knew of reggae before anybody. I used to fly to Jamaica to get reggae records. Mickey booked Bob Marley and it blew my mind. I went every night. Nobody knew who they were, so I could watch them with ten people and they were raw and vital then. By the last few nights everybody was saying, "This music is insane, what is it?" They were trying to disco- and rock-dance to it. Peter Tosh, Bob Marley, Bunny Wailer, night after night.

**MIKE APPEL, BRUCE SPRINGSTEEN'S EX-MANAGER:** I remember Bob Marley opening up for Springsteen at Max's and I had never heard reggae music before that. Bob Marley came up to me at one point during the evening and he said, "Hey man, what do you think of our music?" I said, "I don't know, I like that *aut et chck a unt etckcka unt*—it just goes on like that it seems that's the only song you guys know." Chris Blackwell was familiar with it long before I was, but I liked it right from the get-go....The first place Springsteen played by himself in New York was on MacDougal Street with his guitar and then a few days later he played talent night at Max's....If you were any-body at all and you were coming to New York, you played Max's Kansas City.

Country Joe (photo by Lilly Hou)

Bonnie Raitt (photo by Lilly Hou)

Emmylou Harris and Gram Parsons
(photo by Lilly Hou)

**SAM HOOD:** One of my most enjoyable times was when John Hammond Sr. called me. He was the person I respected most in the music business. He called and asked if I could take the time to personally audition someone that he was in the process of signing to Columbia Records. He said, "I think he's going to remind you of someone that we are both familiar with. And if you could do that I would appreciate it." I said, "Sure." It was Springsteen. Springsteen came down and did a private audition. We had dinner upstairs at around five o'clock before the crowd came in, and Bruce came in and just played the piano and the acoustic guitar. He did around forty-five minutes for us private-ly. We were just absolutely blown away. I mean, you had to be. So I asked him to come back the next week and I'd invite some more people. Then I talked to Mickey about it and we had twenty or thirty people to the next private audition, friends of ours and friends of the house. That was one of the nicest evenings ever in the place. I worked with Bruce a lot later at Columbia. He remembered those days fondly. Actually Springsteen and Bob Marley played three or four weeks together and they just reversed the billing back and forth from one week to the next. Neither of them at the time had enough of a draw on their own.

Bruce Springsteen (photos by Lilly Hou)

Bruce Springsteen
with Clive Davis,
president of Arista
Records

Bob Marley (Jeff Cathro Photography)

Upstairs at
max's kansas city

NOW thru MONDAY

# BRUCE
# SPRINGSTEEN

· COLUMBIA RECORDING ARTIST ·

also appearing

## THE WAILERS

OPENING TUES. JULY 24

## Ruben and The Jets

JULY 30, 31 and AUG. 1, 2
MON., TUES., WED., THURS.
MIDNITE SHOWS ONLY

## IGGY POP

· COLUMBIA RECORDING ARTIST ·

AUGUST 10, 11 and 12
FRI., SAT., SUN.

## TIM BUCKLEY

OPENING AUG. 15-20

## SYLVIA TYSON

AUG. 22-27
AUG. 29-SEPT. 10

NEW YORK DOLLS
SONNY TERRY
and
BROWNIE McGHEE

213 Park Ave. South at 17th St.
For Res. Call: 777-7870

**Clarence Clemmons**
(photo by Lilly Hou)

**DAVID BOWIE:** I originally went to Max's to see an artist called Biff Rose, a quirky but interesting writer. His performance was all right but not even near my expectations. I stuck around as there was another act on. So this guy is sitting up there with an acoustic guitar doing a complete Dylan thing. My friend and I were about to leave when he started introducing a band who were joining him onstage.

The moment they kicked in he was another performer. All the Dylanesque stuff dropped off him and he rocked. I became a major fan that night and picked up *Asbury Park* immediately.

**CHERRY VANILLA:** I had been Bowie's PR lady. He was a small-scale performing artist when we met him in London. He had just made Hunky Dory and he had come to America. I had the biggest mouth and the patience to talk to the press, and all these friends at Max's who were rock critics, that's how it all started. One night Springsteen was playing upstairs at Max's and David Bowie didn't know who he was and we couldn't convince him to go. Bowie knew the headliner and on the strength of that we convinced him. He went bananas over Springsteen. We brought him backstage and introduced him. Then he returned to London to Trident Studios and recorded a couple of Springsteen's songs, based on his visit to Max's and meeting him there.

**JIM LALUMIA, ROCK WRITER / MUSICIAN:** My favorite gig would be a tie between the Bruce Springsteen and the Steely Dan gig. I think Loudon Wainwright, believe it or not, was actually headlining. Steely Dan had one single out, one Top 40 record. They did not become the much-heralded

high on

band until much later. Donald Fagen, shortly thereafter, never performed live, and so this Max's gig was one of the only times when he actually performed, when this first single was first hitting. And they got tacked onto the bill, I believe, with Loudon Wainwright, and Loudon, I think, was writing his own big single at the time which stunk. So that was an interesting bill and the historical significance of the Steely Dan didn't surface until years later. With their success with the critical press, Donald Fagen had become the Howard Hughes of rock-and-roll, and just wasn't going to perform anymore and all he did was issue albums. They just never performed, so this Max's gig was just like a one-shot lucky moment.

**DAVE MARSH, ROCK CRITIC:** I saw Iggy with the cut glass. I had a drink with Billy Idol there, and I saw Patti there, but this is the greatest thing: Bob Marley and the Wailers were in town and I went to review them for *Newsday*. It was like August or September and I go to see Marley and the Wailers and it turns out that there's this opening act that I vaguely want to see. So I go in and I really want to see the Wailers because they are the kings of reggae and it's amazing that they are in New York. The capacity was about 125 people. So I go in but instead of the opening act being the opening act, the opening act is the Wailers. They are playing the first set and they play and they are terrific. So then the second act comes out, which should have been the opening act, and it's Bruce and the E Street Band. The first time I ever saw Bruce was at Max's. People can talk about CBGB's and clubs elsewhere, there was never anything like Max's.

There was a night I was walking outside on my way to Max's and these guys who looked like musicians were walking to Max's. I started a conversation with them....They said, "We are the Grateful Dead and we're here in town to play the Fillmore East opening up for Joplin. Although she should be opening up for us and this is the last time we intend to be opening up for anybody. From here on in we get top billing." Then we all walked into Max's to have a good time.

Upstairs at
max's kansas city

Now thru Sunday

**JOHN HERALD**
& The Honkies

and

**GARLAND JEFFREYS**

Mon. April 2 — Thurs. April 5

**IF**

| | |
|---|---|
| Apr. 6-8 | **TIM BUCKLEY** |
| Apr. 6-9 | **Special Guest** |
| | **MARTIN MULL** |
| Apr. 3-8 | **Fraser & De Bolt** |
| Apr. 11-16 | **BONNIE RAITT** |
| | also |
| | LITTLE FEAT |
| | adva |
| Apr. 18-23 | TOM |
| Apr. 25-30 | ODET |
| | also |
| | BILL QU |

rebellion

**DANNY GOLDBERG, RECORD EXECUTIVE:** Lillian was so great to me. She was the person who would introduce you to everybody and make this absurdly exaggerated fuss over me and make me feel important and confident. She did that with countless people. The one thing you had to do was be nice to her Australians [Lillian was from Australia]. She'd say, "This is the leading banker or leading something" and she always took them to Max's. And she brought Germaine Greer to Max's for the first time. She said, "This is my friend Germaine and she's going to write this book, she is really important, she's really famous in Australia," and she introduced her to everybody and it ended up with Germaine being on the cover of *Life* magazine. That was all Lillian.

**LENNY KAYE, ROCK MUSICIAN/ROCK CRITIC:** The very first press party I ever went to was for Lillian Roxon's *Rock Encyclopedia*. She took me under her wing and encouraged me. She'd tell me how all the young rock writers are like rock stars in themselves, etc. Then Lisa [Robinson] introduced me to her husband, Richard, and there was Danny [Fields], so it became like a little rock writers' circle. At the time, rock writing was so new and had such a feel of *Crawdaddy* about it that it was one of the most creative literary mediums you could get.

**LEEE BLACK CHILDERS:** Lillian Roxon was very influential in launching my career—she and Lisa Robinson. The way I met Lisa was photographing Lou Reed upstairs at Max's. It was the summer of 1970. The whole summer went by, Brigid Polk was recording it and I was photographing it; Wayne County sitting on the edge of the stage looking up at Lou Reed—"Oh my god, there's a God before us." Some nights were very full and some were relatively empty but I was there every night. The last two weeks of the gig there was no Lou. There were all kinds of rumors as to what had happened to him. Dough Yule, the bass player [for the Velvet Underground] had to take over for those last performances. Lenny Kaye called me shortly after that and said, "I understand you have been photographing Lou Reed. You know Lisa Robinson is looking for photographs." I didn't know who Lisa was. So I went to her with all my photographs and she went crazy over them. She then introduced me to Lillian and they both took me on. Lillian got me into an article in *Esquire* as one of the eighty most powerful people in rock and roll. Then, of course, I went on to manage Bowie and the Heartbreakers.

**STEVE GAINES:** Lillian was the mother of rock-and-roll journalism. She took the music business seriously. She had a marvelous sense of what the fans wanted to know. Lillian was Australian. One night after the opening of *OZ*, which was this newspaper that was banned in England, we went down to Max's. We walked in and this European photographer said something mean to Lillian. And Lillian turned to her and said, "You have a face that looks like it's giving birth." If she liked you, you were so lucky because she was such a good friend. But if she didn't like you, she was the world's most horrendous bitch.

## Lillian Roxon
### The Mother of Rock 'n' Roll Journalism

229

•  •  •

**DANNY GOLDBERG:** Everybody looked up to Gloria Stavers. She was on a pedestal for some reason. She was the editor of *16 Magazine*. Her big thing was that she was one of the last lovers that Lenny Bruce had. She was a little older and a little more serious than anybody else.

**SAM HOOD:** When Kinky Friedman and the Texas Jewboys played Max's, the Jewish Defense league started calling with protests. We had bomb scares. I had to call the police and we had undercover cops there because we had so many death threats. Mickey and I used to have this ongoing debate—the importance of Warhol versus Dylan. One night Dylan came in....I remember introducing him to Mickey and I said, "Now you got to talk to Mickey because he feels that Andy Warhol is a lot more important than you will ever be." And we had this great discussion with Dylan about the importance of Andy Warhol....

I remember we were doing a live show with Iggy and all these record people were supposed to show. He was very fucked up. Here was Iggy laying on the floor in the dressing room asking Clive Davis to piss on him. Iggy completely lost it.

**JIM LALUMIA:** *Rock Scene* magazine was the Bible during that period of time. It had first cropped up, I guess, to dovetail with the success of Alice Cooper, T. Rex, and David Bowie, who all have in common androgyny, gender issues, a flamboyant thing. It had gone from the Grateful Dead, Woodstocky, "we are all one" type of mind-set, to suddenly all these critters were appearing on the horizon saying, "We are not all one, in fact I'm not anything at all like you, and it's going to cost you twenty-five dollars to find that out." And that to me seemed very Warhol, and very fascinating. And also the fact that rock had been so straight, white, male-dominated, up to that point, with the guitar as the phallic extension, meaning "We're going to nail the chicks and the babes tonight at the end of the show, and that's what they're good for and that's all they're good for" type of mentality that was out there.

**SHAYNE HARRIS, DRUMMER:** The night I met Led Zeppelin at Max's, they were starting the 1972 tour and I hung out with Robert Plant, Jimmy Page, and my idol, who at the time was John Bonham. I practically dumped a load in my pants shaking his hand. I went limp. I was like a girl on a first date with the football hero. He said, "What are you looking at me like that for?" I gave him a tape and said, "We did it at RCA, maybe you can tell me what you think?" He said, "Oh, you're another one who plays drums." I had to get up because I was going to shit or I was going to puke.

**LYNN EDELSON:** I went into Max's one night and Led Zeppelin was there. Jimmy Page and this other guy, B. G. Falon, who was a DJ and best friends with Jimmy, came over to me in the back room and asked me to join them at the table. I wasn't a groupie. I was a musician. I would inten-

high on

tionally not sleep with famous people. I joined their table. I mean, anything for a free drink. I wasn't really working. I was making these surrealistic birds on pants and painting denim jackets. I go to the table and we all really hit it off with each other. Jimmy and Robert Plant and this girl that Robert Plant was hanging out with, wanted me to do painting for them on their jeans. I remember winding up at their hotel the next week working in Robert Plant's suite, painting. I got taken to Madison Square Garden in a limo. What a time!

While I was working for Led Zeppelin, one night I did not go to the concert. I'm in Robert Plant's room and this guy Percy said, "Do whatever you want, order champagne, caviar, but don't let anybody in." Well he's gone like an hour and there's this banging and banging at the door and I looked through the peep hole and its Iggy Pop. It was at the Drake Hotel. It was during the *Houses of the Holy* tour. It was Iggy Pop, so I figure what the hell. So I let him in and he's beet red. He's as red as that paint that you have in kindergarten. I hadn't met Iggy before. I could see him shaking all over and he was perspiring, and I feel his head and he must have a 103 fever. And I get really nervous. I said, "What did you do?" He said, "Well I ran out of coke so I shot up niacin." So I'm like, "Oh shit, we've got to get your body temperature down. Take your clothes off." So he takes off his clothes and he lies down on Percy's bed. Now this is getting really bad, here he is lying naked on the bed. I wrapped him up in towels and could feel his temperature going down, and he fell asleep.

A couple hours later Percy comes back and he says, "Who the bloody hell is in my bed?" And he's freaking out. And I just laughed and I said, "Go and look." And there's Iggy totally fucked up with towels all over him. They really thanked me. The next night I think Iggy was playing at Max's and one of Zep's road guys called me at home and said, "All of us want to come down to the show and you know everyone there, can you make sure we have a table in the performance area." So I set the whole thing up and they all came. I think that was the night he cut himself up. Iggy leaning over with the blood at Max's....

Another night, I go into Max's and Joyce Francis comes running up to me and she says, "You're not going to believe who's sitting over there!" And I said," Where?" He was sitting right across from the kitchen at one of the little tables. She said, "Just walk past him, you're going to drop dead." And I walked past him, and Prince Charles is sitting at a table right across from the kitchen. He flirted with me. He winked at me a couple of times.

**Odetta**
(photo by Lilly Hou)

rebellion

**Kinky Friedman and His Texas Jewboys**
(photo by Lilly Hou)

**NICKY MARTIN, ROCK MUSICIAN:** Street Punk was a band for the early seventies. Back then it was all this glitter stuff, this androgynous stuff going on. When the Dolls were dressing in drag onstage, I went onstage in blue jeans and whatever leather jacket I could borrow from one of my friends. And just a few short years after that, that was the Ramones' uniform. Nobody back then was dressing that way. And Street Punk, although not a punk band per se certainly had the attitude of a punk band. They came out later when they really didn't give much of a shit about what anybody thought. We were a reckless lot. Just the name Street Punk brought the word *punk* into the public consciousness. It had never really been used from a musical point of view before that.

I was addicted to heroin at the time. We had very little direction. After KISS was signed to Bill Aucoin Management, Gene Simmons made an appointment for Street Punk, because he thought we were great. We had talent. We went into Bill Aucoin's office and we were offered more money as a salary than KISS but there was already dissension in the band and it just fell apart.

**LEEE BLACK CHILDERS:** Almost from the minute people coined that phrase *glitter* and *glam*, it became horrific to anyone who was being pointed at as that. None of them knew what it was, either. Alice Cooper was upstairs at Max's performing with little paper cones in his woman's negligee simulating tits, wearing high-heeled shoes, fuck-me shoes, in fact. Jackie Curtis sat down and said, "Oh my god, he's wearing fuck-me pumps." Yet when someone finally said to him, "Oh, you're glitter," it made him nuts. It made David Bowie even nuttier. He didn't want to be identified with that scene. It was not a serious scene.

**JEFFREY BRENNAN:** What I remember about Alice Cooper is that he would be onstage drinking pitchers of beer and crying about how he wasn't a star. When Iggy performed he collapsed in my arms, blood coming out of his loincloth. The only thing he said was, "Is there a professional photographer in the house?" The story goes that Jackie Curtis said, "I want to see blood tonight!" I think Alice Cooper, who was in the audience at the time, wrapped him in a blanket and took him to the hospital.

**IGGY POP:** To the best of my recollection, I was only up there twice—that's only what I remember anyway. Once is when I gigged myself—the best way I could put it is trying to do a rock-and-roll show in front of your first-grade class with the teacher present, except all the students had morphed into your critics....It was a very stark and static and strange vibe, but it did bring out such an

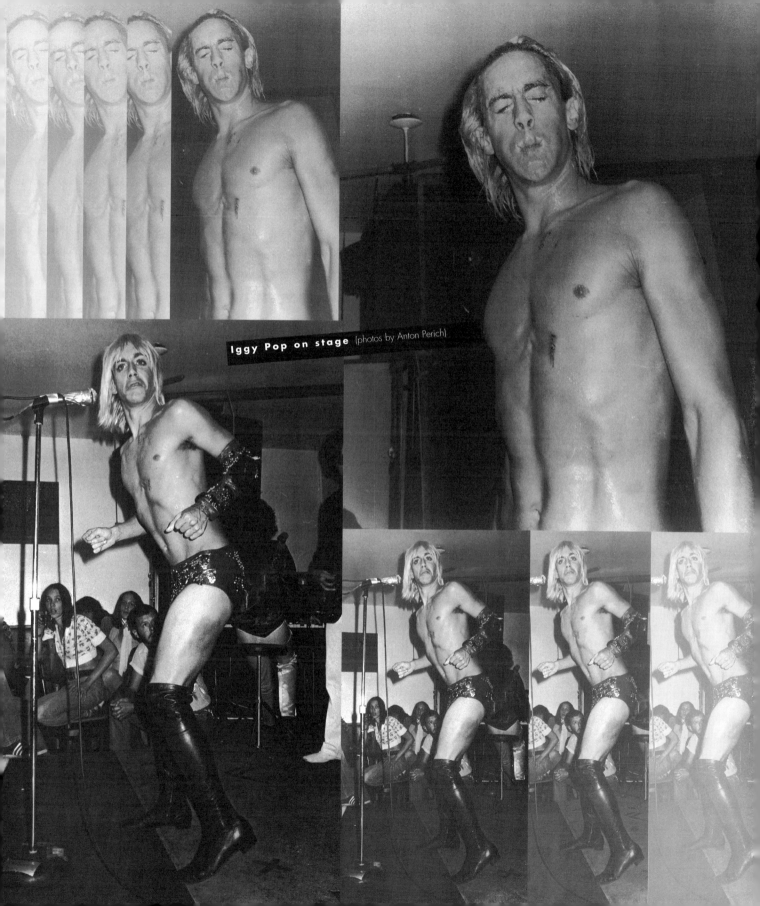

Iggy Pop on stage (photos by Anton Perich)

intensity. It was a room that operated from the neck up. It was not good clean American fun. It was not the room for Aerosmith. I found it a strange place to play. My infamous incident....

**GLENN O'BRIEN:** I think the night Iggy cut himself was a big night. It was at the time of the *Search and Destroy* album and he had this new band—he got that new guitarist who was very glamorous. He had this jet-black dyed hairdo look and the beginning of this makeup thing. And Iggy had dyed his hair silver.

**ALICE COOPER:** The very first time I went to play at Max's [1971, '72], here I was setting up in this very tiny place and we started our set and into the third song all of a sudden the police walk in. They had a complaint because we were too loud. I though it was impossible that the police would walk into that den of iniquity, the den of vipers. There were all these vicious-looking people in there and the police actually strolled through the middle of it to tell me to turn down the volume in the middle of Manhattan at three in the morning. So we had the reputation for being the loudest band.

**SAM HOOD:** Aerosmith were trying to get Clive Davis to come down to hear them—that was also when you let groups arrange for record companies to come down and hear them or audition for their agents. Aerosmith were trying to get Clive Davis to come down, and evidently it hadn't worked out. Nobody from Columbia had seen them. They were desperate for a label deal....Also on the bill that night was John Hall with Orleans. John had gotten a commitment from Clive Davis (who at that point was perceived as every unsigned band's ticket to stardom) that he would come to see him that night. Unfortunately, Clive did show up, before John and Orleans went on, and Aerosmith wedged their way in. Clive saw Aerosmith and the rest is history. He signed them and never even saw Orleans. It was a real blow to John.

**MICKEY RUSKIN:** The only group that ever paid to play the room on a Tuesday night was Aerosmith, because Sam Hood couldn't stand them. They actually paid us, and Leber Krebs signed them to a record deal up there with Clive Davis. I know that Billy Joel started there also, because he eventually bought us out of his contract. We had options in those days for five grand. I remember the Dolls calling me over one day and saying, "Hey Mickey, we're forming a group." I laughed! I didn't know who these kids were; they were just a bunch of hippies to me. Then Leber Krebs took them over, and I believe to this day that Leber Krebs expected the Dolls to be their big group and not Aerosmith, but it turned out to be just the opposite. When Willie Nelson first performed there were only seven of us in the room. We brought Waylon Jennings to perform at Max's. It was his first performance in New York.

**WILLIAM THURSTON:** Waylon Jennings was playing there and I had never seen Waylon Jennings before. I didn't know what he looked like. The band was up there. There was a three-piece

**New York Dolls**
(photo by Anton Perich)

band and they were not too sure of what they were doing and then all of a sudden they started to play. Three-quarters of the way through one song this guy came running through the crowd, almost knocked me over, and ran up on the stage, and it was Waylon Jennings. He was outside, apparently getting high.

**DAVID JOHANSEN:** I wanted to have a band so we got this band together. I think Syl [Sylvain] came up with the name the Dolls and I wanted to call it the New York Dolls. We played Max's like three nights a week for a summer. I wasn't particularly friends with Lou Reed at the time because, you

rebellion

know, we were like the new kids on the block. There was this guy Sam Hood who booked Upstairs at Max's. He was the most miserable man in show business.

**CHRIS STEIN:** I was in art school. I was at the School of Visual Arts and I used to think that the Dolls were a drag act so I never went to see the Dolls. When I finally found out they were a rock band, I went to see them and Eric [Emerson] was playing with them. He opened up for them and I kind of liked him more. I got friendly with Eric and my last year at Visual Arts I got them to play at the school party.

**PHILIP GLASS, COMPOSER:** Mickey must have known my music from the concerts. I was starting to do them in the galleries and museums. The first concerts were at the Whitney and the Guggenheim, but later we did concerts at Leo Castelli's and Paula Cooper's. Mickey had his favorites. They had opened the upstairs and they were booking acts like James White and some fairly radical kumquat stuff. I always thought those James White concerts were interesting because they were so violent. James was one of those guys who liked to insult people. It was weird. He always got into fights with people. This was the beginning of those nihilistic punk groups that were around in the early seventies.

My ensemble was the first experimental group that played in a bar. I mean, now it's done all the time. But in 1972 or '73, when this happened, no one played in bars. No one played in clubs. There was still pretty much a conscious division between the experimental music which you played in lofts, and maybe museums, and then there were pop groups that played in bars and discos, but we were the first actual experimental group. Like, people would say, "Classical music?" Not really. I call it experimental music, that actually played in a bar...Now it's very common to do it. But at the time that we did it, a lot of people really thought it was very *déclassé* to do that. They thought it was very vulgar. Actually, the deal is, Mickey said, "Look, I can't pay you. You get the door." It turned out to be a decent-enough deal, because we invited all our friends to come, filling the place, and whatever the money was, it couldn't have more than three or four hundred dollars, we split with the band. Which in 1972, it wasn't bad. I mean, it was fun to do. That led to my playing in a lot of places.

**DANNY FIELDS:** I resented the music upstairs, I thought that we were the show downstairs and that we really didn't need to put in acts up there. I remember the disco. I loved the disco. I like the option of going up and dancing or totally leaving the dancing and going downstairs. It was a totally different world I thought the live performers would be an intrusion and forever change the character of the place, and it did. I was conservative in the beginning. It was like your club was being invaded by show business and they were letting in people that you didn't approve of. And they did, because paying customers were suddenly there. Anybody could pay and get in, and it was never like that before.

**ARTHUR GORSON, MUSIC MANAGER/PRODUCER:** When we first opened the upstairs at Max's, there were a lot of people coming around for payoffs. And one night the police staged some kind of event with someone with a gun in the stairway and all to kind of scare us into paying kickbacks.

**ABBIE HOFFMAN:** I saw the last show of Phil Ochs' upstairs and then I went underground after that. I was sitting in the back room with him and he was one of the few people I was telling that I was going underground. But he broke a glass in his hand while I was telling him and cut his hand, so I changed my mind. I didn't think he was the best person to know all my plans. It was beyond drunk with Phil.

**JEFFREY BRENNAN:** Patti Smith and Phil Ochs were on a double bill. It was a sing-talk-sing kind of deal. It was real sad because Phil Ochs was sort of a hero of mine. I was a folkie in the early sixties and he was pretty much into alcoholism by that point, and drinking these gigantic planter's punches in the big bell glasses, and snorting. It got worse and worse. It was the Christmas, New Year's Eve week and New Year's Eve, he was actually lying down on the stage, and just screaming about guns and bombs.

**BOB FEIDEN:** I saw Elliot Murphy, Patti Smith. She did poetry with Lenny Kaye playing bass behind her. I brought her to the attention of Clive Davis at Arista. When I went to work at Arista, I had known of Patti Smith because of seeing her all the way back then at Max's....

I saw the Velvet Underground play there and it was nice to hear music of that quality at such close quarters without a lot of volume. It had sophistication to it. It had a certain confluence of things going on that was pretty unique to the times.

**OLIVER RISH:** When I used to go to Max's and the Velvet Underground would play upstairs, they would perform the song "Heroin," and during the long instrumental part of the audience would empty out and go into the bathroom and shoot up and come back out and nod out through the rest of the set.

**JIM JACOBS:** My favorite shows were the Velvet Underground. I was in love with Nico. I had an affair with her. I had an affair with Susan Hoffman [Viva] too. Nico was a six-foot beautiful blonde with a great sultry voice, sexier than anything I'd ever seen then or since. I nearly died the first time I saw Nico. I followed her to Paris....She didn't have any money and I had money. That was how our affair began. I stayed in Paris. We had an affair for about three months. That's pretty good for Nico.

**SYLVIA MILES:** Larry Rivers did this movie called *Tits* and we had a party upstairs at Max's. That is actually where I got friendly with Lou Reed.

rebellion

the velvet underground

Lou Reed (photo by Dustin Pittman)

Sterling Morrison (photo by Dustin Pittman)

Doug Yule (photo by Dustin Pittman)

Billy Yule (photo by Dustin Pittman)

**AL GOLDSTEIN, EDITOR, *SCREW* MAGAZINE:** We had the first *Screw* anniversary party at Max's in 1969. We had it upstairs. It was jammed. The idea of a pornographic paper making it was extraordinary, so we threw a big party. We had all the hookers who advertised. All the weirdos; all the performing cocksuckers. It is the first place I could open a charge account for *Screw*. Only Mickey would do that. There was a waitress named Nancy who became famous as a cock-caster. She did Lucite copies of cocks. And we got several writers from Max's.

**TOM PUNZIO:** Tom Fields, who was the manager at the time, and I were working the service bar upstairs. They were having a party for *Screw* magazine and there was a woman and a guy serving drinks naked. So I'm behind the bar lining up the well and all of a sudden a breast popped in my face and she says, "Are you Tom?" Well, I figured that she was really looking for Tom Fields, but I was also Tom so I said, "Yes!" There she is stark naked and she replies, "So what would you like me to do?" " Ah could you, um…cut the limes for me?"

**ESTELLE LAZERUS, PUBLICIST:** The Grateful Dead were promoting an album and I was doing publicity for Jim Mahoney and they were on Warner Records. It was decided that we would have the party at Max's upstairs. The night of the party came and I had everything set up with the food and the open bar. Somebody came over to me and said, "Be careful, don't drink anything." I said, "Why?" He said that the Grateful dead spike all their drinks. I said, "But what about the new bottles?" I was panic-stricken. He said, "Well, you never know." So I wouldn't even drink the water, I was so terrified. I didn't take drugs, and I was afraid of anything connected with drugs.

**VIVA:** I went to David Amram's publishing party upstairs and Kris Kristofferson showed up, and I had made a movie with him. We got along really well, in fact, I was madly in love with him, but I was pregnant so I did not admit my attraction. I told Kris I needed money and he said, "Call my manager tomorrow," and I did. I think he sent me over some money.

**DAVID AMRAM:** I wrote an autobiography called *Vibrations* that came out in 1968, and Macmillan gave me a book party—actually there were two parties. Jane Passanon in the press depart-ment said, "I know you want to have all these diverse people and all these established people that you have worked with…and I think it would be difficult for us to get as great a variety and cross-sec-tion that you write about in one room. It might be self-defeating and frightening to some of the more conservative people. What we did, we had a party in two shifts. People who worked in radio and TV, publishing, and the arts organizations could come and have some hors d'oeuvres, and the second shift could be just a big bang-out, hang-out, bash-out, get-down good time. The way it was organized, all the people were gone from the first shift when the second shift came in. I'll never forget the look on some of the faces when they were leaving and saw some of these wild-looking people starting to show up. We had it at Max's because it was the one place that could handle such a great cross-section of

"To celebrate the third anniversary of its survival, Screw Magazine threw a huge birthday party for its friends and enemies at Max's Kansas City. More than 1600 people thronged the place to share the joyous celebration. Unexpected guests like Gore Vidal and fifty Cockettes showed up

**Unidentified woman** (photo by Anton Perich)

**Nude waitress at the _Screw_ party**
(photo by Anton Perich)

for color. A nude couple strolled around non-chalantly while the celebrities, cops, and robbers mingled in democratic revelry. All in all, the party had to be listed among the outstanding social events of the seventies."

—Screw newsletter, 1971

people. I also knew what a great host Mickey was. He usually had a calming effect on people.

It was one of the best parties I ever attended: Carlos Mosley, the manager of the New York Philharmonic, Francis Robinson from the Metropolitan Opera, both came, and really enjoyed both Max's and the party. Joseph Papp came, whom I wrote music for at the Shakespeare Festival for twelve years. Gerry Mulligan came with Sandy Dennis and stayed on for the second part and played the saxophone. Paul Desmond came, he was playing with Dave Brubeck, he stayed and jammed with us. Bob Dylan came to the first party and stayed through the second. George Plimpton came. All these people were picking up free copies of the book and browsing through it. Jay Cameron, a great sax player and friend from Paris walked in and said, "Dave, what page am I on?" There must have been two hundred musicians there that I mentioned in the book: jazz players, musicians from symphony orchestras, folk musicians, Latin musicians, Middle Eastern musicians, and American Indian musicians. It was sort of like a United Nations of different kinds of people, plus all the people I knew from Max's, Bradley's, and Caseys. It ended about three-thirty in the morning. We also had dancing where people danced to jazz, which was almost unheard of at that time.

**Cyrinda Foxe**
(photo by Leee Black Childers)

d Lettingwell (photo by Anton Perich)

Ruby Lynn Reyner (photo by Anton Perich)

Martin Mull (photo by Lily Hou)

Jane Forth (photo by Anton Perich)

**Max's facade, second incarnation** (photo by Bob Gruen)

**a**s 1974 approached, Mickey's most successful watering hole began to wear on him. The bar went up in a sea of debts. The glitter-rock crowd had taken over the nightly scene, which drove the artists away. Many of them who were now older and had gained some notoriety, were not hanging out as much. Mickey became bored with his own party. He had filled too many stomachs without filling his own pockets. This combination of factors—the fires, thefts, unpaid tabs, and drugs—contributed to Max's demise.

**ROBERT POVLICH:** Mickey came up to me one time while I'm sitting in one of the booths, and my bar bill was over $1,200. That's the equivalent of $3,600 now. Mickey says, "I'm getting a little tight on the financial end," and I say, "Oh my god, I don't know how that happened." And he said, "Let me give you a clue, you invite people to dinner, you sit down at a table with them, everyone has dinner and they give you the money for their dinner, and you keep the cash and then you sign the check." What he didn't do for people! Chamberlain's tab was over $9,000. It was a time when the art scene was going really bananas. Larry Poons was getting all kinds of money. Christensen was making money. Zox was making money. The art scene was going crazy, everyone was painting, and it was just a matter of time until you were going to make it. And what happened, different artists came on and people started folding up a little. You become accustomed to a lifestyle, and all of a sudden, it starts drifting off. That's what happened to Mickey. All of a sudden the money disappeared. Then the crowd changed, and it turned into a different scene, and that really knocked the shit out of Mickey.

**LARRY RIVERS:** Mickey let a lot of people run up bills, like $1,500. Picture what he was giving away. I didn't run up a tab—I had no reason to. Not to show off or anything like that. Maybe I did for a while, to prove that I was a regular, or loyal until the end. And I knew him so well, that I actually started to feel affectionate toward him, but he was boring, in the sense that he was so hung up in

photo-collage by LEEE BLACK CHILDERS

# Announcing!
# Max's East
# Rock Festiv

**Second incarnation at Max's** (photo collage by Leee Black Childers)

RADIO CITY
STATION

NEW YORK, NY 100
APR 7
PM
1976

PRAY
FOR
PEACE

USA 13c
PROCLAIM LIBERTY THROUGHOUT ALL THE LAND

Amanda Schuster
Island Records
1860 Broadway     Room
*New York* 10019

rebellion

his business. And if you did have any kind of intellectual discussion with him, he had very soft notions of things. But his continual loyalty gets to you finally....

I was sending out the bills. Mickey would bring home the books, two big black books that were like Bibles, that had everybody's invoices, everybody's tab, in it. And the biggest tabs were John Chamberlain's and Neil Williams'. There was an obvious exchange for art, but the exact money value was never stated. I was just trying to collect the money, but Mickey instructed me that Neil and John were not to be hassled.

**TAYLOR MEAD:** I told Mickey one of the last days of Max's, that for one thing, the people working there were robbing him blind, and it wasn't just the bills that we owed, and he said, "Taylor, I knew that, the last four years were just a party for my friends. I got bored with this place four years ago."

**FIELDING DAWSON:** Mickey got bored with everything. He couldn't stay in one place more than five minutes. What did the guy want? He was like a baby. he needed constant action. He got bored making money.

**SCOTT COHEN, WRITER:** In the final days, from late 1973 until it closed, Max's was still the in-spot, based mostly on the reputation of what it had once been. Candy Darling, Eric Emerson, Andrea Whips Feldman, Lillian Roxon were dead. Alice Cooper, Iggy Pop, and Bobby Neuwirth had moved away, and the Warhol crowd had long stopped coming; glitter and platform shoes replaced the sophisticated and cool ambience of the back room; art was replaced by glam rock; and Mickey seemed terminally bored. Max's only connection to its past were a few regulars like Danny Fields, Fran Lebowitz, Terry Ork, David Johansen and Cyrinda Foxe, Larissa, Ronnie Cutrone, René Ricard, Ritty, Taylor Mead, and, of course, John Chamberlain, Neil Williams, and Frosty Myers. When Max's ended, an entire era ended with it, and there has never been anything like it since. For a period of about a year, there was nowhere to go until Mickey became a partner at the Locale, which was something like a Rathskeller on Waverly Place, where NYU students formerly hung out.

**BETSEY JOHNSON:** By the time I got back to New York, it was like the Beatles' White Album. Everybody was going into caves. By the time I got back, Max's wasn't the same; not that Max's had changed, but the times had changed, the people had changed, the whole world had changed. It just wasn't prime time anymore. It dropped dead with a needle in its arm.

**MICKEY RUSKIN:** I never smoked a joint until 1968 except for going to a guy in 1963 who was a disciple of Leary's and doing a couple acid trips under total supervision. I had never done any drugs in my whole life, then Yvonne turned me on to smoke. I did that for a while and one night there was a fire at Max's and I was high on smoke and it took me two hours to get my head together. So after that

I was really paranoid when I smoked. I didn't start doing cocaine until about 1972, '73. So anybody that says it was my doing drugs that put me out of business is ridiculous, because as much as I might have spent in the last year of Max's, it was seven years before that I spent $5,000 just taking my softball team to California. The drugs were actually more of a symptom of the fact that I was just tired of the place and should have gotten out. I sold the place. This guy Soviero was supposed to take over and pay me $10,000 cash plus $500 a week for many years. After about three months I stopped getting the weekly checks, and within another three months I took Max's back. When I arrived, Con Edison was taking out the meter. There was actually money in the tax account which I could have pulled, probably to meet the bill and figure out how to pay the taxes later. People by this point had also started drifting away. When I left, the gross had been about $20,000 a week, by the time I came back which was only like three or four months later, it was already under $15,000. He turned everybody off. He had no concept whatsoever.

**ANDREW WYLIE, LITERARY AGENT:** I was beaten up by the Hell's Angels upstairs. At one point after Mickey left Max's and Don Soviero took over, he brought in the Angels to create disipline for about four nights. The first night I went up there to check it out, and I got hit with brass knuckles right between the eyes. I still got a scar.

**SHAYNE HARRIS:** When Mickey finally closed Max's, we had called a friend and said we were going to Max's. My friend said, "No, it's closed." I said, "What do you mean, it's closed?" We got in our car and we drove down there and the windows were already soaped up. My wife Debbie and I sat in front of the place and cried. It was the end of an era.

**KERRY RIORDAN:** When Max's closed, Laurel Delp and I were sitting there and we were looking outside and we were devastated, and she looked at me and said, "Our sex life is over." Essentially, that was true. You went in and you slept with everybody.

There was no big party for Max's when it closed. It was a very sad closing. Mickey was trying to turn it over to somebody; he was basically going to sell it to somebody slowly, but while it was still in Mickey's name, the guy he was selling to had run up lot and lots of bills. And Mickey came back in and decided he was going to give it one last go, but he really had no interest at that point. Joe Bird, who was the bartender from the very beginning until the very end, got a whole crew together and they came back in—for Mickey—to give it one more stab. Then he got a letter from Con Edison that said they were going to turn off the electricity. Mickey walked out and never walked back in again. Mickey declared bankruptcy, and Tommy Dean, who was a restaurateur from New Jersey, got wind that there was this empty space just sitting there. He reopened it as Max's Kansas City and ushered in the era of punk.

**David Johansen and David Bowie**
(photo by Bob Gruen)

In late 1975, Max's started living its second incarnation under the ownership of Tommy Dean. A new generation of young people were passing among the ghosts of the 60s as they came to hear bands like Blondie, Talking Heads, Television, Lance Loud's Mumps, the Dead Boys, and the Ramones. Along with CBGB, Max's became one of the premiere venues for punk music. Some of the new patrons knew what had gone on inside those walls; others were oblivious to its past, but many of the new musicians had been hanging out at Max's for years, soaking up the influences of the New York Dolls, the Velvet Underground, and Iggy and the Stooges. Tommy Dean's Max's lasted six years and closed in 1981.

**LEEE BLACK CHILDERS:** I went back when Tommy Dean reopened Max's after Mickey closed it down....He got a lot of people down there including me to tell him what the old Max's was like. His original idea was to reopen exactly as it had been. He never understood why no one went in the back room when he ran it. He just couldn't figure it out. It was a real Long Island concept as to how to do a bar. Mickey's idea was to set up something comfortable for himself and his friends. Tommy saw it strictly as a money-making enterprise. There was no way of telling him what made us all go back there. He used to tell us he'd pay us if we'd sit back there so other people would go back and join us. He did not have the personality or charisma.

So Max's was reopening up as this really tacky place with stained glass hanging over the bar, just really awful. And no one really thought anything. Max's had been Max's and we'd been brilliant and we'd all fashioned our lifestyles from being there and then it closed—that's the way life is. You get divorced. You lose or win a war. It was over....Inside it was like Thank God It's Friday's....It was bartenders and waitresses in little white shirts and bow ties, that kind of look.

I think it was Peter Crowley who walked in and just said, "Oh my god, this place stinks and I can make you a lot of money." And he certainly did. He said, "Get rid of the stained glass, get rid of the waitresses and the bow ties, and let's do rock and roll here." And to Tommy Dean's credit he said, okay.

**JIM LALUMIA:** Peter Crowley at that time came on board as the music booker. He basically came

high on

on board as Wayne County's manager, and since Wayne was the DJ and was an attraction at Max's, Crowley became insinuated and sold himself to the Deans, who I think really didn't know the music at that point. He came on board and did the actual bookings and we formed a kind of alliance at that period of time. This was when a tradition did continue—whether it was KISS, or Queen, or Paul McCartney, or whomever had played Madison Square Garden a few hours earlier, would then pop in and make the rounds to be seen at Max's during that period of time. I think a lot of that again was based on the mythology of the first administration. So they were running on fumes at that time, on all the mythology that had gone down from the Ruskin era, still carried over. Because McCartney, or Queen, probably didn't really stay on top of who was in charge of Max's at that period of time. It was just that the mythos had been set in place about Max's and that this was the place to go. This was the place to be seen, this was where all the cutting-edge activity, mixing and mingling, was going on.

**LEGS MCNEIL:** I was about sixteen years old. I had gone to Max's when I first heard about it, but when I went there it was during the day. We didn't have any money and I couldn't hang out. We weren't hip at all. We didn't know anything. We weren't hip. So, I didn't go back until punk started happening.

**CHRIS STEIN, GUITARIST FOR BLONDIE:** We started seeing things around that said, "Punk is coming," and we all thought it was a band with a bad name but it turned out to be the magazine. That's when I met Legs.

**JIM LALUMIA:** Around 1975, I think Punk magazine came into existence, and I think in the very first issue, they ran an editorial that was maybe two paragraphs long called "Death to Disco Shit," because disco at that time had become the predominant pop music on the scene. Disco had evolved out of being an underground gay, black, Latino city thing into mainstream Top 40, dominating and sweeping everything in its path. I saw that issue of Punk magazine, I loved it and I especially loved the "Death to Disco Shit" editorial. Of and by itself, it was never mentioned again. This Death to Disco thing stuck in my head because I had already developed relationships as a writer with WABC-AM, which was the huge Top 40 superpower at that time and I was constantly campaigning on behalf of

**Richard Hell** (photo by Stephanie Chernikowski)

rebellion

Debbie Harry's records, the Ramones, Television's records, to try to get them played, and I was running into a brick wall. There was no room. Radio put up a complete wall, did not want to know about this New York rock scene that Lisa Robinson wrote about coming out of Max's Kansas City and CBGB's. So this Death to Disco thing stuck in my head and I went into the button and bumper-sticker business and I started marketing Death to Disco buttons and Death to Disco bumper stickers, started selling them at Max's with a little copyright logo underneath, even though I didn't really copyright, so I just figured that by using it I would go on record as the Death to Disco guy. And I did, and it became a little rage.

**LEEE BLACK CHILDERS:** In the Mickey Ruskin days, there were certainly bands upstairs— Alice Cooper, Iggy, and Lou Reed. But there was still downstairs, which you almost had to carry yourself away from to see the Velvet Underground....Holly Woodlawn said, "We didn't care about anything, we just wanted to get high and get laid." And she was totally right. So when the new Max's came along, it was just another opportunity to get high and get laid.

**ELDA BRANCH:** We were one of the first bands to bring an audience to CBGB's. I think we played Max's once when Mickey owned it. That was right before the changeover. You were able to sense that there were some problems going on at Max's. It kind of got really cold for a while and one night I was in the back room and Terry Ork said, "Hey guess what: I'm managing a band, Television, they're really cool and they're playing down at this club called CBGB's and Patti Smith is reading poetry down there." I knew Patti because I had been in a play with her, Jackie Curtis's Femme Fatale back in in 1969, when I got pregnant. I booked the Stilettoes to open with Television and we brought the crowd into the place. And the only reason we brought the crowd is because I knew so many thousands of people from being at Max's....

When the old Max's closed down, Eric freaked out. He destroyed the loft he was living in over it. He was so upset that Max's closed down, it was like his life had ended. Then he died in '75. By 1979, every musician in the band was a junkie except for me. Except for Tish and Snookie—they weren't in my band but they used to perform with me from the Sick Fucks and they were fabulous. They had Manic Panic. You didn't really hang out at Max's anymore in the second incarnation, you went to see bands.

**LEEE BLACK CHILDERS:** But suddenly we were just swept along. The place was packed. To quote Jayne County: "The place was packed and the groupies were all lined up." It was just like suddenly it was crazy and everyone was dressed up and everyone was there every single night. Tommy Dean, bless his heart, he certainly didn't know what was going on around him. He didn't know how to handle it. Thank goodness for Laura, his wife, she just stood there at the door taking the money in.

**ANTONIO DE PORTEGO, SINGER:** I saw Walter Steding by himself with a drummer and a bass player and I thought, These people are so out there, I want to be in that band. They need a singer like me who can sing so high. A week later I was in the Tomato Bar and I sat next to this guy and we started talking and I was talking about the show I was telling him about this band I saw and the guy started laughing and it turned out he was the drummer with the band, Lenny Ferrari. He said, "Come join our table." A week later I ran into Walter in the elevator and he mentioned they were playing at Max's. He told me to dress funky, and when I got there he invited me onstage to perform with them. That was my debut onstage in New York. Then I performed a lot with Blondie because Debbie and Chris Stein would come and guest-star with us. I performed many times at Max's also with the Contortions.

**JIM LALUMIA:** The biggest mainstream type of action that happened there later on were acts that grew out of the Max's scenario that then when on to mainstream album success: Patti Smith, Iggy Pop, Television. At that point I think Peter Crowley was closely guarding who got in and who didn't. What had come to exist at this point in '75, '76, there was Max's and there was CBGB's. Max's represented the more sophisticated, more knowing—in my mind anyway. CBGB's was more of the nuts and bolts and those who hung on to more of the status quo. And after a while the bands started bouncing back and forth between the two.

**LEGS McNEIL:** I usually went to CBGB's every night and I went to Max's if somebody was playing. I think in my poor-white-trash mind I thought Max's was a bit more upscale and out of my league. So at CBGB's you could always get someone to buy you a beer. I knew more people. And Max's still had that leftover kind of glitter, junkie crowd. So junkies weren't going to buy you beers. There were probably as many junkies at CBGB's as there were at Max's. But somehow I always associated Max's as more of a junkie scene and CBGB's as being more of a whiskey scene....I'm sure for the artists, the rock-and-rollers did ruin the scene at Max's. Later, when artists started coming to CBGB's, it ruined it for me. That whole No Wave. Those really bad bands. The music wasn't as good. When you've got the Heartbreakers onstage playing with Richard Hell and Johnny Thunders and Dee Dee and the Ramones, I mean, that's great fuckin' music. That's great rock and roll. Then it became noise, then it became hardcore. There was about two years where the music was just brilliant.

**ELDA BRANCH:** The Stilettoes had separated from Debbie and I was doing a solo thing and then Eric died in 1975. I was devastated by that. When I got back on the stage, the world was a different place. I was certainly angry enough to fit into that punk scene. I was really pissed. That was the last thing that should have happened. Now Tommy owned the club and Peter Crowley was booking it. I had Cheetah Chrome in my band. In those days Sid Vicious used to come and see me. I watched Johnny Thunders die before my eyes practically. I remember he locked himself in the bathroom on the dressing room floor. We couldn't get him out for three hours. He was gonzo.

**CHRIS STEIN:** I remember seeing Devo there. The first time they were in New York was at Max's. They were so influential to everything. They lost it. They got shuffled around and fucked

rebellion

253

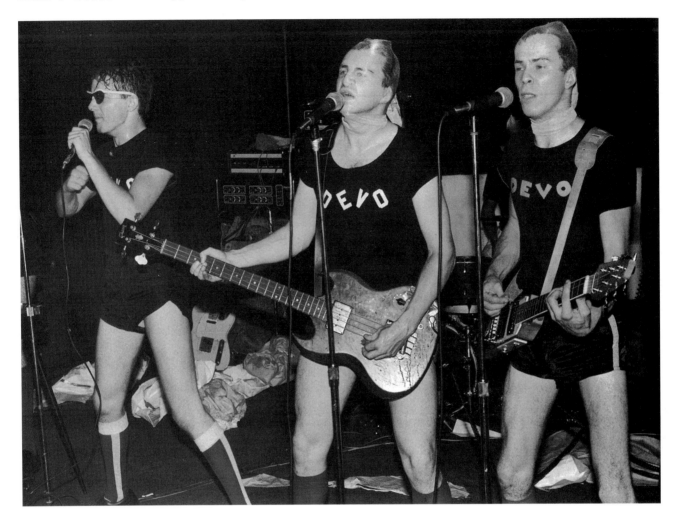

**Devo** (photo by Ebet Roberts)

over dramatically....I remember Richard Hell's last show with the Heartbreakers.

**LEGS MCNEIL:** The Ramones were my favorite group that performed at Max's. I remember probably the first year the Ramones were going and we took Lester Bangs to see them. And it was the first time Lester had seen them. Lester was really a drag that night. We were all excited about taking Lester and we got there and it was like, "Oh, I don't want to go." Lester was really a drag. I said, "Come on, we're going to see the Ramones." We were all excited and wanted to have fun and get drunk and pick up girls and that's when we discovered that Lester was not like his writing.

**DEE DEE RAMONE:** I used to go back and forth between CBGB's and Max's. Wherever they would take me. That's just the truth. I'm greedy. That's just the way it goes.

high on

David Johansen, left, and Dee Dee Ramone outside of Max's (photo by Anton Perich)

**MARIA DEL GRECO, WAITRESS:** I remember the second Max's was a little rougher and harder…more raunchy.

I didn't know what I wanted to do with my life at that time. I started waitressing at Max's. Dinner was slow but you had your regulars. Weekends were packed with young kids, Hell's Angels, kids from the boroughs, everybody…people nodding out at the tables. A lot of drugs—mostly pills, Quaaludes—more downs than ups….It started with the junk but not as much. There was a lot of shooting dope. The Sex Pistols came a lot. Patti Smith was there all the time.

**JIM LALUMIA:** I was mostly upstairs seeing bands. Originally it wasn't really punk, in what I would call the guttersnipe period. I call it guttersnipe. I don't know why. I call that period prior to the

*rebellion*

Lance Loud and friend (photo by Anton Perich)

Johnny Thunders (photo by Anton Perich)

Sex Pistols exploding in London, which is where the terminology for "punk" really first entered the vocabulary, because when the Ramones were first playing and everything, there was the New York rock scene and this is evidenced by any old issues of Lisa Robinson's Rock Scene magazine.

**MARIA DEL GRECO:** They still had a lunch hour and a cocktail hour, plus they still had the chick peas. The kids that worked in the neighborhood that wanted to hang out started drifting in, and by nighttime you had all the musicians. I remember Squeeze there when they couldn't afford a cup of coffee and I used to sneak it to them. The Damned, of course, Robert Gordon, the Cramps. It was really important to me. Tommy did give some credit to certain people. I stopped going there after 1980. It started getting worse and worse and there wasn't a scene going on anymore, the bands weren't any good and the pinball machines started coming in. It went from Quaaludes to junk....

When I first met Wayne he was Wayne, and for the show he would dress up and wear the lampshade and it was a great entertaining show. And he would spin

**Cheetah Chrome, left, and Mary Anne Christiano**
(photo courtesy of Mary Anne Christiano)

records on a Tuesday, Wednesday night, and he would come in as Wayne then, without the wig. He'd wear a T-shirt and fatigues....He was soft-spoken and he did his shows on weekends. Then he went away to England and had decided that he wanted to become a she. He came back and he came to my place, he wanted to do a different kind of set like Edith Piaf, the French singer. He wanted a little black dress and they wrote us up in the New York Rocker. Supposedly at that point he was going to have a sex change. She had gotten the breasts, but not the sex change.

There had been a friendly rivalry between Max's and CB's for a number of years. Wayne County symbolized Max's to a lot of people. There was also a gender phobia rising, including in the pages of Punk magazine, that was not very positive toward this gender thing. There was a band called the Dictators, all about White Castles, girls, and fast cars. And they came to be championed by a lot of people including the guys at Punk. They were signed to Epic with their first album. They sold about five thousand copies nationwide and were dropped. And the lead singer Dick Manitoba started hanging out at CBGB's drunk all the time. When the Talking Heads played he harangued Tina Weymouth: "Ah, you're an ugly little dyke!" When the Heartbreakers played he was screaming at Johnny Thunders, "You sucked with the New York Dolls and you still suck." He was taking out his hos-

**Johnny Thunders**
(photo by Ebet Roberts)

tility on the world. Then one night Wayne County played.

**LEGS MCNEIL:** When Wayne County hit Handsome Dick Manitoba over the head with the microphone at CBGB's there was a big division in New York punk between gay and...I don't even know what it was—heterosexual and gay—and Max's championed Wayne County and CBGB's championed Handsome Dick Manitoba. So I guess the Dictators, of course, were blacklisted from Max's and Peter Crowley blamed Punk magazine, all us heterosexual guys. So there was a real split. It was real messy and ugly. I don't think Handsome Dick was gay-bashing Wayne, I just think he was being an obnoxious prick like we all were. I think Wayne overreacted. I think it became this big heterosexual versus homosexual controversy, when it really wasn't about that at all. So people were blacklisted. There was a benefit at Max's so all the people who played the benefit—you know—there were battle lines drawn. And you weren't supposed to go to Max's because it was a big mess.

**LEEE BLACK CHILDERS:** In the front, sitting at the tables because they'd heard that Max's Kansas City was the coolest place to go, were kids. They were kids from New Jersey. And suddenly Jayne is walking across their tables in high heels, fishnet hose, and three wigs all pinned together. And she's not just walking across their tables and turning their drinks over, she's turning their tables over in their laps. Turning their chairs over, hitting them, smacking them, and they didn't know what to do. They had never been involved in a situation like that. Suddenly there's this big drag queen just standing on their tables and rocking them and they think its part of the show, when—*BANG!*—the whole table goes over. And they didn't know how to deal with that. Were they supposed to hit her? The Cramps did the same thing. Levi and the Rockats did that too....

When Jayne was charged with assault, every single band played at the benefit to make money to pay her legal fees, which didn't in the end need to be paid because all charges were dropped. But Blondie, Robert Gordon, Divine, and everybody rallied to her defense because—and even Dick Manitoba would probably tell you this nowadays—if you're onstage, you're a target, so if you defend yourself, you're defending yourself, that's what it comes down to. And Jayne may be wearing negligees

high on

but she can pack a wallop. She wasn't gonna be maligned. She wasn't gonna be treated badly.

As far as Max's was concerned, Jayne was the DJ, and Tommy Dean wasn't going to fire or even lay her off because she had a fight at CBGB's. Tommy Dean and Hilly Kristal [owner of CBGB'S] had a very good understanding that they actually supported each other....Everybody played both of them. Although the fight had taken place at CBGB's, Tommy couldn't fire Jayne even though she was wanted by the police. She got a black wig and a black wig moustache and she continued to be the DJ as this kind of Mexican-looking person.

**MARIA DEL GRECO:** I was working on a Friday night and it used to get really busy and really crazy. This was downstairs, I was waitressing, and I remember there were these biker guys who kept ordering bottles of champagne and steak and they were really running up a bill, so I was trying to keep my eyes on them because I was afraid they might walk out. Meanwhile these kids from Long Island walked out on me and I ran to the front and I said to the cashier, "I just had a walkout." I went after one of the guys and grabbed him by his shirt and pulled him away from the crowd and the bouncer came over and harassed him. About a half hour later there were all these people at the bar and one of the kids from that group took a brick and threw it through the window. Luckily no one got hurt but Warhol had signed that window. I felt it was one of the last replicas left from the old scene so I always felt bad about it.

**JUDY STRANG, BASS PLAYER FOR PULSALLAMA:** One night there was a band called Red Transistor....I met this guy and he said he had been asked that night to play in this band called Red Transistor as a drummer. He had never met these people before, but they needed him to play that night. I was upstairs in the dressing room and the the leader of this band played several instruments, that at the end of each song he actually graduated from having an ax—not a guitar, something you chop wood with—to chopping keyboards and the guitars with this ax, pieces were flying in the audience. It was actually terrifying. Later on the drummer who was playing with them that night told me that everybody in the band was on LSD.

**STEVE KLEIN, ARTIST:** James Chance was up on the stage doing his thing and he was just spitting and spurting and there was one of the Jersey guys or whoever in the audience and some saliva got on him and it turned into a brawl. He dragged James Chance offstage. He beat him up. [James Chance] got back up onstage bleeding and continued the show.

**CHRIS STEIN:** All those instances of violence were few and far between. If you put them all together it looks like the whole scene was very violent but it wasn't. I remember when Jerry Nolan was sitting down in the foyer and the whole thing was covered with blood. My memory is that he was rolling around with some guy on the floor wrestling and he rolled on broken glass and got his femoral artery cut. Legs said he was stabbed. Those are the memories that stand out.

rebellion

**Tish and Snookie in the Sick Fucks** (photo by Mike Leben, courtesy of Tish and Snookie)

**TISH AND SNOOKIE, OWNERS OF MANIC PANIC:** We used to play at Max's. We were Blondie's backup singers....The bill was always the same—it was Television, Talking Heads, and Blondie....We didn't sing with Blondie anymore when we opened our store. We opened the store in '77. We were still playing at Max's, but we were playing with the Sick Fucks, a punk band.

**SNOOKIE:** Laura Dean loved my boyfriend, Robert Gordon. When he played she'd bring her panties and throw them at him. I think I actually met Robert when he opened for us when we were performing with Blondie. He was starting with this band Tuff Darts, right before he had his own band, he was in this pseudo punk band....

Patti Smith came into our store when she first started getting famous and gave us this big pile of badges and xeroxes of her poetry and signed them and told us we could sell them to help pay our rent.

**TISH:** When we moved into our store, in 1977, it wasn't a shopping area. It was a burnt-out druggie-hippie dead area, and we opened the first punk boutique in America and made it into this wonderful shopping area. By the time we left it was starting to get creepy because people were selling all the knockoff stuff on the street.

**LEGS MCNEIL:** Blondie really sucked in the beginning. They were considered the worst band on the scene. But they were so nice. Chris and Debbie were great. Then they got better and better. That's what was nice about that time. You watched people actually evolve.

**LEEE BLACK CHILDERS:** Peter Crowley got a crowd no matter who he booked. He filled the place no matter what, and to his great credit, he booked people I didn't even know were alive or I didn't even know were legendary. He booked a whole weekend of Victoria Spivey, who was from the 1920s, one of the great blues singers. She couldn't get work. Where was she gonna work? Nowhere. He booked her in Max's Kansas City and the place was packed. And they cheered her. He also had Edith Massey there.

People like Pere Ubu would have gone nowhere if Peter Crowley hadn't said, "Pack your bags, come to New York, I'll book you. You're totally unlistenable, you're totally weird, you're totally unattractive physically. I'll make you a star." And he did. Even with the Cramps. They were all monumentally so unattractive; their music was discordant in the extreme, but Peter Crowley saw something and I don't even know what he saw—he could see something in these people....Lux Interior had this pudding-

**Debbie Harry in Blondie** (photo by Ebet Roberts)

# Punk Rock: Contortions, a Quin

THE CONTORTIONS, who were at Max's Kansas City last weekend, count as one of the leaders of what is being called the New York "no wave" school of progressive punk rock. Whether that's apt is open to question — categories of this sort are like slogans, and about as appropriate. But the Contortions are interesting for a couple of reasons, not all of them positive.

The quintet's music is ab...
disjunct, cha...

ing of the others, the band's leader. His singing is mostly of the frenzied howl variety, but effective as such. What causes problems is his stage act.

Mr. Chance espouses overt hostility in performance (perhaps he's *genuinely* hostile in "real" life; if so, so much the worse for him). This hostility expresses itself in stage me...
combine Mick...

lishing a certain
it has helped win
a following amo
Mr. Chance's p
treme and limit
imagine the Cont
evolve from here

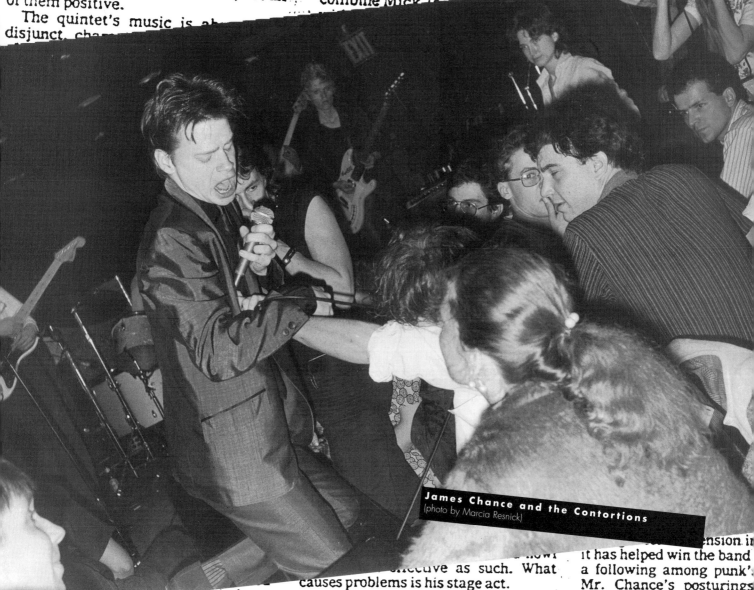

**James Chance and the Contortions**
(photo by Marcia Resnick)

...school of pro-
...ressive punk rock. Whether that's apt is open to question — categories of this sort are like slogans, and about as appropriate. But the Contortions are in-

...howl
...ective as such. What causes problems is his stage act.

Mr. Chance espouses overt hostility in performance (perhaps he's *genuinely* hostile in "real" life; if so, so much the worse for him). This hostility expresses itself in stage moves that

...ension in
it has helped win the band
a following among punk'
Mr. Chance's posturings
treme and limiting that
imagine the Contortions w
evolve from here.

bowl haircut and skin that looked like a "before" ad. Ivy looked awful. I just stood there and thought, "What is supposed to be going on here?" And it didn't take long until something was going on. Suddenly they were great, and Peter Crowley gets a lot of the credit for that. He brought them out of Ohio, He got them on the stage in New York. He made sure they could eat, pay the rent, and function until they found out who they were. He did that with a lot of bands and that's one of the important things the second Max's did.

There were other bands. There was one performer called Honey Davis. He was so beautiful. Maybe that was his downfall, he was so pretty before he got onstage that all anyone wanted to do was fuck him.

**GLENN O'BRIEN:** The first time I ever saw the B-52's was at Max's. It was their first gig ever in New York. There was a very brilliant kind of semi–drag queen that was hanging around who went by the name of Sylvia, whose real name was Jerry Aries. He was friends with all of those kids from Georgia. He wrote me a letter saying, "You have to go check out my friends." I thought they were incredible and we became friends immediately.

**JUDY STRANG:** I started going to to Max's around 1977 and the first band I ever saw at Max's was the Ramones. These girls were jumping across the table and it was the loudest music I had ever heard in my life. At the time I was married to someone in the Fleshtones, Keith Strang, the guitarist and co-leader. All of us were from Queens. As a result of that we were all playing Max's and CBGB's and the Mudd Club. I was playing in a band called the Cosmopolitans, and eventually I was the bass player for Pulsallama, We were on Y Records. It was an all-girl percussion band. There were seven girls. There was this DJ in L.A. who had this disease called Tourette's syndrome and we had this record that was called "The Devil Lives In My Husband's Body" about a woman whose husband had Tourette's syndrome. It was one of the first videos on MTV. I think that the punk scene started as an anti–big rock star kind of a thing. When the B-52's came to town, one of the first places they played was Max's.

It was the most fun, unusual, artsy, free-form, exciting time that I can remember. Every kid's dream is to get up and play onstage, and in the seventies you could get up and be playing in bands though you could barely play.

**JIM LALUMIA:** There were three bands that drew me to Max's as a fan, as a journalist, and later as a fellow performer and band person, and those were the core Max's bands in my mind. The ones who could still headline on a weekend and pack the rafters no matter what, and that was Wayne County, Cherry Vanilla, and Johnny Thunders....Patti Smith had found a welcome home at Arista, Blondie found a home at Chrysalis. Cherry went over to England along with Wayne and Thunders and they were very well received. In fact Cherry's band at that time included the Police's Sting and Stewart Copeland. Cherry landed in England with her boyfriend Louie who played guitar, and Zecka

**Max's Kansas City, fall 1977**

**B52s** (photo by George DuBose)

**Lydia Lunch** (photo by George DuBose)

"I saw Lydia Lunch
fronting the band
'Teenage Jesus and
The jerks' opening
up for the B52s'
NYC debut. Loved the
Bs, hated 'Teenage
Jesus.' Photographed
both of their first
album covers."

—George DuBose

Chris Spedding (photo by George DuBose)

Patti Smith (photo by Ebet Roberts)

Tom Verlaine and Patti Smith
(photo by Anton Perich)

the keyboard player. The Copeland brothers were managing a band called the Police who were very mainstream and really didn't fit into punk, they were looking for a way to get in. Vanilla was signed to RCA England, and the Copeland brothers said, "We'll cut you a deal. If you allow the Police to open for your RCA-supported tour, we'll supply you with a bass player and a drummer." The bass player was Sting and the drummer was Stewart Copeland.

Cherry had foolishly signed with RCA in England, the label that also had David Bowie. Cherry had alienated the RCA people because of representing Bowie, so when it came time for her record to be issued in America on RCA they said, "We don't even want to hear her name." She had worked for MainMan as Bowie's press lady. So Tony Defries would send Cherry into RCA making demands for Bowie. The reason Defries took all the Max's people and made them MainMan staff is because he knew record-label guys were used to dealing with other record-label guys when they were negotiating. But when you had Leee and Cherry stumbling into the RCA offices, they never knew what hit them or how to deal with them. Leee was the vice president of MainMan. Leee became the resident photographer at Max's. He was living with Wayne. They were roommates. Because of his past experience dealing with Iggy, Lou Reed, and Mott the Hoople, he became the manager for Johnny Thunders and the Heartbreakers. He took out a full-page ad in the Voice for a weekend headliner that they did at Max's, and it's still not paid for. This was the ad that was supposed to get them a deal.

**CHRIS STEIN:** Johnny Thunders was a real creative entity no matter how screwed up he was. He was a major influence on so many people. Stylewise, he influenced me. Most of my playing I just copied from people. I learned all the solos from the first couple Stones records.

**LEEE BLACK CHILDERS:** The line which was printed in the Village Voice was, "See them now before they die." And it became the thing. The place was packed, thinking it would be the last Heartbreakers show. Well, the Heartbreakers took it to heart. And every show was the last Heartbreakers show. They went crazy. They went over the top. They were junkies, everyone knew they were junkies. And they didn't know that complete legendary status was still waiting for them. They were just a band at Max's Kansas City. They didn't know that they were gonna be on the road with the Sex Pistols and it was gonna get completely nuts....They were gorgeous, they were young, and if the audience was packed to the rafters waiting to see their very last show, well, then, they were going to give them a very last show. And they did it. Every time.

**KENT CARTER, ROCK MUSICIAN:** The bands that I would be either performing with or going to check out included, Gina Harlow and the Cutthroats, the Spaces, Sorcerer, Blowgun, Pookie and the 70th Precinct, ReMod, as well as some fun audience time with James Chance stage-diving and the weekly adventures of the Heartbreakers—would Johnny find his way to the stage? These episodes were usually answered after a quick trip to the ladies' room located on the stately second floor next to the bar. You see, the men's room didn't have a stall, so most of the bands would do the drugs in the ladies' room. Johnny Thunders was not exactly the stoned-out junkie that his reputation foretells. He would arrive early, usually while it was still a bit light outside, for what would amount to a *Killer* soundcheck where everything went really smoothly and well. It was just when stage-time was approaching that a kind a stage fright or something would take hold and the chemicals would kick in at the same time and he would find himself lying on his back onstage looking up during most of the set. As a favor, the band members would unplug his guitar, yet he wouldn't know the difference throughout the set....

Neon Leon was also there many nights in his high heels looking around seven feet tall. I caught up with him at a club one late night on Forty-second Street, where we exchanged amusing stories that we liked concerning the infamous third-floor dressing area at Max's, where anything would happen. Neon always had a rule to never get the ice from the ice machine on the third floor because many times he caught most of the Dead Boys pissing in it after throwing back close to a keg of beer. It was a long walk down the stairs and you had to be in the crowd to use the restroom, so why bother?

I told him of a tale that was spread around the upstairs room for many years which still visually horrifies me when I think of it. Some girl got terribly twisted on Quaaludes (yes, at the time they still made those) and was wearing close to nothing—I think perhaps it may

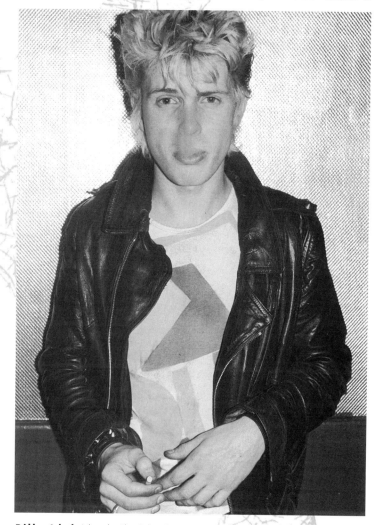

**Billy Idol** (photo by Ebet Roberts)

have been one of those little string bikinis. Well, one of the band members got kind of scared that it was the big H that she was doing, so to try and revive her—he thought that she shouldn't be sweating and may have had some sort of "jungle fever," so to try and bring down the fever he put the sleeping princess inside the ice machine to help. Shades of Norman Bates, can you just picture that girl waking up after a blackout and finding herself in a pitch-black box with freezing cold ice cubes coming down on her near-naked body? Ohhhh, I'm glad I was somewhere else that night....

Doing songs about washing your dogs and drying them in the microwave were not only sly and amusing at the time, but quite fashionable to everyone there. The point of shock value was expect-

rebellion

**Backstage with Johnny Thunders, Wayne County, Cherry Vanilla, and Jim Lalumia**
(photo courtesy of Jim Lalumia)

ed there—I mean, did you really expect to get major radio play and sell truckloads of records with songs like "Fifi Goes Pop"?

I would always have more fun playing those Gina Harlow and the Cutthroats shows. You see, Gina was what I would like to call one of those "movie stars" (you know the type, spend a quarter) as well as a dancer, and would make it a point of inviting all of her "movie-star friends" to the second show each night (yes, we would play two sets). She would then take off most of her clothes during the show. That was expected.

**LYNN EDELSON**: One night I was at the bar at Max's and Cheetah Chrome and Gyda were having this huge fight. A knockout, screaming, throwing-each-other-around-the-place fight. They were both incredibly drunk. They hit one of the wall photos and the thing cracked and there was glass everywhere. Because I had gotten so conditioned to this dysfunctional behavior, I remember this

high on

changed my life in the worst direction possible. I was thinking, Wow, I wish I knew someone who liked me that much.

**Sid Vicious and Nancy**
(photo by Stephanie Chernikowski)

**ELDA BRANCH:** By 1979, I formed a band with my son called the Brattles. Tommy Dean let them play at Max's to help them get experience. They were eight to twelve years old. They were the youngest rock band to play their own instruments. Inside of a year they opened for the Clash. Syl Sylvain used to come down and help them with the guitars.

**JIM LALUMIA:** Max's started becoming dependent on the bridge-and-tunnel people. What I

rebellion

269

viewed as the campaign to obliterate the memory of Max's, had succeeded on several levels. The press was merciless after the big Wayne-Manitoba thing and were totally dismissive of Max's. First administration and second administration all blurred into one. The bottom line was as though Max's never happened, which was an insult to the memory of the first administration as well as the second. They succeeded for quite a long time. I remember doing an interview with Joey Ramone when he said, "Oh, we only played Max's once or twice," when I remember seeing them a lot more.

**ALICE COOPER:** Max's Kansas City is gone now. It's good and it's a shame. After Mickey bailed out and Tommy Dean took over in its second reincarnation, it turned into a depressing glitter-groupie hangout filled with everybody who had carfare from Brooklyn. But years ago, in the late sixties and early seventies, it was a haven of decadence of the unreal, Theater of the Absurd becoming Life of the Absurd at the time the infamous back room at Max's was restricted: "Freaks Only." Mickey Ruskin, who owned Max's, didn't care if the place was empty. If you weren't hip enough to belong there you had to sit upstairs with the tourists. It was the Algonquin of its day. This was a topsy-turvy world where drag queens and leather boys were held in esteem. There was no other single place that you could be accepted—even lauded—for being different. To the people in Max's, being different was a creative effort in itself.

**PATTI SMITH, POET/ROCK MUSICIAN (QUOTE FROM *THE INDEPENDENT*):** When I saw the deli that took over the space that was once Max's Kansas City, I stood there and cried. Even now, when I shut my eyes and see that red table and Mickey rushing back and forth, it gives me a certain pang.

**LEEE BLACK CHILDERS:** It was a bar. All bars are made to make you feel welcome. It's been in a million movies, it's been in a million plays before that. Greta Garbo saying, "Gimme a viskey and don't be stingy, baby." A bar is where you…can sit down if you've got the price of a drink— and you're okay. Well, that's all either Max's was. A bar. The fact that it's gone down in history as legendary, neither owner intended and neither owner even encouraged. It was a bar. You'd go in there, you'd sit down, you knew you were welcome. You might sit next to David Johansen; you might sit next to Patti Smith; you might sit next to Nancy Spungen, and she would be talking to you very frankly, like people do in bars all up and down Third Avenue. That's what happens in bars. People talk to each other very frankly. The big difference in both Max's was all the people who went on to become famous. So the fact that Nancy Spungen was a junkie with track marks all up and down her arms and bleached blonde hair with roots and was talking with me about "Oh, Jerry Nolan won't fuck me, what's his problem?" while drool was coming out of her mouth and she was sloshing her drink off on the bar…visually, she wasn't any different from any other junkie prostitute all up and down Third Avenue, except she went on to become one of the most famous murder victims of history. That's it. I solved it. That's what made Max's famous.

**KENT CARTER:** I found myself coming back to the Union Square location years later, working in the office building right next door to where Max's first started. I couldn't care less about the job then, but always had a great time at lunch where, I would announce every day when I was leaving for lunch that "I'm going to Max's for lunch." Many at the workplace did question what I was talking about and I had to explain that the deli where they stopped each morning for coffee and donuts originally was a haven for most of the art-deco crowd in New York City. I didn't bother telling them that the second floor where I religiously ate each day next to a big gold-and-orange fish was the site of many performances and that I might have wished to feel the magic and the ghosts of the room swirl around me as I ate lunch. I would almost wish that I were in a kind of Twilight Zone adventure where I would close my eyes and all of the sudden be at the club again as it was *before* the deli took over. My mind just fogged at lunch hour and I would constantly run scenarios through my mind of how easy it would be to reopen that stairwell and forgive and forget....

Shortly after Mickey closed Max's he became acquainted with Richard Sanders, who had a restaurant on Waverly Place. The restaurant was not doing that well and Mickey had a huge following, and could not open a place in his own name for a few years since he declared Chapter 11. He had the steam and Richard had the place, and that's how it started. A year or two down the line, Mickey got antsy to branch out again on his own and the Ocean Club on Chambers was born. The Ocean Club was fabulously laid-out; Frosty designed the lighting. And once again some of the top new acts like Television, the Talking Head, the B-52's, and Patti Smith were featured there, but the location on Chambers Street was just a little bit ahead of its time. There wasn't much going on down in that neighborhood.

**HOWARD SMITH:** Mickey called me—very rare for him to do it—and he said, "You know I've been on my ass and I'm now going in as a partner with Richard Sanders at the Locale. Could you put something in the column that would let everybody know very quickly that this is where the hangout is?" It was so rare for Mickey to ask a favor.

**NATHAN JOSEPH, ARTIST:** My relationship with Mickey really didn't get close until the Locale. I split with my wife, and he knew I was upset about it and all of a sudden I was drinking, and one day Mickey comes over to me and says, "How would you like to work for me?" I never worked in a restaurant before. I said, "What do you want me to do?" And he said, "I want you to be the bouncer." "The bouncer? How am I going to bounce anybody up two flights of stairs?" I had a feeling he just wanted to keep an eye on me. I never really understood why. So I said, "Great, why not." I was hanging out in the bar anyway so I started working for him. But it was never really like working for him, he said, "Just be here." You see, his theory about the restaurant business was never to really 86 anyone unless it was absolutely necessary. He had this Zen quality of talking people out of the place.

rebellion

The way he looked and talked, people just didn't want to tangle with him. He just bored you out of the place, and I did basically what he did.

Mickey and Richard split up and Richard kept the Locale and Mickey opened the Ocean Club. Those two were partners by handshake. They actually liked one another. They liked one another's shortcomings. Neither one of them was about money and they both liked people. Obviously they didn't worry about money because everything went through their fingers.

Then when Mickey opened the Ocean Club, he said to me, "I want you to be my manager." I knew nothing about managing a restaurant. But the funny thing is, he knew nothing about running a restaurant as long as he'd been in the restaurant business. He just knew about people. He kind of liked certain people and having them around.

**DANNY FIELDS:** When Mickey opened the Ocean Club he got me my apartment down near the Ocean Club. I was going there and I wanted to move from Eighteenth Street. It was this nine-room apartment that I always hated. I lived there for two years. It was jinxed; it was horrible. Then the Ocean Club closed on me. I used to think, There's nothing in this goddamn neighborhood at all, but thank God at least there's the Ocean Club down the block so I can always go there—and then it closed and then there was nothing. I really felt betrayed when the Ocean Club closed.

Mickey Ruskin and Gerard Malanga at Lower Manhattan Ocean Club
(photo by Gerald Malanga)

**GLENN O'BRIEN:** I went to the Ocean Club every night with Scott Cohen. There was the Ocean Club and Barbarus Rex. The first time I saw the Talking Heads was at the Ocean Club. The X-Men played there early on. I saw Television or maybe Tom Verlaine, Patti Smith. It was definitely a little ahead of its time, but it was busy.

**NATHAN JOSEPH:** I didn't know Mickey was doing any drugs. Mickey, in fact, had a reputation of not drinking or doing any drugs. The first time I heard about it was after Max's. Even then he was discreet about it. It wasn't part of his outside routine. But as things moved along, there was just no deny-

high on

ing it, you see, because everybody was doing it. But you really couldn't tell Mickey was doing drugs unless you saw him doing them. Then he started drinking. He'd drink tequila at the Ocean Club, and he'd he'd do some coke there too, but you didn't see him doing it. I think he got into them because the constituency of that bar in the early eighties was just a drug culture. You couldn't run an "in" restaurant business without accommodating all those guys, and at that point he became one of the guys. He still didn't stay out all night; he was still a family man. But all the people he admired were doing drugs, so I guess he didn't think there was anything wrong with it.

**SAM HOOD:** I paid the rent on the Ocean Club for about six months toward the end. Mickey came to me really desperate.

**NATHAN JOSEPH:** Richard and Mickey hooked up again at One U, which was Mickey's last club. They had to bring in this guy V., because neither one of them had money. V. had made some money investing in porno films. he was from another era. He was more a friend of Richard's. I don't think he and Mickey ever got along.

**RICHARD BOCH, FLOOR MANAGER AT ONE U:** When I was about fifteen, or sixteen, sometimes friends and I would sort of sneak into the city cause we weren't suppose to come into the city yet by ourselves. We'd go to the Fillmore or hang outside the Fillmore. We came in from Long Island. We'd wind up making our way over to Washington Square, and then Union Square and then up to Park Avenue, and we'd hang outside Max's sometimes, and when we'd get really courageous and we'd see a group of people going in we'd just sort of try to slide our way in. Sometimes it would work for about fifteen or twenty minutes, and sometimes we'd get smiled at by Mickey as we'd go in the door. Sometimes we'd last about thirty seconds, or wouldn't even get through the door.

I moved into the city and started getting involved in the club scene downtown. CBGB's, then later working at the Mudd Club, and after the Mudd Club, through coincidence, I wound up being a manager at Mickey's last restaurant, One U. So it took on this whole full-circle thing. That's where I really learned how to do what I still do today.

One U was real different than Max's. It was bright instead of dark. It had evolved, the scene had evolved. The scene had certainly changed. Some people had grown up. There was a lot of new faces. A lot of the punk rock and what was to become the New Wave crowd. On a given night sure you would see artists who were at Max's fifteen years ago: Robert Rauschenberg, Larry Zox, Gerard and Ronnie Cutrone from the Warhol crowd; occasionally you'd sit down with Jackie Curtis if she were still alive; in a rare moment you'd even see Holly Woodlawn dressed down in jeans and a sweater....One night you'd see Abbie Hoffman having dinner with David Bowie at One U when that would have been two different factions ten years previous. You'd see people from the newer bands like the Clash, Patti Smith Group...a different kind of drag queens—you'd see Terry Toy instead of a Candy Darling, but it was still the same thing, going where the artists and the freaks

273

rebellion

went. There were still always interesting people. And the way Mickey was at the door, he taught me how to work the door, even though I had been doing it at the Mudd Club for two years prior to One U, I still learned sort of a finesse. There was this subtlety about Mickey that there was a certain way to do it, and you really didn't stray from that certain way and that certain eye that Mickey had. But at the same time there was a way to do it. I learned a lot about working a room. It was more intimate than Max's and the Mudd Club. It was more of a controlled chaos than One U.

Mickey was already looking for the next thing. He was talking to me. He would call me up, and I'd go meet him around the corner at a coffee shop because I wasn't supposed to be working at One U anymore and he would say, "I want you to go look at some spaces for me." He had this idea of doing the next level, possibly with rooms, or suites where people could go privately for short or extended periods of time. Sort of the kind of thing that Ian Schrager is doing, a small boutique hotel which was way ahead of its time in 1981. He was always ahead of his time.

**MICKEY RUSKIN:** I'd been three years at One U and I was already making plans for other things. The one thing I learned between Max's and the Locale is that I couldn't run more than one restaurant at one time. Throughout all those great times when some of the greatest moments in Max's were occurring, most of the time I was standing in the middle of the room totally depressed. I can count without giving specific examples, I feel if I had ten happy moments in my life then I'm ten points ahead of 99 percent of the population.

**PHILIP GLASS:** I followed him around. I didn't hang out as much as other people did, but I always knew where Mickey's club was, and my friends always went. The last time I went there, when I went to see him just two weeks before he died, I saw that he was actually very sad. People weren't coming anymore. He would say, "Our crowd isn't here."

**JOHN CHAMBERLAIN:** What goods I gave Mickey over the course of the years essentially paid for the tabs. Evidently he figured he wouldn't have been in that business if it weren't for people like myself. For some reason, Williams and Myers and myself were some kind of inspiration to him. I kept asking him, up until the time he checked out, "What is it I did that made you treat me this way, all this freebie number?" He never did say. I'm not so sure he knew. I guess everybody had the people that they liked or admired, or who saved their day or saved their life or saved their year or whatever; he kept asking if he had done any good, and I always tried to tell him how many people he made happy.

**CHARLES YODER, ARTIST:** I'd been calling One U "Death Cafe" because so many people were dying around the place, either overdosing or being robbed and mugged, or getting sick with all the stuff that had crept into the drug life. I had often sat in the back room with Mickey, talking, smoking cigarettes, and snorting coke. I never saw Mickey do heroin, but it was well known that he did just about anything he wanted to.

# max's after mickey, mickey after max's

Another time I was sitting at One U at the round table just outside of the game room. I'm with a group of six or so people and we're inhaling nitrous oxide. Someone had brought in a large box of the canisters, and we were drinking and snorting these things and laughing insanely, Mickey came into the restaurant and walked up to the table. "What are you people doing? Trying to get me into trouble? Put that shit away." I said, "Mickey, it's legal." "Well, in that case, move over," he said, and sat down, took one of the canisters and took a deep inhale and started to giggle.

**DONALD LYONS:** Unfortunately, when you get a period where all the old restraints have gone down and people are allowed complete freedom—complete freedom is a very dangerous drug, the most dangerous drug of the sixties. At the time there was no kind of system to tell you to slow down— to tell you to use your energies and to conserve them and channel them in the right way. But there was this explosion of energies, and sadly a lot of energy burnt itself out very quickly with and without drugs, mainly due to the age-old human insufficiencies and self-doubts. This made it a dangerous period.

**BENNO FRIEDMAN, PHOTOGRAPHER/ARTIST:** Toward the end Mickey was definitely getting strung out. More and more of his personality was subject to the things that I knew from personal experience. He always had trouble sitting in one spot and talking to anybody for any length of time. He was always moving around, but the more blow he did, the more that intensified, where he couldn't even look at you while he was talking. His eyes would be going in thirty-seven directions and he was already somewhere else before he even got there. There was this skittishness where it became harder and harder to get any relaxed and honest moment from Mickey. It was all chemistry talking to you rather than Mickey. It was very evident to anybody who was into that stuff what was going on. It became part of his greeting but he remained true to himself up to the very end. He did art shows that were high quality—he was still involved with artists and cared about them in whatever way he could. The drugs tend to disassociate you except with those you are doing the drugs with. He was a risk taker and an outsider. Probably not intentionally a visionary, but he was. He would probably minimize his role in this and he probably wished himself to be an artist but he felt he didn't have the skills, so he wanted to surround himself with those people. He was an innkeeper, that was his art.

**NATHAN JOSEPH:** The last time I saw Mickey was on May 15, 1983, at One U after seeing Scarface. I wanted to go home and go to sleep and I knew Mickey was having trouble going to sleep, because of all the troubles he was having, so he always had Valium. I just wanted to go down there and get a Valium. I went down there and asked where Mickey was and they said he was in the office, don't go in there. So I sat at the bar. And then he came out and I asked him what he had and he said nothing, he couldn't get anything. So I sat a couple more hours and this guy John Neeham came in, out of the blue, in fact. John used to own the Spring Street Bar. So they went into the office. They were similar characters. They were both well educated and rejected their education and denied their background. But they didn't like each other.

After a while they came out of the office and sat down at the bar where we had at least six or seven grilled-cheese-and-bacon sandwiches, and Mickey was shooting down tequilas. I had worked for both these people and became good friends with both, and this was one of the few times where those two were having a good time together, which was interesting because they were always countering each other. Then Mickey said we should go to the L'Express, which was owned by an Algerian named Rashid, who I think Mickey suspected was going out with his wife Kathy. So I got in the Pacer with Mickey and John followed in his Cadillac. Mickey. We sat down and ordered asparagus. Then Mickey started telling me the best way to go to sleep was to take three Valium and a couple of hits of tequila. He was slobbering the aspara-

Julian Schnabel, left, and Bob Williamson at One University, 1979 (photo by Alan Kleinberg)

gus and I was stunned. So we left and sure enough, it was about five o'clock, and Rashid pulls up and Mickey's thrilled that Kathy's not with the guy. Then Mickey got in the Cadillac with John and I drove the Pacer. We drove by the Chelsea Hotel, and he jumps out and gets the New York Times, gives me one, gives John one, gives me a package of M&M's, and he was like the sweetest guy. Mickey never liked to show his sweet side. Then he got out and I told him what a prince he was, and that was the last time I saw him.

I was managing a recording studio at the time. I was in the studio with one of my customers when the phone rang. It was Kathy. She told me Mickey had just passed away. I froze! I let out such a cry, I scared the guy in the room. I thought I would die on the spot. I thought my heart might stop beating. He was my Knight in Shining Armor. My hero. He was never going to die. He was the father of my children. We were devastated for so long. It had such a tremendous effect over our lives from that day on. It took me years and years to get over it. Only now am I beginning to find some closure.

**LI-LIAN OH, ACUPUNCTURIST:** I was with Mickey and Kathy in Jamaica the week before he died. Michael Arlin had rented a place in Jamaica and we all stayed in the house. It was really great. All we did was swim, sit, eat, and read. Mickey was so healthy. When we all came back I went upstate. I got a call a week later from my friend in the city. She

"I met Bob Williamson at Max's. He usually arrived at one in the morning and I was always glad to see him. I loved talking with him because I felt we were doing something constructive. . . . Bob was not a painter, but he knew a lot about art. He seemed able to see what was going on inside of a painting, into what it was or what it could have been. He had an encyclopedia mind. . . As we sat in our booth—him knowing everything and me knowing nothing—we judged all. We gave ourselves that power. We were ruthless and efficient and we argued with everybody."

—from *Paint Job* by Julian Schnabel

rebellion

said, "Are you sitting down?" I said, yes, and then she told me. I was in shock.

**RYDER McCLURE:** Mickey was a moral man with a sense of right and he became addicted. His system just died on him. He was delivered late in the morning. Two people brought him home. He was all fucked up, drunk and drugged....He turned blue and Kathy couldn't revive him. The clothes he wore on the final day at the funeral, the kids picked out. The guy called from the funeral parlor and said, "I think the bags were switched, these clothes he has on are all torn and trashy." Kathy said, "No, that's right. That's what he would have wanted to wear."

**JOSEPH KOSUTH:** I had been with Mickey hours before he died. I was back in the office hanging out with him. The next night I went in there and the place, I had never seen it feeling so weird, it was just in the air. And I went and sat down, and I said, "What's going on here?" And he had died and I didn't know. They came over and told me, and I just remember sitting at the table just crying my eyes out. Like when René Ricard ran over to me one night yelling, "They shot John Lennon tonight."

**RYDER McCLURE:** Your heart is usually a victim of your head and if you look at anything in history, there is a time to sell to get out. It's the classic story of riding a dead horse. To me that's what Mickey never really got. He never could understand how it happened. He was never really particularly overjoyed that it did happen until it was long gone and then he claimed not to give a shit, but I never for one second believed it. It was the time of his life. And ours too.

**HOWARD SMITH:** When a painter, a sculptor, a poet, or a photographer dies, the space that is left can often be assessed; with a spirit like Mickey Ruskin, the depth of the hollows is more difficult to perceive.

VOICE JUNE 21, 1983    38

## JOEL OPPENH

# Friends

There's a story Myron Cohen use guy who comes home and smells cig on a frantic search through the hou wife's lover. He ends up in the bathr closed shower curtain which he rips culprit, standing in the tub, the ciga "What are you doing here?" the intruder says, "Nu, everybody's got
. . .

When you're young and eager and this city of dreams, that somewhere to be a saloon. It ain't only a place to to score. It's also your home awa extension of your living room, your and maybe even your bank.

I've been lucky. I've had three wi in the Cedar Tavern, waiting there o spring in 1953, because Franz Klir earlier, "Kid, when you get to the cit and sit there and nurse a beer. I'll ge I sat from one until four, slowly worki and by God, he did show up. "Hi kid you tell them you were looking for m of the evening I knew the bartend waiter, and a dozen people who wou the next 10 years.

And for the last 15 years I've ha even though I've not had a real dr years. Still that was the place I lived life—and there were times when I c phone number to P.S. 3 or I.S. 70 emergency number, because it was home.

In between those two places ther place. I knew Mickey Ruskin from house days, but it wasn't till the porarily and drove us all out in the drinking at the Ninth Circle and friend. Then he left there and we sta

**Mickey Ruskin: a death in the family**

a year or so later when he called and asked me over to his house for dinner it wasn't a special occasion, but just friends eating together. He said, after the meal, that he was opening a new joint and asked did I have any ideas for a name. That night—despite his misgivings about my choice—Max's Kansas City was born.

When I got married, Mickey gave us the upstairs at Max's for the ceremony in the afternoon and a hell of a good party that night. He even conned the Sangria salesman into donating a barrel of the stuff, because "There's this famous poet getting married and the elite of New York's drinkers will be there, and you'll get 200 new customers!"

Mickey was an entrepreneur, clear and simple. He loved to take places that had never been successful, or were in some location no one'd ever gone, and he'd make them work. Max's was a dismal Chinese restaurant that I never would've taken a chance on, and the Ninth Circle had had a new owner every week before he got to it. The Locale, which came after Max's, was downstairs and dark and the two times I'd been in it before Ruskin got it had been enough for a lifetime as far as I was concerned. Then there was the Lower Manhattan Ocean Club, again breaking new ground, and, finally, Chinese Chance, at 1 University. In between there'd even been a stab at uptown with Max's Terre Haute.

The one thing all the places had was Mickey, yelling at the waitresses, a bitch to work for but an angel with his friends. Painters and writers, layabouts and scoundrels all, there was a home for us. I walked in one night with a date, and Mickey bounced Huntington Hartford from a table so we could sit down. You could love a guy like that, and I did.

The only problem with Mick was that he got bored as soon as a place caught on. He wanted the risk, the dare of opening up where everybody said you couldn't. He wanted to see could he make it work—no, that's wrong, because he *knew* he could make it work.

And he liked to try things out. A couple of years before the state legislature passed the law about making legal jargon readable, Mickey called me and asked me if I'd take a stab at rewriting his legal documents in real English. When the banks started offering "scenic" checks, Mickey had Max's checks underprinted with a faint but discernible shot of John Chamberlain, Neal Williams, Frosty Myers, and me lounging at the bar. He paid us each a fee of 99 cents, made out on the first four checks, and mine still hangs on my wall at Westbeth, framed. I often meant to ask him if the accountant had gone crazy over the uncashed check but I never got around to it.

Now I can't any more. He's gone. I got the call a couple of weeks ago, from my son Dan, who'd worked for Mickey at Chinese Chance a couple of years ago. He was the day waiter then, and Angus Chamberlain, John's son, was there at the same time, behind the bar. John and I said it was the least Mickey could do for us after we'd supported him for so long.

I couldn't get down from New Hampshire for the funeral. I couldn't hear John and Neal eulogize him. I spoke to John the night before the funeral and he was outraged that he'd have to say something. John's like his sculpture, big and rough, and he keeps thinking words are alien materials. "What the hell is a eulogy anyhow, damn it?" he screamed. "Beautiful words," I said. "Just say some beautiful words about the good times, and let the bad times go." And I hear he did just that. Well, that's what it's about, the good times, and you keep the bad times quiet, and just think about how somebody like Mickey bailed you out of so many of them, of the loans, and the time he bought a gen-u-wine manuscript poem because he knew you were broke, and the times he paid for a meal or bought you a drink because you needed it.

The one thing I wish he'd been able to do was to prevail on the Cornell Alumni magazine to do a cover of Max's with him (a real graduate) and the dozen or so of us who were all Cornell failures lined up in front of the joint. He thought it would have made a pretty good shot. ∎

# 130 FABULOUS FACES
## by Leee Black Childers

1. David Johansen
2. Divine
3. Danny Fields
4. Donna Jordan
5. Ahmet Ertegun
6. Paul Stanley
7. Sable Starr
8. Miki Starr
9. Ekaterina Sobechoskaya
10. Ron Asheton
11. Robert Mapplethorpe
12. Paul McCartney
13. Patti Smith
14. Pristine Condition
15. Lou Reed
16. Rosey Ross
17. Tim Hauser
18. Richard Hell
19. Ian Hunter
20. Jimmy Destri
21. Tally Brown
22. Syl Sylvain
23. John Collins
24. Daniella Parma
25. Viva
26. Bobby Alessi
27. Billy Alessi
28. Maria Smith
29. Tony Zinetta
30. Alice Cooper
31. Allen Paul
32. Jim
33. Richard Robinson
34. Eno
35. Lisa Robinson
36. David Bailey
37. Jimmy Page
38. Dee Dee Ramone
39. Joey Ramone
40. Keith Moon
41. Eric Emerson
42. Ruth Karsh
43. Andy Warhol
44. Shayne Harris
45. David Cassidy
46. Jane Forth
47. Lewis Furey
48. Amanda Lear
49. Salvador Dali
50. Prindiville Wells
51. Patti D'Arbanville
52. Pat Luvcazo
53. Truman Capote
54. Simon Turner
55. Larissa
56. Rod Stewart
57. Marianne Faithful
58. David Essex
59. Geraldine Smith
60. Jonathan Richman
61. Lizzie Mercier
62. Chris Franz
63. Peter Brown
64. Howard Bowler
65. Cindy Lang

66. Allen Ginsberg
67. Holly Woodlawn
68. Leslie Gore
69. John DeSalvo
70. Lenny Kaye
71. Tom Verlaine
72. Elvis Presley
73. Kathlyn Black Stone
74. Anthony Ingrassia
75. Wayne County
76. Mick Ralphs
77. John Lennon
78. David Bowie
79. John Waters
80. Jane Hutcherson-Simpson
81. Toby DuPrey
82. Debbie Harry
83. Mick Jagger
84. Cyrinda Foxe
85. Robert Gorden
86. Michael Gray
87. Cherry Vanilla
88. Iggy Pop
89. Andrea Whips Feldman
90. Freddie Buretti
91. Jim Clifford
92. Jackie Curtis
93. Rio Grande
94. Mitchell Dancik
95. Ruby Lynn Reyner
96. Jimmy Marcus
97. Jed Johnson
98. A mannikin in a store
     window
99. Candy Darling
100. Paul Zone
101. Earl McGrath
102. Jim Bouton
103. Michael Dean
104. Duncan Hannah
105. Johnny Paley
106. A boy from 53rd & 3rd
107. Taylor Mead
108. Col. Tom Parker
109. Rocky Roads
110. Joe Perry
111. Peter Frampton
112. Johnny Thunders
113. Miss Christine
114. Andy Paley
115. Angela Bowie
116. Gary Valentine
117. Rick Derringer
118. Liz Derringer
119. Peter Noone
120. Geri Miller
121. Bunny Eisenhower
122. Richard Lloyd
123. Lance Loud
124. Janis Cafasso
125. Gene Simmons
126. Jacqueline
127. Mick Ronson
128. Suzi Quatro
129. Steven Tyler
130. Roger Daltry

**GEORGE ABAGNALO:** assistant at Warhol's Factory

**DAVID AMRAM:** composer, musician, writer

**CARL ANDRE:** sculptor

**MIKE APPEL:** Bruce Springsteen's first manager

**PENNY ARCADE:** actress in the Playhouse of the Ridiculous; performance artist; recently staged an autobiographical one-woman show titled *Bitch! Dyke! Faghag! Whore!*

**EVA BABBITZ:** writer, author

**JOAN BAEZ:** singer/songwriter in the early folk-rock movement which included Bob Dylan; well-known for her anti-Vietnam War stance and socially/politically conscious lyrics

**BENEDETTA BARZINI:** model

**DAVID BEHRENS:** reporter, journalist

**JIM BELL:** entrepreneur

**LARRY BELL:** painter, sculptor

**RICHARD BELLAMY:** art dealer; director of Park Place Gallery

**AGNES BENJAMIN:** fashion editor at *Harper's Bazaar*; married Marjoe Gortner.

**CAROL BERGE:** poet

**BRIGID BERLIN:** outrageous Warhol Superstar; credits in Warhol movies include *Chelsea Girls, Tub Girls, Loves of Ondine, Bike Boy,* and *Nude Restaurant.*

**RICHARD BERNSTEIN:** artist/Illustrator; designed covers for *Interview* magazine during Warhol years.

**PETER BERRY:** Max's bartender

**JEANNIE BLAKE:** painter's and art dealer's assistant

**SUSAN BLOND:** artist; later became a publicist, first at United Artists Records, then at CBS, where she was a vice president; now owns her own PR agency, Susan Blond Inc.

**MEL BOCHNER:** painter

**RICHARD BOCH:** former doorman at the Mudd Club; former floor manager at One University; presently manages a French bistro on the upper east side.

**VICTOR BOCKRIS:** former publisher of Telegraph books; writer/biographer whose books include *Uptight: The Velvet Underground*; *Making Tracks: The Rise of Blondie*; and *Keith Richards: The Biography*

**SUSAN BOTTOMLY:** Warhol Superstar

**DAVID BOWIE:** songwriter/performer/rock star; one of the progenitors of the glitter-rock scene in the 1970s. Famous for alter-ego stage personas such as Ziggy Stardust, Aladdin Sane, and The Thin White Duke; went on to a side career in acting; starred in films such as *The Man Who Fell to Earth* and *The Hunger*; starred in *The Elephant Man* on Broadway in 1980. Bowie is still recording albums.

**BOB BRADY:** actor/teacher at School for Visual Arts

**ELDA BRANCH:** singer/performer; founding member of the all girls group the Stillettos; had a child with Eric Emerson.

**JEFFREY BRENNAN:** doorman for Upstairs at Max's rock club/disco.

**MEL BROOKS:** film director/producer; films include *The Producers, Young Frankenstein,* and *High Anxiety.*

**GREG BROWN:** filmmaker

**JACKSON BROWNE:** well-known popular singer/songwriter; famous for his boyish looks

**TIM BUCKLEY:** folk/rock musician. Died from a heroin overdose on June 29, 1975.

**DAVID BUDD:** painter

**BEBE BUELL:** model, rock-and-roll manager and singer. Longtime companion of Todd Rundgren; girlfriend of Aerosmith's Steven Tyler; mother of Liv Tyler. Former lead singer of the Gargoyles

**DONALD BURNS:** graphic artist/photographer; photographed old steam engines

**WILLIAM S. BURROUGHS:** author of *Naked Lunch* and *Junky*; usually considered a seminal member of the group of writers known as the Beats. Recently deceased.

**JOHN CALE:** co-founder of The Velvet Underground. Continues to record and perform as a solo artist.

**DEREK CALLENDER:** photographer's assistant

**STEVE CANNON:** poet/writer

**JACQUES CAPSUTO:** Max's regular; now owns Capsuto Frère.

**LEO CASTELLI:** art dealer and gallery owner

**TED CASTLE:** art historian and writer

**ROSEMARIE CASTORA:** painter

**JOHN CHAMBERLAIN:** sculptor; best known for his works in crushed sheet metal, works resembling "car crashes"

**LEEE BLACK CHILDERS:** rock-and-roll manager and photographer

**DAN CHRISTENSEN:** abstract expressionist painter

**SCOTT COHEN:** freelance writer; editor for *Circus* and *Interview* magazines

**IRA COHEN:** photographer/poet

**COLETTE:** environmental artist and painter

**ALICE COOPER:** legendary "shock rocker"; progenitor of "spectacle" rock shows, and forerunner of such acts as Marilyn Manson

**WAYNE COUNTY (NOW KNOWN AS JAYNE COUNTY):** transsexual rock performer and former drag queen

**ROBERT CREELEY:** poet/writer

**PILAR CRESPI:** fashion model

**PETER CROWLEY:** booking agent for Upstairs at Max's during the Punk era ,1975-81

**JASON CROY:** hairdresser for many artists and Max's regulars

**ROBIN CULLINEN:** Max's manager

**PATSY CUMMINGS:** Max's waitress

**JACKIE CURTIS:** drag queen; Warhol Superstar; wrote the play *Glamour, Glory and Gold.*

**RONNIE CUTRONE:** painter

**JOE DALLESANDRO:** Warhol superstar and movie actor

**DAVID DALTON:** author of biographies on James Dean, Janis Joplin, Sid Vicious, and Marianne Faithful

**SUSAN DALTON:** writer

**CANDY DARLING:** drag pioneer and Warhol Superstar. Died in 1974 in New York City.

**FIELDING ("FE") DAWSON:** poet/author

**MAXIME DE LA FALAISE:** contour designer

**MARIA DEL GRECO:** clothing designer; worked at Max's second incarnation.

**ANTONIA DE PORTAGO:** singer with Walter Stedding

**FRANK DIBENEDETTO:** Max's bartender; the only bartender who remained through all the incarnations of the space

**WALTER DEMARIA:** sculptor

**LIZ DERRINGER:** journalist

**ELIZABETH DESALES:** artist

**DIVINE:** actor and transvestite; featured in John Waters' films, including *Pink Flamingos, Female Trouble,* and Hairspray; deceased

**RITTY DODGE:** Max's maitre'd

**SUSAN DOUKAS:** Max's waitress; actress

**CATHY DREW:** Max's waitress

**BOB DYLAN:** folk-rock legend. Continues to write and record.

**JOE EARLY:** poet/writer; managed Max's softball team.

**LYNNE EDELSON:** harmonica player; performed with various bands.

**PAUL EDEN:** Max's maitre'd. Deceased 1998.

**MARSHALL EFRON:** actor/screenwriter/author

**JOE ELETZ (AKA JOE BIRD):** Max's bartender; painter

**ERIC EMERSON:** A-list back-room personality and Warhol Superstar. Died from heroin overdose in 1976.

**BRIAN ENO:** musician and record producer; pioneer of "ambient" music; produced the Talking Heads and Devo.

**AHMET ERTEGUN:** president of Atlantic Records

**FABRIZIO:** Max's maitre'd and manager

**RITA FECHER:** artist/teacher

**BOB FEIDEN:** RCA record executive

**ANDREA FELDMAN (AKA ANDREA WHIPS, ANDREA WARHOLA):** the "Showtime girl" in the back room at Max's; Warhol Superstar; deceased

**FEDERICO FELLINI:** revered filmmaker; worked with Nico on *La Dolce Vita.*

**JACKIE FERRARA:** painter

**DANNY FIELDS:** record executive/manager; a mainstay in Max's back room

**NAT FINKELSTEIN:** photographer; took many photographs at Warhol's Factory.

**ANNIE FLANDERS:** clothing designer; founded Abracadabra clothing store.

**JANE FONDA:** daughter of Henry and sister of Peter; award-winning actress in numerous films; Vietnam War protester ("Hanoi Jane"); aerobics and fitness guru

**JOHN FORD:** prominent fashion photographer

**JANE FORTH:** Warhol Superstar; had a child with Eric Emerson.

**JIM FOURATT:** record-company executive; editor of *Gay Power* magazine

**CYRINDA FOXE:** actress; Max's back-room regular; formerly married to David Johansen and Steven Tyler.

**BENNO FRIEDMAN:** photographer/artist

**MYRA FRIEDMAN:** former Columbia Records executive in publicity; wrote biography of Janis Joplin, *Buried Alive.*

**FUDGE:** Max's regular and sometime bouncer

**STEVE GAINES:** author of books including *Me Alice, Marjoe,* and *Halston*

**GYDA GASH:** musician

**MEL GEARY:** Max's manager and contractor for Max's

**HENRY GELDZAHLER:** commissioner of cultural affairs in New York City

**ALLEN GINSBERG:** seminal beat poet; author of *How.* Died in 1997.

**JOHN GIORNO:** poet, writer; books include *You Got to Burn to Shine.*

**GISELLA:** Max's regular; artist

**PHILIP GLASS:** composer/musician; influenced such bands as Sonic Youth

**CARL GLIKO:** Max's bartender; painter

**ELLEN GOFEN:** Max's back-room waitress

**DANNY GOLDBERG:** former rock critic

# cast of characters

**AL GOLDSTEIN:** founder of *Screw* magazine

**MICHAEL GOLDSTEIN:** founder of publicity company, Goldstein Management; founder of the *Soho Weekly News*

**RICHARD GOLDSTEIN:** writer for the *Village Voice*

**RICHARD GOLUB:** celebrity attorney

**SHEP GORDON:** manager of Alice Cooper

**ARTHUR GORSON:** music manager, record producer

**TONY GOULD:** Max's manager

**BILL GRAVES:** Max's bartender

**JULIE GREENFIELD:** painter; creative consultant

**FRANCIS GRILL:** president of Click Modeling Agency

**MICHAEL GROSS:** writer; author of book on the fashion world, *Model*

**ELAINE GROVE:** model, artist

**BOB GRUEN:** photographer; directed the New York Dolls video, *Looking for a Kiss*; his books include *Listen to These Pictures—John Lennon*; *Chaos*; *The Sex Pistols*; *Sometime in NYC* (with Yoko Ono); and *Crossfire Hurricane—25 Years of the Rolling Stones*.

**HALSTON:** fashion designer; deceased

**HELEN HARRINGTON:** Max's waitress; artist; married painter Brice Marden.

**SHAYNE HARRIS:** drummer with band, Luger

**LYNN HARRITON:** Max's waitress

**DEBBIE (DEBORAH) HARRY:** early Max's waitress; singer, songwriter, actress; lead singer with Blondie

**ROSE (BUNNY) HARTMAN:** wrote for the *Soho Weekly News*.

**JOHN HAYES:** journalist

**CLAUDE HAYN:** road manager for John and Yoko, and Elephant's Memory

**ROBERT HEIDE:** celebrated off-Broadway playwright. His play *The Bed* was filmed by Andy Warhol, and he appeared in Warhol's *Camp* and *Dracula/Batman*. Author of twelve books with John Gilman on American popular culture, everything from Mickey Mouse to Greenwich Village.

**BARBARA HODES:** fashion designer

**ABBIE HOFFMAN:** famous Yippie and 1960s radical; well-known author of books such as *Steal This Book* and *Revolution for the Hell of It*; deceased.

**BILLY HOFFMAN:** artist, illustrator

**SUSAN HOFFMAN (AKA VIVA):** Warhol Superstar, actress, and author of *Viva*

**SAM HOOD:** former owner of the Gaslight; booked Upstairs at Max's.

**DENNIS HOPPER:** film actor since the 1950s; costar of *Easy Rider* (with Peter Fonda and Jack Nicholson), *Blue Velvet*, and *True Romance*

**JERRY HOUK:** Max's bartender

**TONY INGRASSIA:** playwright and theater director

**PHIL JABARRA:** songwriter, actor; deceased

**JIM JACOBS:** artist; manager for Joan Baez

**GARLAND JEFFREYS:** singer/songwriter/performer

**DAVID JOHANSEN:** lead singer of the New York Dolls; actor and solo performer; now performing as his musical alter-ego, Buster Poindexter.

**BETSEY JOHNSON:** one of Americas preeminent fashion designers.

**JILL JOHNSTON:** feminist writer; former writer for the *Village Voice*

**BRIAN JONES:** former guitarist for the Rolling Stones; died in England in 1969.

**DONNA JORDAN:** model, back-room regular

**NATHAN JOSEPH:** painter; managed the Ocean Club in lower Manhattan, owned by Mickey Ruskin.

**ARTHUR KANE:** bass player in the New York Dolls

**ED KANE:** attorney for Guardian Life

**IVAN KARP:** art dealer; gallery owner

**RICK KAUFMANN:** art dealer, gallery owner

**LENNY KAYE:** former rock critic; guitar player with the Patti Smith Group; formed the Lenny Kaye Band; produced Suzanne Vega.

**PIA KAZAN:** fashion model

**PAUL KILB:** model/carpenter

**BILLY KLUVER:** scientific architectural designer for EAT, Experiments in Technology

**ED KOCH:** former Mayor of New York City

**JOSEPH KOSUTH:** painter

**PAMELA KRAFT:** Max's waitress

**MARILYN KRAUSS:** Max's regular; photographer

**ANTHONY KRAUSS:** sculptor; painter

**BOB KRIVITT:** partners with Mickey Ruskin in the Ninth Circle Restaurant

**LAURA KRONENBERG:** artist

**GERALD LAING:** painter

**JIM LALUMIA:** musician; founder of group the Psychotic Frogs; currently a freelance music writer

**JENNY LANDFIELD:** Max's waitress; married to Ron Landfield

**RON LANDFIELD:** abstract expressionist painter

**LARISSA:** fashion designer and muse to other designers

**JOHANNA LAWRENSON:** photographer, model, organizer; married to Abbie Hoffman

**ESTELLE LAZARUS:** publicist

**ELSBETH LEACOCK:** Max's waitress

**TIMOTHY LEARY:** world-renowned for being among the first to experiment with LSD; directed the movie *Cheech and*

high on

*Chang's Nice Dreams*; recently deceased

**ED LEFFINGWELL**; assisted John Chamberlain on films and sculptures.

**LES LEVINE:** conceptual artist. Levine's, one of Mickey Ruskin's restaurants, was Les Levine's concept

**JEFFREY LEW:** painter, photographer

**JACKIE LEWIS:** Max's waitress; model

**ROY LICHTENSTEIN:** Pop artist

**STUART LICHTENSTEIN:** Max's manager

**PHILIP LOCASCIO:** Max's maitre' d

**JOE LOGIUDICE:** art dealer, gallery owner

**CATHERINE LOMBARD:** Max's waitress

**CHARLES LUDLAM:** founder of the Playhouse of the Ridiculous

**JILL LUMPKIN:** Max's waitress

**DONALD LYONS:** professsor of literature at Rutgers University

**GERARD MALANGA:** poet, artist, and photographer; performed with the Nico-era Velvet Underground.

**MANOLO:** Max's busboy; one of" the three Bananas"

**ROBERT MAPPLETHORPE:** controversial photographer; early collaborator with Patti Smith. Well-known for portraiture, male nudes, and still lifes; deceased

**BRICE MARDEN:** abstract expressionist painter

**MARISOL:** painter

**EMMARETA MARKS:** Max's waitress; performed in the Broadway musical *Hair*.

**DAVE MARSH:** writer for *Creem* magazine; author of several books on Bruce Springsteen

**JULIE MARTIN:** administrator at EAT; married Billy Kluver.

**NICKY MARTIN:** formerly lead guitarist with the group Street Punk

**RYDER MCCLURE:** artist/sculptor; designed functional scupltures

**LEGS MCNEIL:** cofounder of *Punk* magazine; freelance writer; recently authored *Please Kill Me*, an oral history of punk rock.

**TAYLOR MEAD:** poet, actor who made numerous films with Andy Warhol, including *Lonesome Cowboys*, *Nude Restaurant* and *Imitation of Christ*, as well as John Schlesinger's *Midnight Cowboy*. His most recent book is called *Son of Warhol*.

**JONAS MEKAS:** poet and director of the Film Anthology Archives

**ALAN MIDGETTE:** actor

**SYLVIA MILES:** film actress; appeared in *Midnight Cowboy*, *Psychomania*, Warhol's *Heat* (directed by Paul Morissey and costarring Joe Dallesandro), and *Superstar: The Life and Times of Andy Warhol*.

**GERI MILLER:** Warhol Superstar

**JIM MONTE:** curator for the Whitney Museum; painter

**JIM MOORE:** fashion photographer

**MARIE MORREALE:** author/writer

**JIM MORRISON:** lead singer of the Doors; died in 1971.

**STERLING MORRISON:** guitarist in the Velvet Underground; died in 1995.

**PAUL MORRISSEY:** filmmaker; collaborated with Warhol on several films, including *Andy Warhol's Dracula*, *Andy Warhol's Frankenstein*, *Flesh*, and *Heat*; also wrote and directed *Mixed Blood* in 1984.

**TIGER MORSE:** brilliant fashion designer; invented the electric dress; deceased

**DENISE MOURGES:** dancer/singer; Max's regular

**BILLY MURCIA:** first drummer for the New York Dolls; died of a drug overdose in 1972.

**GAIL MUTRIX:** art and film research; now has her own film production company.

**FORREST (FROSTY) MYERS:** sculptor; designed the laser beam at Max's, as well as several of Mickey Ruskin's restaurants.

**LYNN MYERS:** Max's waitress; deceased

**BILLY NAME:** artist; photographer; staff photographer at Warhol's Factory

**JULIE NEUFIELD:** fashion advertising art director; now artist

**BOBBY NEUWIRTH:** painter/songwriter/musician/producer; has recorded several albums.

**JEREMIAH NEWTON:** writer, screenwriter; received credit on the 1996 film, *I Shot Andy Warhol*.

**JEFFREY NICKORA:** Max's cashier

**NICO:** Teutonic chanteuse; model; actress; sang with The Velvet Underground; a true icon; deceased

**NOANA:** Max's doorlady, waitress

**DICK NUSSER:** author; former writer for the *Village Voice*; member of the Living Theater

**GLENN O'BRIEN:** former editor of *Interview* magazine; presently writes for several publications; recently published his first book, *Soapbox*.

**TERRY O'CONNER:** Max's bartender

**OCTAVIO:** one of "the three Bananas"; Max's regular

**MICHEL O'DARE:** filmmaker

**TOM O'DONNELL:** balloon vendor

**LI-LIAN OH:** acupuncturist

**ALFA-BETTY OLSON:** screenwriter/author

**ONDINE:** worked with Andy Warhol at the Factory; starred in Warhol's movie *Loves of Ondine*; deceased

**JOEL OPPENHEIMER:** poet, writer; named Max's Kansas City; died in 1986.

**JERALD (JERRY) ORDOVER:** attorney to art dealers and artists

# cast of characters

**AL PACINO:** famous film actor; star of *Dog Day Afternoon, Serpico, Scarface,* the *Godfather* movies, and more recently, *Carlito's Way* and *Scent of a Woman*

**ANDY PALEY:** musician, producer; formed the group the Sidewinders.

**BOB PAULS:** business consultant

**SIERRA PECHEUR:** actress; member of the Playhouse of the Riciculous

**DONALD PHELPS:** poet, writer

**MICHAEL POLLARD:** actor; movies include *Bonnie & Clyde, Dick Tracy,* and *American Gothic.*

**LARRY POONS:** abstract painter

**IGGY POP:** punk pioneer; formed seminal punk-grunge band the Stooges; went on to a prolific solo career; appeared in John Waters' film *Hairspray,* as the beatnik husband of Pia Zadora.

**VALERIE PORR:** fashion designer; artist; teacher at the School of Visual Arts

**ANDREA PORTEGO:** ballet historian; fashion model

**ROBERT POVLICH:** abstract expressionist painter

**DAVID PRENTICE:** painter

**JOHN PUMA:** former record producer; movie agent

**TOM PUNZIO:** Max's bartender; played on Max's softball team

**MIKE QUASHIE:** "The Limbo King"; performer; innovator

**DIANE QUINN:** Max's waitress; model

**J.P. RADLEY:** Max's accountant; business consultant

**DEE DEE RAMONE:** bassist and founding member of the Ramones; currently playing in his own band, the Remains.

**JOEY RAMONE:** lead singer and founding member of the Ramones

**LOU REED:** songwriter, performer, musician; lead singer and founding member of the Velvet Underground; wrote the classic rock-and-roll songs "Walk on the Wild Side," "Sweet Jane," "Rock and Roll," and "Heroin."

**PETER REGINATO:** painter, sculptor

**RUBY LYNN REYNER:** actress in the Playhouse of the Ridiculous; won the Drama Desk Award for her acting in *La Bohemia;* lead singer in her band, Ruby and the Rednecks, who have recently performed in various New York clubs

**RENÉ RICARD:** poet/writer; actor in the Playhouse of the Ridiculous

**KERRY RIORDAN:** model

**OLIVER RISH:** Max's regular

**LARRY RIVERS:** painter, musician; East Hampton socialite

**ROCCO:** Max's back-room regular

**DOROTHEA ROCKBURNE:** painter

**NILE ROGERS:** formerly a member of the dance-music group Chic; one of the preeminent music producers of the 1980s

**ABIGAIL ROSEN:** Max's first coat-check girl and doorlady

**DEBBIE ROSS:** Max's waitress

**GASTON ROSSILI:** actor

**RAEANNE RUBENSTEIN:** photographer; has contributed to many publications, including *Rolling Stone, People Magazine, Pulse, Vanity Fair,* and *Vogue;* new books include *Honkytonk Heroes, Mug Shots,* and *Gone Country.*

**TODD RUNDGREN:** rock musician, singer, songwriter, and record producer

**MICKEY RUSKIN:** creator and sole proprietor of Max's Kansas City; died May 16, 1983.

**BOB RUSSELL:** Max's bouncer

**JOHN RUSSELL:** attorney; Max's regular

**RUSSELL RYAN:** worked at Feigan Russell art gallery; great storyteller

**TOM RYAN:** painted the interior of Mickey's restaurants, including Max's.

**GIORGIO ST. ANGELO:** fashion designer

**BILL SALANO:** fashion photographer

**ED SANDERS:** poet; publisher; formerly a member of the Fugs

**TONY SHAFRAZI:** artist, art dealer, gallery owner

**JULIAN SCHNABEL:** painter, filmmaker, author

**CAROLEE SCHNEEMANN:** painter; performance artist

**IRA SCHNEIDER:** filmmaker

**EDIE SEDGWICK:** actress/model; Warhol superstar. Died in1971.

**CAROL SHAW:** drummer for rock group Isis

**SAM SHEPARD:** Pulitzer-prize winning playwright (*Buried Child*); cowrote *Cowboy Mouth,* a play about a couple searching for the new rock-and-roll savior, with Patti Smith.

**JACKIE SHERMAN:** Max's waitress; married Robin Cullinen, Max's manager.

**ALAN SHIELDS:** Max's busboy; now an artist

**JIM SIGNORELLI:** director, producer, filmmaker; presently with *Saturday Night Live*

**DAVID SMITH:** Max's bartender

**GERALDINE SMITH:** Max's back-room regular; Warhol superstar

**HOWARD SMITH:** wrote the "Scenes" column in the *Village Voice* for a number of years, produced the movie *Gizmo,* and made a documentary, *Marjoe.* He is currently working on a novel.

**PATTI SMITH:** rock-and-roll poet/songwriter/musician; lead singer of the Patti Smith Group. Published books of poetry include *Babel* (1974) and *Seventh Heaven* (1972). The 1975 Patti Smith Group album, *Horses,* is considered one of the great rock-and-roll records; in 1993 she came out of "retirement" and is enjoying a much-heralded comeback.

**ROBERT SMITHSON:** earthworks sculptor

**VALERIE SOLANIS:** founder of SCUM (the Society for Cutting Up Men); published *The SCUM Manifesto*; shot and nearly killed Andy Warhol in 1968.

**CHRIS STEIN:** bass player and founding member of Blondie; ex-husband of Debbie Harry

**JUDY STRANG:** bass player with all-girl group Pulsallama

**MARJORIE STRIDER:** painter

**RON SUKENICK:** author of *Down and In*; currently teaches at University of Colorado

**INGRID SUPERSTAR:** invented the word "Superstar"; a Warhol Superstar

**BILL THURSTON:** building teacher; contractor

**FRANCINE TINT:** painter; costume designer

**CORY TIPPIN:** hair and makeup stylist

**ED TISCH:** cab driver for the Max's regulars and employees

**TISH & SNOOKIE:** creators of the punk store and hair-dye and makeup company, Manic Panic; members of the punk group the Sick Fucks in the 1970s

**OLIVIERO TOSCANI:** fashion photographer

**MAUREEN ("MO") TUCKER:** drummer with the Velvet Underground; has recorded as a solo artist.

**STEVEN TYLER:** lead singer of the rock band Aerosmith

**JOHN VACCARO:** director of the Playhouse of the Ridiculous; his plays include *The Mokeeater*, *La Fin du Cirque*, *La Bohemia*, *Nightclub*, *Heaven Grand in Amber Orbit*, and *Son of Cockstrong*.

**KEN VAN SICKLE:** photographer, filmmaker

**CHERRY VANILLA:** actress; recording artist on RCA; formerly publicist for David Bowie's Management company, Mainman Ltd.

**ULTRA VIOLET:** Warhol Superstar; actress and art collector; author of *Famous for 15 Minutes*

**JOAN VOS:** Max's waitress; worked at Warhol's Factory.

**LOUIE WALDEN:** Warhol Superstar, actor

**ANDY WARHOL:** facilitator of the New York celebrity–society scene; founder of the Factory and *Interview* magazine; pop artist and filmmaker. Held court in Max's back room. Deceased.

**JOHN WATERS:** probably the most influential underground filmmaker ever. Brought Divine to the big screen in his films *Female Trouble*, *Pink Flamingos*, *Polyester*, and *Hairspray*, among others. Has published several books, including *Crackpot*.

**WILLIAM WEGMAN:** painter, photographer, filmmaker; famous for his photographs of his dogs, especially Man Ray

**TONY WEINBERGER:** Max's regular, carpenter, writer; managed Max's Terre Haute.

**ALICE WEINER:** Max's waitress; married Lawrence Weiner.

**DORY WEINER:** Upstairs at Max's doorlady; formerly part of the Mainman Management team

**LAWRENCE WEINER:** sculptor

**CAROLE WILBOURN:** Mickey's friend; former teacher and *Playboy* bunny; now a cat therapist

**NEIL WILLIAMS:** painter and Mickey's mentor

**HOLLY WOODLAWN:** Warhol Superstar; best known for her role in Warhol's *Trash*; author of *A Low Life In High Heels*

**MARY WORONOV:** Warhol Superstar; actress

**ANDREW WYLIE:** former owner of a bookstore and publisher of Telegraph Books; now a literary agent

**CHARLES YODER:** painter

**WENDY YUJUICO:** Max's waitress; married Tex Wray.

**TONY ZINETTA:** formerly part of Bowie's Mainman Magagement team; author of *Stardust*, a biography of Bowie

**LARRY ZOX:** abstract expressionist painter

Yvonne Sewall-Ruskin met Mickey in the fall of 1967 after graduating from college and while applying for a waitressing job at Max's Kansas City. They became a couple in the beginning of 1968 and had two children together, Jessica and Michael. During this time, Yvonne completed her Master's degree in Education at N.Y.U. and began a teaching career. While at Max's she was instrumental in helping to create "Upstairs at Max's," which showcased many of the unsigned bands that have now made history. She also selected singles for the jukebox and advised Mickey of new promising talent on the scene. She got George Thorogood booked into Max's for his debut appearance in New York City.

After separating from Mickey, Yvonne continued to work in the field of music, promoting and managing various recording studios, including Bearsville Studios, as assistant manager, then, in New York City, 39th Street Music, Evergreen, and Celestial, and was the sales rep for Atlantic Studios. She started her own company, I Contact, the first audio production service to exist in New York, representing engineers, producers, and recording artists, as well as brokering studio time. Presently Yvonne is selling real estate in downtown Manhattan and is planning to open a new concept of Max's Kansas City downtown.